Praise for *Mules, Mules and More Mules: The Adventures and Misadventures of a First Time Mule Owner*

Rose Miller has done it again! In her new book, *Mules, Mules and More Mules* Rose takes us on her trip down the Grand Canyon wall and into the next chapter of her life with equines. Learn along with Rose as she discovers the difference between horse training and mule training. I laughed out loud at mule antics and deeply sympathized when Rose "bit the dirt" after she was pitched off one of her mules. I loved this book and have recommended it to all my animal lover friends. If you already own a mule you will definitely appreciate Rose's experiences with her mules. If you don't own a mule you will be tempted to start looking for one. I know I am.

Connie T. Orland, IN

I enjoyed this book! I especially liked the little mention that Hoosier and I received. *Mules, Mules and More Mules* is a cute story about one woman's quest for the perfect mule. The author learns to love and learn from the mules she encounters on this journey, and readers can benefit from her trials and tribulations along the way. It is a good read for anyone planning on going "mule shopping," and anyone who has ever been, will be able to relate to Rose's tale. Rose is right when she says that mules are like potato chips: "You can't eat just one." And readers will be closer to understanding why.

Cori Basham
Mules and More Editor
www.mulesandmore.com

Rose Miller's book: *Mules, Mules and More Mules*, contains a great deal of information that will be interesting and helpful to mule and horse owners. Every new mule owner, and those who are considering buying their first mule, should definitely read her story.

John Hauer, author of *The Superiority of Mules* (The Lyons Press 2005)

I thought *Mules, Mules and More Mules* was very well written. The descriptions of things and events made them easy to understand. This book held my attention all the way through, and I thoroughly enjoyed it. Most people that have purchased a mule have gone through some of the same experiences. I especially think that people who haven't had mules very long will appreciate these stories and be able to relate to them. The main message I got was: if you take the time to understand your mule and learn to work with it, you'll have a wonderful companion.

Loyd Hawley
Owner of Hawleywoods Mule Farm
Charter member, Past President & Chairman of Rules Committee for the North American Saddle Mule Association (NASMA)

Rose's all-true mule adventure begins with a gripping mule ride down a wall-clinging switchback trail into the Grand Canyon. I found myself leaning away from the precipice as I read her matter-of-fact and thrilling prose. Her life with mules unfolds as a great true adventure for any reader, young or old.

Laura Leveque, aka Jackass Jill, *Whoa you donkey...WHOA! Adventures of a Lady Prospector*

Rose accurately describes the challenges and rewards of mule ownership. The abundant details put the reader by her side as she and her mules try to reach an understanding. I enjoyed reliving our own trip down the Grand Canyon on mules through her trip. A person would not want to trust his life to a horse on that trip! A mule is smart enough not to want to get hurt and the rider is the beneficiary. However, it takes a mule longer to trust the rider than it does for a horse. And a transition to a new owner can be very difficult for the mule and for the new owner. The transition can take 3 weeks to 3 years. During the transition the mule may seem to have "forgotten" all the manners and skills he has demonstrated with the original owner. So the bottom line is, if you have developed a relationship in which the mule trusts and respects you, the mule will be a great companion. If not, keep looking . . .

John Niebruegge, Gaited Mules, www.jandbpasofinos.com

At 83 I regularly ride my mule, Scooter, all over mountain trails, and I drive my mini mule, Macho Man, at least once a week. Because I am a mule lover, I read Rose Miller's book with interest. It left me with several impressions:
1. Reminiscences about the ride I once made down into the Grand Canyon with my family on mules. It is one of the most extravagant scenic experiences possible in life.
2. Rose's book made it clear to me why my imprint training method, now in use all over the world, has been more widely accepted the by mule breeding industry than by any other "breed" of horse. I had a couple of mules before I started breeding my own and imprint training the foals. Those 2 mules had behavior quirks, just as some of Rose's did. My imprint trained mules have been flawless, better than any of the horses I have raised. It works with horses; it works even better in mules!
3. I was glad to read about my friend Steve Edwards. He *is* a mule man!

Robert M. Miller, D.V.M. Author of *Imprint Training of the Newborn Foal, Natural Horsemanship Explained, Understanding the Ancient Secrets of the Horse's Mind* and many more. www.robertmmiller.com

Mules, Mules and More Mules: The Adventures and Misadventures of a First Time Mule Owner

Rose Miller

Copyright © 2010 Rose Miller

ISBN 978-1-60910-493-1

All rights reserved. No part of this publication may be reproduced, stored in a retrieval system, or transmitted in any form or by any means, electronic, mechanical, recording or otherwise, without the prior written permission of the author.

Printed in the United States of America.

BookLocker.com, Inc.
2010

Cover photograph

Rose and Grand Canyon Charlie at Phantom Ranch
Photo by Robert Whitney

This book is lovingly dedicated to my husband Hal who has unselfishly encouraged me to follow my dreams and aspirations to become a horsewoman, and open my heart and our home to many diverse creatures—great and small.

Also by Rose Miller

The Horse That Wouldn't Trot: A Life with Tennessee Walking Horses, Lessons Learned and Memories Shared

TABLE OF CONTENTS

Introduction by Meredith Hodges 1
Chapter One: "His Name is Charlie" 3
Chapter Two: Down We Go 8
Chapter Three: The Kaibab Trail 24
Chapter Four: Mirabella 41
Chapter Five: Mirabella the Trail Mule 52
Chapter Six: Samson - One Big Mule 62
Chapter Seven: Miss Ellie 69
Chapter Eight: Four-Wheeling on a Mule 75
Chapter Nine: Samson Goes to a Show 84
Chapter Ten: Mirabella Comes Home 91
Chapter Eleven: Samson Makes His Presence Known 99
Chapter Twelve: Sugar n' Spice 106
Chapter Thirteen: Miss Ellie Goes to Boot Camp 119
Chapter Fourteen: Maybellene 127
Chapter Fifteen: Adventure in Utah 138
Chapter Sixteen: Bryce Canyon and the Hoodoos 146
Chapter Seventeen: Mirabella Is Sold 157
Chapter Eighteen: Ornery Samson 163
Chapter Nineteen: Reclamation 172
Chapter Twenty: The Cow Pony 181
Chapter Twenty-one: On Again, Off Again 184
Chapter Twenty-two: Soul Searching 188
Chapter Twenty-three: Ruth Ann 195

Chapter Twenty-four: Born to Jump 214
Chapter Twenty-five: Not This Again! 222
Chapter Twenty-six: Rescues 229
Chapter Twenty-seven: Ah, Spring 232
Chapter Twenty-eight: Summer Daze 238
Chapter Twenty-nine: Divorce 242
Chapter Thirty: Lessons Learned 249
Chapter Thirty-one: A Solution for Ruth 253
Chapter Thirty-two: Lucinda 257
Chapter Thirty-three: Lucinda, Part Two 264
Chapter Thirty-four: Reflection 271

INTRODUCTION BY MEREDITH HODGES

Mules are wonderful animals! They are smarter and more versatile than horses with much smoother and more forward gaits. They are more resistant to parasites and disease, more surefooted and require less feed for good health. Mules are less likely to hurt themselves and are therefore cheaper to keep. The mule inherits the best characteristics from each parent. From the jack, mules inherit strength, intelligence and thickness of bone and from the mare: beauty, athletic ability and height. For this reason, the mule is always stronger and more athletic than his dam (the horse), and quite capable of ALL equestrian endeavors depending on the proficiency and methodology of the trainer.

Mules come in as many diverse personalities as do people, so it is important to consider a mule that is compatible with your own personality. It is vitally important to buy a mule with this in mind. Generally speaking, mules do not take kindly to the fragmented training techniques that are prevalent with most horse trainers, resulting in bad behaviors. For instance, if you play horse "games" with a mule, he will most likely turn the tables on you and will be "gaming" you. Fortunately, mules and donkeys form separate relationships with people and although they may have been misunderstood, or mistreated by one person, they will not be soured on all people, just suspicious. With the correct approach, those mules who have been abused can often be taught to trust and love again, and disappointed owners might still find the "Mule of Their Dreams."

Rose Miller has written quite eloquently about the foibles that can occur while looking for that "Mule of your Dreams!" Her journey of discovery unlocks the mysteries of the mule in a warm and personable way, one mule at a time, and reveals that which is uniquely mule...a case of Mule Fever! Those who have mules will tell you, "It's terminal!"

Chapter One: "His Name is Charlie"

It was a gorgeous morning. The grass was lush with spring green that only April can sport. My ride on Sunday Praise, one of my retired Tennessee Walker show mares, had been delightful, but carefully planned. The previous May I had tried to help a horse get up who was stuck down in his stall. When he lurched to his feet, he knocked my right leg, hyper-extending it. I was devastated, not only because of the excruciating pain, but it coincided with the birth of my first grandchild, a little girl. What kind of Grammy was I going to be? I could hardly hobble, let alone carry a new baby.

Over the next year, the knee slowly healed, but bending it to ride a horse was tricky. My stirrups had to be just the correct length and time in the saddle was of short duration, but to someone addicted to sitting on a horse, any time was quality time.

As I was unsaddling my horse, Bob walked into the barn with his dog Hershey.

"Hey Rose, what would you think of taking the mule trip down the Grand Canyon with me?"

I nearly dropped my saddle as I turned to look at him in consternation. I was barely able to ride my horse on flat ground, how could I possibly ride for the hours it would take to do the steep ups and downs of the Grand Canyon?

Bob, who had come to stay with our family while he completed his MBA at a local college, had never left. He was the same age as our oldest daughter, loved the farm and county life, and we all sort of adopted each other. Bob had a special love for the Grand Canyon and had hiked it three times.

Seeing my surprise, he grinned and said, "Well, you should really think about it—before you get any older!"

I was astounded he would be willing to ride a mule. He didn't ride our horses; I never got the impression he even liked them. He preferred walking the farm trails with the dogs.

"Okay, let me sit down and we will talk about this crazy idea."

"The thing is, we need to schedule a year in advance. The ride is very popular and has limited openings. If you can't go when the time arrives, we can cancel."

That made it a possibility, but what would my husband Hal think of this venture? For thirty plus years he had been extremely tolerant of all my horse activities, such as traveling miles with our daughters to horse shows and breeding and raising horses. Now that I had retired from both endeavors, I think he was hopeful life might be quieter and he could worry less about my exploits.

As it turned out, Hal just rolled his eyes and smiled, and another phase of my equine life was about to unfold.

We decided on the two-day ride, going down to the bottom and staying at Phantom Ranch for dinner and the night, and then riding back up and out the next day.

During the succeeding year, my knees made great progress, my back stayed together and nothing else happened to make me hobble. I researched all I could find on the Internet about the rides, and read several experiences of other riders. It appeared that I could do it, if only my knees would hold together. It is very stressful on knees going downhill as we would be doing.

Late evening on May 11, 2006, we arrived at the El Tovar hotel on the south rim of the canyon. Between car and air travel we had been on the road thirteen hours and I was exhausted.

"Look down there," Bob said. "There's the Tonto Platform with Indian Garden within it. That's where we're going and will have our lunch."

I shaded my eyes against the setting sun. It looked so very tiny and far away—*down*. The Garden Creek area could be spotted by all the green cottonwood trees that were growing along it. It looked like an oasis in the middle of the desert. The Grand Canyon is actually two canyons: the upper one that can be seen from the rim, and the deeper inner canyon that can only be seen as a hiker, river rafter, or mule rider. We would be among a small percentage of Grand Canyon visitors who saw the inner canyon and the Colorado River.

The sun was making spectacular shadows and sunlit areas on the canyon wall. I have seen many pictures of the sun rising or setting over the Grand Canyon, but although the pictures are beautiful, they cannot create the same feeling as seeing it in person. The canyon looked painted in light mossy green horizontal strips mixed in with the red of the rocks. The color was different from the clumped darker green of bushes and trees. I asked Bob what made it look like that. Was it like the famed Painted Desert, the color coming from sand?

"No," he answered, "it is vegetation." That was amazing. It looked as if it had been created by an artist's brush. I would get to see for myself soon enough.

The next morning we were to be at the mule corral by 6:45. After waiting for half an hour, Bob pointed out the mules coming back across the road from their barn and pens. There were several wranglers each leading a group of mules. The mules were tied to each other with about two and a half feet of rope between them. As the mules came across the road, traffic stopped and waited—and waited. It takes awhile for thirty mules to slowly cross a road.

I wondered how they would all fit in the small corral, but the wranglers packed them in with only inches between them. Some mules had a few disagreeable looks for their neighbor, but mostly they stood, ears flopped off the sides with a sleepy look in their eyes. They'd been here before and seen it all. The wranglers poked and pushed mule butts over and squeezed in to tie them up with their rope halters. Each mule had his bridle hanging on the saddle horn.

Next, Marilyn, the petite blond mule boss, started her speech about the rules of the trail.

"Be sure you drink plenty of water from your canteens that you have been given. Dehydration is definitely possible because today is predicted to be in the 90s." We all hung around the corral and listened raptly, not wanting to miss anything.

"The mules have the right of way," she continued, "hikers must stand aside and let you pass." She paused for emphasis and swatted her leg with a riding switch. "The most important rule is that all the mules must be ridden close to each other. A tight compact group is ninety-five percent of the safety of the trip. If your mule lags behind, it will miss its buddies and will run to catch up. Then the ones behind that one will run too."

I got the picture. Having greenhorn riders on running mules could be a disaster.

Marilyn continued waving her riding crop and said emphatically, "You have all been given a switch. We call it the 'Motivator.' You must use it to keep your mule close behind the next mule. No gentle taps will work; you need to *mean it*."

That should pose no problem for me; I was, after all, a veteran horseperson.

I will remember *that* rule to my dying day.

I had already decided to not utter a word of my rather vast experience. I had ridden, trained, and shown horses for thirty years. I had bred mares, standing at stud seven stallions at one time or another, foaled mares, and broke young horses. At different times on our farm I had up to fifty horses for which I was responsible. Nope, I wasn't saying a word. I thought if I did, they might give me a mule that could need some extra ability and I was on vacation. I didn't want any kind of challenges.

There were two "day-ride" groups which would only go part way down, have a sack lunch and then return. Each group was called in to the center of the corral separately, lined up in a row, and a mule chosen especially for the individual rider. I don't know how Marilyn decided who rode which mule, but later I would have reason to want to ask her that question. Next, we overnight riders were given our mules. There were two groups of six with their wranglers. These groups were limited in number because Phantom Ranch at the bottom could only accommodate a certain number of guests at one time.

Bob and I were in the last group of overnighters, and were the last two to be assigned a ride. First Marilyn called Bob out for his mule, and I was wondering which of the remaining mules would be mine. As I stood alone in the middle of the corral, I turned back to look at Bob, who was now seated on Sleepy, his mule. I thought I discerned a fleeting look of "What the heck am I doing up here," on his face.

Finally, Marilyn led a mule over to me. "His name is Charlie" she said, and I was about to embark upon a splendid adventure.

Rose and Charlie getting instructions

Chapter Two: Down We Go

First, however, I had to get up on Charlie. At home I use mounting blocks, which I've placed somewhat advantageously around the farm. My knees simply won't bend well enough, and my five-foot-four-inch frame graced with short legs won't reach high enough to get on without one. Getting on and off would prove to be the hardest and most ignominious part of the whole trip. I felt like a sack of potatoes being hoisted into the saddle. That was another reason I was grateful I had kept my extensive riding experiences to myself.

Patrick, our guide and wrangler, led us out of the corral and headed down the Bright Angel trail. The three ladies in our group followed him, and the three men brought up the rear. After we had gone a few hundred feet, which included some gentle switchbacks, I was aware of the most amazing feeling of delight welling up inside me, one that brought tears to my eyes. Here I was on an equine, one of my very first childhood loves, enjoying one of the absolutely most magnificent creations of God and nature—The Grand Canyon. How could I be so blessed?

From then on there were no more thoughts of worry about my capabilities. I only felt extreme appreciation for my sure-footed mule Charlie, and the breathtaking vistas.

Soon after experiencing my flush of pleasure and negotiating a few sharper downhill switchbacks and rough footing, I realized, yes indeed, we were several mule lengths behind Patrick and the other two ladies. There was no way on earth I was going to ask Charlie to hurry up while we were proceeding through this part of the trail. Finally, the path leveled out, relatively speaking, and I tapped my mule smartly on his behind. He responded with a nice little jog trot to catch up. Of course, that meant the ones behind us had to do the same thing, but I didn't hear any sounds resembling fear. Okay, so far so good.

Pretty soon a gap of several mule lengths again appeared between Charlie and the second lady rider. This time we were going around a switchback, which meant that a rider above could see us below. I heard someone say, "Git up there, Charlie." It was another wrangler who had been bringing up the rear of our group. Oh great. We were only thirty minutes into our ride and already I was causing a problem. I tapped Charlie again and we were off at a little trot to catch up. The wrangler at the rear said "Adios," to us, and our little group was now alone with our guide, Patrick.

I talk to my own horses—mind to mind—as well as in words, indicating appreciation for them and berating them when necessary. I was talking to Charlie, too. He was very sure footed, and he did not "walk the edge." The lady's mule ahead of me did, and I held my breath for them. She looked around several times, and by the look on her face there was no doubt she wished her mule would not. We had been told some mules walked very close to the edge, and we were not to compensate by leaning in towards the other side. That could make the saddle slip, or worse. She was a good trooper, sitting straight in her saddle, but definitely not looking over the edge at any scenery.

I was beginning to feel a real rapport with Charlie by now. I knew from the start that you did not guide them; you just let the mule go and held onto the reins. A rider definitely had to trust her animal, and I did indeed trust Charlie. I rubbed his neck from time to time with my hand and told him softly that he was a good boy. But again we lagged behind.

Charlie catching up

Going downhill was interesting to say the least. Some parts were smooth and the walk was easy—except for me and the rest behind me—we were jogging to catch up to the others who had again gained several mule lengths on us. Some parts of the downhill ride consisted of steps, some quite deep from the dirt being flicked out of them by many mule feet. The steps were held in place by wood poles so they were very stable, just steep and sometimes deep. Charlie sort of hopped down the steep ones stiff legged so I got a nice jolt each time. But I was glad to be riding and not hopping down them with my own knees. Each mule had britching straps that went around their rear end to keep the saddle from slipping forward. Coming back home up the trail, they were not used.

The rocks were abundant and naturally "cemented" in the path, requiring the mule to pick and choose its way through. I noticed that each mule seemed to have a preference as to footsteps. Charlie did not always step into the same little spaces that the mule ahead of us had.

Mules, Mules and More Mules

There were places that didn't have rocks, and there again, Charlie and I, leading our little group of stragglers, were trotting to catch up. After the first two times of tapping Charlie's butt, he trotted on his own to catch up as soon as he had a clear path. I thought that highly intelligent of him. He was not worried in the least about losing his forward companions and his trot was slow and controlled. Apparently Charlie hadn't listened to Marilyn's admonition about worried mule laggers.

After a few looks over his shoulder at our little trotting periods, I sensed that Patrick wasn't quite as pleased as I was. I also suspected the fellows behind Charlie were not enjoying their trot as much as I did.

One of the rock formations at the beginning of the ride down Bright Angel Trail looked like an Indian gazing out towards the canyon. Patrick told us the native Indians considered it to be a spirit that looked after the canyon and its inhabitants. We passed under a rock with ancient Indian drawings upon it that indicated the long history of the trail, maybe as long ago as 10,000 years.

The trail lies along Bright Angel Fault that creates a natural break in the cliffs and gives access to Garden Creek 3,500 feet below the rim. This is where we were headed for our box lunch, and where the day riders would turn around and go back up the same trail.

As we rode lower and traveled through several climate zones, it got hotter and hotter and soon was 90 degrees. The heat was unusual for the time of year, but the whole spring had been strange. Patrick told us that in April, a snow storm closed the upper part of the trail at a switchback with two feet of snow. Problem was, there were day riders at the bottom that needed to come home. He and several others had to go down on mules and shovel the snow off the trail. The other trips down were cancelled.

As we rode the mules down the trail, the trees changed. A thousand feet below the rim we found the slow growing pinyon pines (which reminded me of the feathery white pine trees in my own Indiana back yard), and the denser, scrubbier and shorter junipers. Another thousand feet brought us to the Tonto Platform and desert scrub like blackbrush. Later as we enjoyed the last part of our ride to the river and Phantom Ranch, we would see more desert-like conditions and plants such as brittle brush, honey mesquite and cat claw acacia. The heat and the change in rainfall made the difference.

Bob said it could be snowing or raining at the rim and when the moisture reached a certain depth in the canyon, it just stopped—evaporated. He had wanted to come at this time of year because we should see wildflowers and cactus in bloom.

"Oh, Bob, look!" I pointed with my motivator to a spot about fifty feet high on the canyon wall. "See that one lone magenta cactus growing out of solid rock?" It was a stunning sight and unnoticed by the group ahead, but if you were riding a pokey mule like Charlie, you might as well enjoy the sights....

As we got closer to Indian Garden, the tiny green oasis I'd seen from the top of the rims, the trail leveled out. True to form, Charlie and I had dropped behind again. The path was level, but still rocky; I didn't want to make him hurry up through bad footing so the distance got to be about seventy feet between us before there was a nice place trot to catch up. I gave just a little squeeze and he trotted pleasantly off. A mule trotting on the trail makes quite a lot more noise than just walking. As Charlie trotted on, so did the three mules behind us. Problem was, however, they weren't through the rocky place. Apparently that didn't deter the sure-footed animals, but I heard several exclamations from the riders as their mules hurried to stay attached to Charlie's tail.

Of course, four mules trotting along make even more noise than one, and Patrick quickly turned in his saddle to see what the clatter was about. I was truly embarrassed this time. I had committed the cardinal sin of canyon mule riding. Fortunately, it was on level ground, but I don't think the guys behind were very happy with Charlie and me. Patrick seemed more surprised than anything, but I was glad I couldn't read his mind.

After traveling a little over two hours down the decline into Indian Garden, we stopped for lunch. The day group had proceeded on to Plateau Point, where there was a sheer drop to the Colorado River and a splendid view, and then they would return to the top.

Mules, Mules and More Mules

The first group of the two-day-riders was already eating, their mules tied to the hitch area. Their guide's name was Frosty. He had been wrangling the canyon mules for sixteen years, and had decided this would be his last year. He looked every bit the cowboy, which he always had been. A tooth missing, deeply tanned, with glinty eyes, he wore spurs with what looked like three-inch rowels. Tall and slender, he walked with spurs clanking just like cowboys in the old west movies. Frosty rolled his own cigarettes while riding his mule. My one and only conversation with him didn't go quite as I had hoped.

We all were munching on the lunch items, like chips, fruit, and snack bars, things that could be easily carried down on the mules, and Frosty was chatting with a couple from his group. They were right beside me, and I thought I would tell Frosty about gaited mules. These mules were from Tennessee Walking Horses, Paso Finos, Racking Horses, or any mare that did a smooth gait. Bred to a jack (a male donkey), the mare sometimes produced a gaited mule. They are a big hit with trail riders, and I thought he would find it interesting.

I introduced myself as being from northern Indiana where we raised Tennessee Walking Horses. With a look of pure disgust on his face, Frosty said, "Why, I wouldn't have anything to do with those horses. They are only good for shooting." Seeing the look of total surprise and dismay on my face, he added, "Well, they might be good in parades."

My face burned with embarrassment, and I muttered something about hoping he never came to northern Indiana and that was the end of the conversation. Before we mounted back up to continue our ride, it hit me that he was probably thinking of the padded, chained, and sored "big lick" show Tennessee Walking Horse. Of course, he would only have total disdain for those poor creatures. It was too late to explain that I was talking about trail horses, as he had already headed back out on the trail—and I'm not sure I would have braved his ire again, at any rate.

This was where Patrick told us we would be sprayed from the hose to be cooled down. I was more than ready. While being hosed down, I asked Patrick if the mules would be watered. There was a big trough available.

"No," he answered, "they wouldn't drink anyway. They will be fine until we get to the bottom." He further explained that mules rehydrate quickly, so dehydration wasn't as big a problem with them. We, however, were admonished again to drink, drink, and drink from our little water canteens. Patrick told us he had extra water with him if we needed it.

We were allowed to give our mules the apple cores from our lunch if we desired. I quickly grabbed two that weren't mine—I had been given an orange—and Bob and I gave Sleepy and Charlie a treat. At least I thought it would be a treat. Both mules took the apple like it was a job they had to do. My own horses almost jump up and down in glee at the thought of an apple. Their eyes widen, ears prick forward, nostrils flare. Not these fellows. They chewed slowly with their ears still flopped off to the side, eyes half closed. I hoped the treat might entice Charlie to walk faster—but no such luck.

The gentleman of one of the married couples in our group asked Patrick if they could ride together instead of the three women in front and the fellows bringing up the rear. That was fine with him, so all of us decided to ride with our own buddy. Someone else asked how he wanted the group to go. He answered, "It doesn't matter." The mules were lined up at the hitch line with Bob's mule Sleepy and Charlie together at the end of the line, and I *think* that is how we ended up at the rear of the group. Either that or everyone else scrambled to get away from slowpoke Charlie.

The rider who had been right behind Charlie rode a mule named Nora. She was a big fat long-legged black mule. She absolutely loved to eat and rather than have the riders fight with her all the way, she wore a "grazing muzzle." I use the same type on some of my fat— and getting fatter horses. They can drink, eat several blades of grass at a time, and breathe easily through it. Nora liked to boogie on. She was forever on Charlie's tail, or with her head a little past it, along his side.

Her rider had complained about this to Patrick at one of our stops. Patrick's reply was, "That's fine; just don't let her pass him." I think both Nora and her rider had had enough of Charlie's rear end and seeing their chance, got in line ahead of Charlie. I know that was fine with Charlie too. He was tired of turning his head to the side and giving Nora dirty looks. So off we went, with Bob and me bringing up the rear.

Patrick rode an eye-catching mule named Norman. I had noticed him that first morning being led across the road to the mule corral where we would be given our mules. He was a light brown color, almost creamy. He had a beautiful head, which is what I noticed first, and walked smartly along. I thought the wranglers rode their own special mules—mules that were perhaps smarter, better trained, and even better looking. That turned out to not be the case. Norman was only four years old. I think that alone spoke of his intelligence. Patrick said he was almost ready for a customer to ride. What a lucky person that would be.

As Norman and Patrick rode ahead, here and there I could see Patrick's boot with his spur tapping Norman's side. Patrick's spurs were not big as Frosty's, but they were efficient. The mule responded by moving sprightly on. In my mind I begged Patrick to not use the spurs. *Darn, you are already leaving us in the dust. I really don't think you need the spur. Maybe I could borrow them?*

The ride from Indian Garden into the inner canyon was breathtaking. It followed the water for some way, so the cottonwood trees were green and provided a little shade from the heat. Many cacti appeared ready to bloom, but we missed seeing those. There were several species of cacti and Indian paintbrush blooming vibrantly with gorgeous orange and red blooms, and brittlebush with bright yellow flowers. One of the strangest of all was the dantura flowers that seemed to grow splendidly out of the granite walls. They looked a little like our morning glories. It seems strange to say, but that was maybe my most favorite spot on the ride. It was shady, the creek bubbled along beside us now and then, the flowers were especially bountiful, and it was *green*. I know one does not go the Grand Canyon to see green, but I delighted in it. This little green oasis could be seen from the top rim of the canyon.

Again Charlie lagged. It was getting harder and harder to encourage him to trot to catch up. Whack, *whack*—nothing much happened any more. We had two hours left to get to Phantom Ranch and my feelings for Charlie were turning into a sort of love/hate relationship. I appreciated his carefulness and steadiness, but goodness, couldn't he possibly walk just a little faster?

Sleepy did fairly well at keeping up with Charlie most of the time. We certainly were going slowly enough. We crossed the little creek several times, and at one of the crossings, Sleepy decided to have a drink. I had turned around to check on them, and told Bob not to let him. Not that it would have hurt the mule, and I did feel like a total heel not letting him drink, but Charlie had fallen quite far behind again, in fact, I couldn't see anybody ahead at the moment. If we waited for Sleepy to drink in his slow methodical mule-like manner, we would really be behind the rest. Bob pulled his mule's head up and I told him we had to hurry.

"Is there an easier way to ride this darn trot?" Bob asked. "My rear end hurts."

"Stand up a little in the stirrups and maybe it won't be so bad. I am really sorry, but this is going to be a long one." The path ahead was relatively smooth and flat and somehow I got Charlie into a trot. As we came rattling up behind the group, Patrick didn't even turn to look. Neither did the others. Everyone knew who it was and who had caused it.

At Indian Garden I had apologized to Patrick for Charlie's slowness. He said Charlie always did that—slowed down the ride. I told him I was an experienced rider and that although I couldn't get him to walk faster, I was not afraid of riding him to catch up. That seemed to relieve Patrick's mind. He answered, "I won't worry so much about an experienced rider." But that didn't cover poor Bob who was destined to bounce along behind us.

The green ride was short but sweet and soon we were going down again. The inner canyon is narrower with steeper sides. Instead of vegetation, we saw stunning rock formations of different colors and sizes. It was on this portion of the trail that Bob had a heart stopping experience with Sleepy. As Marilyn had told us, mules have the right of way. Hikers must hug the wall side of the trail, or step into or onto an out-of-the-way spot. We had traveled past several hikers, including one who was safely positioned into an indented part of the stone wall. We all trooped by, but when Bob and Sleepy at the rear passed by, the hiker stepped out a little too soon and his walking stick hit Sleepy on his rear end.

There had been about twelve feet between Charlie and Sleepy—too far to be correct, but maybe good in this case. Sleepy jumped ahead and closed the gap in a second.

"*Whoa!*" Bob shouted. It would have given me alarm and I am a rider of spooky horses at home. True to form, though, Sleepy did not head for the cliff's edge, just the comfort of Charlie's rump.

Bob was busy snapping photos of the plentiful and colorful flowers. As I rode first, I pointed with my motivator to show Bob something I wanted to be sure he spotted. We enjoyed the plants; in fact, if Patrick had heard us talking, he would have been convinced the reason we were so far behind was not Charlie's fault, but rather our fascination with the flora of the region. But of course, he could not, and again we were quite far behind.

After descending another thousand feet or so, Bob said, "Just wait, soon you will see the Colorado." Sure enough, after going around another bend in the trail, there it was. We were nearly at its banks, but still above the big river a little. From a distance we could see a rubber raft coming toward us. That was another way to see the spectacular canyon and river, but not for me. I'd stick to the mules. Ahead in the distance we saw a bridge spanning the river.

We knew we were going to cross on one, but Patrick yelled back that this one was not ours. We would cross farther on. It was disappointing. All of us were ready to cross the river and be at Phantom Ranch. We were hot, tired, had sore bottoms, and I was becoming worn out from trying to coax Charlie to move faster—which simply wasn't happening. Patrick knew we were all weary and tried to keep us encouraged. "Just a little farther and soon you will have ice tea or lemonade."

I shifted my weight from one very numb buttock cheek to the other. *Oh goody.*

The trail now followed the river, but it went up and down along the side of a mountain. As I looked down from the narrow path, the swirling green water of the Colorado made me feel dizzy and disorientated. Some of our group waved to the big raft as it got closer, but I kept my eyes on the trail ahead except for a quick glance now and then. It was along this path that Charlie noticed a hiker backed into a cleft of the mountain. He had passed what seemed like hundreds of them before and never even turned his eyes. For some reason this particular man was noteworthy. Charlie hesitated a step, and pricked his long ears forward. My heart skipped a beat, but the rest of me was too tired to feel any anxiety. Then just as quickly, he decided the man posed no threat and walked on.

After I reached home with my mule fascination in high gear, I read that mules take more after their sires, the donkey. A donkey does not have the extreme "flight" response to situations that a horse does. He will stand and look the situation over, deciding if he should run, fight, or just remain still. That was wonderful—a thinking equine. Charlie showed that he was thinking several places on the ride.

Finally we saw our bridge. I think we all almost broke out into song—or tears. Glory be! We were almost there.

When I got home I also researched this bridge. It is an architectural marvel, in a way. Everything to build it had to be brought down the trail by foot or mule. Before the bridge, everything had to swim the river or use a boat to get to the other side. Also before this bridge, enterprising men with their trusty mules had built a slow and treacherous cable-way completed in 1907. In 1921 a swinging bridge was constructed allowing mules and men to cross. However, wind sometimes turned the bridge upside down, so although it was better than the cable car, it was not ideal either. In 1928 a rigid suspension bridge was built. The cables were 550 feet long, weighed 2,300 pounds, and couldn't be carried by mules. Forty two Havasupai Indians were hired to lift them on their shoulders around the curves.

We saw the bridge quite a ways ahead before we would cross. First, were more rocky ups and downs. The path followed the river but not in a straight line. Bob mentioned that as hikers, he and his friends were quite disheartened to realize they had more climbing to do after reaching the bottom and the river before they could cross to the other side.

The Colorado, tunnel and The Bridge!

We entered a tunnel that was not long, but had a bend in the middle of it, which made the center dark as night. Charlie did not falter as he traipsed after his fellow mules. Thankfully, somehow he actually was on the tail of the one ahead. Almost as soon as we exited the tunnel, I saw the bridge.

It was quite a sight, not only because it signaled the end of the journey, but it *was* an engineering marvel. Suspended high above the frothing water, it looked like two fourteen-inch planks in the center for the mules to walk on with just inches to spare on the sides. The substantial sides were made from steel with a wire fabric attached to it. Relating the impending crossing to one of my horses, I knew I would never make it across, but on Charlie's back I didn't feel at all frightened, but neither did I look down. Charlie hesitated just for half a breath before stepping on the boards, checking it over to be sure it hadn't moved since the last time he had been there.

On the Bridge

The end was finally in sight. It had been quite an adventure; however, I would be glad to dismount from my trusty, but slow, mule. Charlie put his head down a little and looked at the end of the bridge too, just for half a second. My Charlie *was* careful.

I turned in my saddle and plaintively asked Bob, "How much farther?"

"Just a little more. Hang in there."

People were fishing in the Colorado with campsites along the river's banks. Even a tent looked good at this point. We passed by Hopi Indian ruins, the remains of five families' dwellings. The stone sides were visible with the fire pit close by. And then around another bend was the level path into Phantom Ranch. I breathed a deep sigh of relief. We had arrived.

I saw a building ahead, and all of a sudden our mule string came to a sudden, complete stop. It was like a traffic jam. After Charlie caught up, I craned my head around to see what had happened and saw Patrick encouraging Norman with his spurs to keep going. What in the world was that about?

We started up again, and Charlie and I came to the spot where Norman had wondered about continuing. Two big black plastic garbage bags sat close to the path. We have those monsters in Indiana too, and our horses are not likely to go past without some questions, but I was surprised about the mule. I figured they were used to anything. But those big black things had not been there last time. Charlie cocked his ears and turned his head, but didn't miss a step. Good old Charlie.

Finally, we stopped. Although eager to get out of the saddle, I wasn't sure I could straighten and move my legs. After we were pried and hauled off our mules, we endeavored to walk out of the little corral. Everyone except Patrick and the mules appeared to be lame.

Phantom Ranch was like an oasis with a bigger stream flowing beside it and several little ones running through and around the cabin area. Our guides led us to some benches where we sat with water softly misting over us. Talk about simple pleasures: a seat that didn't move and cooling water. Heaven!

"I know you are all tired and hot," Patrick admonished, "but don't do the thing I know you all desperately want to do—lie down. If you do, you will become very stiff. Walk around a bit and limber up and get the circulation moving in your legs."

Bob and I limped off to our delightful rustic stone air conditioned cabin and immediately took a nap. So much for following directions.

We awoke starving (and not stiff) and ready for our home cooked meal. Our supper was scheduled for 6 p.m. They served two meals, and seating was assigned. One would not want to miss supper.

Bob told me that the added air-conditioning was new; the last time he had hiked down only "swamp coolers" were used. We had arrived around 2 p.m. and the cabin was pretty warm with the sun beating down on the uninsulated metal roof, but by 5, the sun was starting to slide behind the tall mountain, and it began cooling down.

Bob and Rose at the Phantom Ranch Cabin

A clean shower area was provided with nice fluffy towels, all the more impressive when I remembered that all the items had been carried by trusty pack mules for our pleasures. Refreshed and clean, I wandered toward the canteen to find Bob. My stomach growled.

Time for supper didn't arrive any too soon. What a supper it was— thick tasty steaks, big baked potatoes, salad, a vegetable and chocolate cake. Golly, I have been hungry before, but food never tasted this good.

My dinner companion to the left was a gentleman from Bakersfield, California. We started talking about the ride. He and his wife Jeannie had been in the first group with Frosty. He related that his wife had a horse and rode at home, so she was in better shape than he was. My ears pricked up. A fellow horse person. Someone to talk with about the mules!

The four of us lingered after dinner and had a delightful conversation. Jeannie and I had much in common with our mules. Hers was named Betty, and Betty was a slowpoke like Charlie. I had seen Frosty's group now and then as they wove their way ahead of us on switchbacks. Frosty was ahead of his group many mule lengths, next a black mule followed, and then the rest of the pack. They were strung out too. I tried to tell myself that I was not the only one with a laggard mule, but it hadn't helped much. It was a blow to my self-worth as an experienced horse person that I couldn't encourage Charlie to keep up with the others.

Jeannie said that Frosty's mule had refused to go by the black garbage bags and he had to get off. Her mule Betty then decided to "head for the hills" off to the right side of the path. Fortunately, we were on the bottom of the canyon and there was space to go. With a little effort, Jeannie got Betty stopped and headed back to the path and into the ranch.

Chalk another up for Charlie, the trusty slowpoke; he had walked right by. Thank goodness there were no black garbage monsters along Bright Angel Trail.

Chapter Three: The Kaibab Trail

After a wonderful night's sleep, we were up for breakfast at 6:30. Hikers were fed the first meal so they could get started back up the trail before it got blistering hot. Scrambled eggs never tasted better. Pancakes were light and fluffy, and the bacon was just right. We were told that everyone who worked at Phantom Ranch had to hike down and up. Everything else was carried in on the pack mules and all the garbage—and mail— carried back out by them. The accommodations were especially luxurious considering that fact.

I headed out to the mule corral a little early; I wanted to give Charlie a pep talk. I was already dreading the long ride. We had been slow coming down, what in the world would it be like going back up?

Patrick arrived and saw me gently stroking Charlie's long ears.

"I am trying to con Charlie into walking faster," I said somewhat sheepishly.

"I don't know that conning old Charlie will work. I think you need to use that motivator…."

"Bob can attest to the fact I whacked poor Charlie's butt plenty on the way down, but it did no good," I said, sighing. I was tired already.

Patrick sort of smiled and headed back toward the cabin area, spurs clanking. Frosty's group, with Bob and Jeannie, our new friends, would head out first, and then Patrick's group would follow. It was around 70 degrees and getting warmer by the minute. It would only get hotter as we went up. The ride would be about five and a half hours and seven miles long.

When we were on our mules, Patrick gave us instructions.

"Be sure to drink your water. There is no water on the way up, but I will carry extra. We will stop frequently for mule rests and you can view the magnificent sights and take pictures. It will be hot. Be sure and keep your mule moving…."

His voice sort of trailed off as he looked straight at me, but I saw the half grin on his face and felt assured he wouldn't leave me behind.

Off we went, back across the bridge, through the tunnel, and then up the Kaibab Trail to the left, leaving the Bright Angel Trail that we'd taken down.

I looked up ahead, then down at Charlie's ears. *Oh, Charlie, what's in store for us?* But I knew Charlie knew: it was up and up and up. My legs were already exhausted just thinking about it.

Bob said, "I love the Kaibab trail. It has the prettiest scenery of all the trails. The last time I hiked the Canyon, my friends and I took the Kaibab Trail down and back up. Usually hikers come down the Kaibab and go back up Bright Angel because Kaibab it was steeper and harder to hike steeper."

Up the Kaibab

I saw immediately what he meant. Some of the path was only stone and dirt, with many of the stair steps made from timber to keep the dirt in place. Up and up Charlie had to step, and naturally, we fell more and more behind.

The Kaibab Trail is more open as it follows a ridge line out of the Canyon rather than following a fault line as the Bright Angel Trail does. The views were breathtaking. I could see farther to the sides and down and in a couple places could see the emerald green Colorado River. Patrick stopped the mules for breathers and for us to take pictures. Bob had become rather adept at taking shots as he rode. Only one or two flopped, although a lot seemed to have a view of Charlie's (and my) rear end.

When Patrick stopped the mules to rest and enjoy the views, the riders were to pull their mules' heads and turn their bodies toward the drop-off, and hook the reins over the saddle horn—the mule break. On the way to the top, Charlie was always several mule lengths behind, so when Patrick stopped, it gave time for Charlie to catch up, but it didn't give him much time to stand still, as Patrick soon moved on.

Charlie and Sleepy developed their own method of stopping. Charlie knew that very soon they would be moving again, so why should he turn his body sideways and look out over the side? It took too much effort and several more steps. He just stood still on the path. I left him alone—why bother? Sleepy and Bob saw Charlie standing on the path and did the same thing, which perhaps was a good thing in one instance.

A "Charlie Rest" with other mules correctly facing the drop off

Hikers asked, and were allowed to pass to the rear end of the mules as they stood looking out over the cliffs, hugging the back of the mountain side. Hikers are not usually animal people, I think, and don't realize what a mule might do. My shoulders tensed as the hikers squeezed by, but Charlie was oblivious.

As the last hiker in the group passed Bob and Sleepy, his walking pole hit Sleepy's rear—*again*. By now the mule was sure those guys with poles were not to be trusted, and at this moment he was absolutely positive of it. He jumped forward into Charlie who never flinched, making stones clatter. Patrick looked askance; I can only imagine what he was thinking. I know what *I* was thinking—I was getting worried for Bob.

On we went again, more up and up and more hikers. I was once more glad I was on a mule. Those people looked absolutely worn out. We said "hello," and moved on. Bob almost always said, "Hi, have a safe trip." He knew from experience about the hiking, and I think he was also thinking of himself and Sleepy. I know I was.

Starting up the trail, we had again passed through the Vishnu Schist's beautiful black rock formations, and then into the sandstone and limestone formations, and another switchback.

Bob said, "Look down there."

Two pack mule trains, packed with our garbage and the mail, were moving along at a good fast walk. I raised my eyebrows. *Hmm. I wonder what's going to happen when they catch up?* They had started out quite awhile behind us, and there was no place to pass that I could see.

Mules, Mules and More Mules

Mule Train and lots of switchbacks up and up

Patrick pointed out Little Vista, a view off to both the right and left of us. It was a panorama of rocks and crevices with dark shaded areas and some vegetation here and there.

Bob took more pictures. Around another bend and there was an even larger expanse of visionary delights. We'd come to part of the trail that seemed to be like a bridge between two points. It was down, down, down on both sides. By now the paths and trails, heights and stones in our path didn't bother me. I knew Charlie would navigate them all safely—but bless his heart, we were falling farther and farther behind again.

There was no power left at all in the motivator. All I got was a half hearted swish of his tail, if that. After Bob's last experience with Sleepy and the hiker, every time I halfheartedly hit Charlie, Bob said, "Don't hurry." I nodded. I wouldn't want to be in a hurry on a mule that had done some serious skittering around on the paths either. But there was nothing to worry about: Charley was not going to hurry.

It seemed like days, but it had only been four miles and probably three and a half hours when we reached The Hermit Shale that makes up Cedar Ridge. It is quite an expanse of fairly level ground that was 5,200 feet above sea level and 2,000 feet from the rim—and it was hot. I felt hotter going back up than I had coming down—like I was in direct path of a blast furnace—even though the temperatures were likely the same. I think it had something to do with trying to encourage Charlie to walk uphill faster. It was a tired reflex by now. I tapped his sides with my legs as I would do my horses. Of course, nothing happened. I had given up on the whip long ago.

Patrick took everyone's pictures on our mules with our own cameras and then we dismounted, if you could call it that. As we walked and limped around the site to limber up, the views were absolutely superb. We saw 6,072 foot O'Neil Butte, named for Rough Rider Bucky O'Neil towering above the landscape. It was painted with the same pinks and greens of the canyon.

Mules, Mules and More Mules

Bob and Sleepy with Rose and Charlie at the rest stop

There was a place to go potty, but I sure didn't need it. I had been drinking from my canteen every chance I got, but not while we were moving. Our stops were short because of Charlie's slowness. I had no extra liquid to contribute to the potty.

It doesn't seem like getting a drink from your canteen would be at all challenging, but it was wrapped by its small rope around the saddle horn a couple of times. You were not to just drop your reins; you were to hook them over the horn. By the time I took off the canteen, hooked the reins and then figured out what to do with the motivator, I had my hands full, and my brief "Charlie stop" was over.

Two little Kaibab squirrels were much in sight, hoping for a handout. Feeding any of the animals was strictly forbidden because they would become dependent upon easy food instead of looking for themselves. I sat in what little shade a pinyon pine tree provided, and watched one of the brownish-grey striped critters come closer and closer.

Smaller than our gray or black Indiana squirrels, this one was even more brazen, and actually climbed up on my leg. He got a peanut from me. I don't think I was the first or would be the last to feed him. After we had been pushed back up on our mules and were heading out, I pointed out to Bob a squirrel climbing up on a hiker's pack as she sat totally unaware, under a tree.

"Those little rascals know food is in a backpack and if given enough time, some of them will even undo the zipper and get inside."

I grinned. "Personal experience again?"

He just chuckled.

Before we reached Cedar Ridge, we caught up with Frosty's group, no doubt due to Betty, Jeannie's slow mule. I saw a ray of hope. I remembered that Betty was pokey like Charlie—perhaps we could go in one long, leisurely group and I wouldn't be to blame. But, no, Patrick stopped for a nice long rest, giving Frosty time to move ahead again.

Just a short while after reaching the next rest spot, the pack mules appeared. The wranglers said "Howdy" to each other as they passed, but the pack mules got no rest-stop. I wondered if this was all planned, like a real train schedule. As they trooped by, I noticed that because they were all tied together, the forward mules were "towing" the following ones. Maybe that is what Charlie wanted—a tow.

The pack mules looked none too happy having to march smartly on at a fast walk. Most of the rear ones had their heads up, being pulled along. They were not looking at the ground where they were walking. I was mystified about this, wondering how in the world they could see where to put their feet on the many treacherous spots. When I got home and began to investigate mules, I read that a mule's eyes are placed farther out on the side of his head, more like the donkey. A horse's eyes sit forward and their vision is totally different. I was flabbergasted to learn that a mule can see where he is putting all four of his hooves! That certainly explained part of their surefootedness.

Later I read that mule's eyes are *not* placed differently, and do not see differently from a horse, but since they are more careful about where they place their feet, they are sure-footed. I don't know which is true, but for whatever reason, mules, perhaps because of their strong self-preservation attribute, take more care in where they walk.

After our rest, we were hoisted back onto the mules. It took both Bob and Patrick to push me into the saddle this time; I was getting tired and couldn't help a lot. Part of the problem was the high cantle or rear of the saddle. After I got up I had to swing my stiff right knee and leg over it. My mounting was getting more and more unattractive. I wanted to ask how much longer we had to go, but held my tongue. More switchbacks were in store for us, and it was steep; it would take another hour or so to reach the top.

Final zig zag switchbacks and the top!

My feelings for Charlie had undergone yet another change. I was feeling sorry for him; I knew he was tired. He had broken out into a little sweat; Sleepy, on the other hand, was quite sweaty. By now, he looked around to his rear when any of those strange creatures with poles came near. Bringing up the rear was not a comfortable spot for him any longer.

I had thought about trading places with him. I doubted that anything would make Charlie jump forward, but if Sleepy decided to keep up with the rest of the mules, I would be left totally alone. Patrick might have to send back a scout for me.

Bob and I were not the only riders to have some problem with our mules. The rider on Nora just ahead of me had to cope with her wanting to eat everything in sight, even with her muzzle. Whenever we stopped for lookouts, Nora turned her butt away from the steep downside to hunt up some small grass blades growing on the mountain side, exactly the opposite of what we had been instructed. It seemed her rider was quite ineffectual in stopping her.

I wondered how many gray hairs Patrick got during the ride. I also understood why after sixteen years, Frosty thought it was time to do something else. Regardless of that habit, during one of the few times Charlie and I were actually close enough to hear him, Nora's rider said, "I love this mule. I think I will buy us a couple when we get home."

Charlie was moving as though he had ten pound weights on each foot. Each step seemed an effort. At one of the turns he stepped up, turned, placed his front feet on the path ahead, and came to a complete standstill with his hind feet planted on the step below.

"Come on, Charlie. Don't quit on me now," I said. Sleepy was right at his butt with nowhere to go.

After a momentary pause, Charlie continued climbing. He was not too tired to notice something not quite to his understanding, nonetheless. We saw many hikers coming down from the top of the Kaibab Trail. It was Saturday, and more were taking the trail. A person can trek down to Cedar Ridge and then back up for a short hike if he did not wish to continue down to the Tonto Trail and across to Indian Garden, or on to the Phantom Ranch.

We were approaching a sharp curve in the trail, but fortunately for my nerves, it was not one of those where the mule had to go forward to the edge and then turn. Charlie saw something and pricked up his long ears. I tensed and peered ahead. "Oh, Charlie, what do you see?" I could see absolutely nothing out of place. He did not hesitate, but went on in his slow steady pace. Ears pricked forward on one of my saddle horses at home could mean a spook was on its way, or a quick turnaround at some real or imagined monster. But nothing happened with dependable Charlie.

At one place on the Kaibab Trail, again Patrick was above me on a short switchback. He could see that, yes, there was quite a distance between me and Nora. Looking down, he called, "Come on, Miss Rose."

Talk about embarrassed. I looked up and waved, giving him a nice big grin—but Charlie would not "come on." If Charlie could have actually spoken in words, I'm pretty sure I know what he would have said. I heard them in my mind: *"Miss Rose, don't worry none. I've been up and down these trails so many times I could do them in my sleep. I'll get you to the top. There is no hurry. I know what I'm doing."*

Trusty slow-but-sure Charlie

I think his plan was to conserve his energy rather than have rest stops. At any rate it worked out the same.

That was not the end of my humiliation, however. At another big bend in the trail, all the rest of the mules and their riders were gone from sight. There were many hikers in this section and they had to wait for the mules, as we had the right of way. Patrick must have told them we were coming behind and to wait for us.

As I approached a lady with a big grin on her face, she asked, "Is this Pokey?"

At this point it was rather funny. I laughed and said, "Yes, we are the last mules."

As we continued up the trail, Sleepy had one more electrifying moment for Bob. There was no one behind them and nothing happening that Bob could attribute Sleepy's actions to. There was a scramble, the sound of loose stones or shale and Sleepy took several quick steps toward the side of the mountain. By now I think Bob wanted to get off and hike the rest of the way. Earlier, we had informed Patrick about Sleepy's escapades, and he said one of the wranglers would ride him next time and get him over *that*. Obviously those actions were not the ones for a Grand Canyon mule. Slowpoke Charlie was looking better and better.

We stopped again, for what would turn out to be our last look at the Canyon. I sat and drank in the reds, golds, and mochas of the creation, and felt so small and unimportant in this awesome universe of beauty

Patrick was talking to someone on his two way radio. I heard him say something like, "Ten minutes." I wondered and hoped that meant we would soon be up to the Rim. Sure enough, he told us our ride was nearly finished. Then he looked back at me and Charlie, grinned ear to ear, and said, "Watch Charlie now, as soon as he gets to the top he will take off at a gallop for the mule corral!" It was nice to see that Patrick had maintained his sense of humor.

That was, however, far from the truth. Charlie, Sleepy, Bob and I moseyed in about twelve mule lengths behind, amid some good natured ribbing from the rest of the group.

My first thoughts were that I had done it, but I would never do it again. It would be one of those totally memorable experiences in life to always look back upon in wonder and happiness. Now I was hot, tired, hungry and thirsty, and ready to be done with mules, dirt, sun, and beautiful vistas. This time it was harder to be dragged from Charlie's back and harder to stand. With a final pat on his rump, I said "Good-bye, Charlie," and we were off to the bus, which would take up back to the start of our ride. Bright Angel Trail and the Kaibab Trail do not join. The mules would be hauled in a trailer. Charlie would be ready for his own ride.

After a lunch with lots of cool refreshing water, a shower and a nap, and dinner with our new friends, Bob and Jeannie, it was off to bed.

The next morning I wanted to visit the mule corral and talk to Marilyn about mules in general, and Charlie in particular. We got a late start and I thought they might be gone already, but Bob went to check and told me they were still there. I got there in time to hear Marilyn's talk about using your motivator and sitting straight in the saddle. They were late also.

As I stood around the pipe corral looking for Sleepy and Charlie, I spotted Patrick. I asked him jokingly if he was going to ride Sleepy today.

He chuckled and replied, "Sleepy is at the barn."

I could see why he wouldn't want to use Sleepy today. There were many more riders on Sunday than had been on Friday when we left. Sleepy's antics wouldn't be at all helpful. Trusty Norman was standing, ready to go.

Then I asked him who got Charlie today. This time I swear he looked a trifle sheepish as he said, "He's at the barn too."

I was happy for Charlie—and for the person who would *not* be riding him that day. I questioned Patrick why they didn't put all the slow mules together.

"I really don't know," he answered, "it seems that could be a great idea."

I'm sure much more goes into picking mules for a ride than their speed, but it is a dilemma even with our Tennessee Walking Horses. They do not all gait at the same speed and I learned that to enjoy your ride, you must pick not only congenial people, but similarly gaited horses.

Just a few feet away, Bob had been talking to a hiker who had come up from Phantom Ranch. He said many people were talking about the frightened girl and the mule who had turned completely around on the narrow trail. Oh my, I could just envision it.

What would the guide do with his mule while he threaded his way back to the poor girl? How far back was she? Then I thought it was probably Nora or one like her who turned around for a blade of green to eat. Apparently mules aren't perfect, but I would forget that significant fact as I later looked for mules of my own.

Patrick was already drumming up business for another day by asking us if we were going to do the ride again. I wasn't at all sure, but

Bob said, "Well, perhaps yes, we might just do that." What *was* he thinking?

I looked at Patrick and said, "Well, maybe, but not on Charlie."

This time Patrick actually chuckled a little. "No, we wouldn't do that to you again."

I told Bob that riding the Grand Canyon was a little like having a baby. Right afterwards you are sure you will never have another, but given just a little time, the idea begins to look intriguing again.

We came home and I promptly began investigating mules. Bob began checking out another trip into our nation's beautiful wilderness.

My mule adventures were just beginning

Chapter Four: Mirabella

For thirty-six wonderful years I had bred, trained and showed Tennessee Walking Horses. But after my mule ride in the Grand Canyon, I came home with mules on the brain. I've always been fascinated with them and every now and then I thought about breeding one of my Tennessee Walking Horse mares to a male donkey to produce a mule.

I've always loved horses. I am sure I was born with that affection, sort of a soul gene. When I was four I informed my city-dwelling parents we should move to a farm and raise horses. They thought it really amusing, but we eventually did move because of Dad's school teaching job, and ended up on a farm in north central Pennsylvania. My sister Linda and I had many animal pets and finally two riding horses. It was the beginning of a long road shared with animals, especially horses.

When I married my husband Hal, in due course, we moved to a small farm in northern Indiana. In 1965 the horrible series of tornados that devastated the Midwest also destroyed our farm. My husband, our two young children, Sharon and Roger, and I survived, but all the animals were lost—either killed or sold. I was distraught about losing all my animals and buried that profound love for God's creatures deep within myself.

We built a beautiful house on the Elkhart River and became suburbanites. That state of affairs didn't last too long after ten-year-old Sharon decided she had to have a horse or life simply wouldn't be worth living. Having horses again began to sound good to me, too. After six years had passed, I was getting the horse bug again. We bought and kept three of them on a small river lot that flooded, and soon planned a move to another, bigger farm. On New Acre Farm I was finally able to fulfill that childhood dream of raising horses.

We also added two more children to our family: daughters Michal and Chessa. Sharon, Michal and Chessa went with me to many horse shows in our showing era. Son Roger wasn't as interested and my husband Hal really wasn't able to join us because of his busy one-man chiropractic business.

A few years after Sharon and Roger graduated from college, a friend introduced us to Bob. When I retired from showing and breeding horses, I wondered what would be next. Thanks to Bob and his love of the Grand Canyon, it turned out to be mules.

A friend gave me some mule magazines and I poured over them, getting little else done. It seemed mules had made it into the big time. Depending on what type of horse you cross your choice of jack (male donkey) with, you can have dressage type, Western, English, jumping and even racing mules. Some are gaited, meaning they have a smooth gait of some sort, perhaps a rack, stepping pace, foxtrot, or a running walk. Maybe they just amble, but it's smoother than trotting. All reason pointed to a gaited mule for me because of my back, but they were hard to find. When one of my friends said she knew of a four-year old gaited molly, or female mule, which was started under saddle, I bought her sight unseen. She was delivered to my door on a Saturday evening, and as easy as that, I was in the mule business.

I'd seen pictures of her and knew she was no beauty, but I thought she'd teach me about mules and I could resell her later if I wished.

Young Mirabella

I'd found a beautiful black mammoth jack in Missouri I really liked. I thought I might breed two of my Tennessee Walking mares and raise two little—hopefully gaited—mules from them. But by the time I bred the mares, they foaled, and the young mules were ready to begin riding even gently, it would be three years later. Being the impatient sort, that was too long to wait.

This molly was fifteen hands, which was a popular size for mules, I would discover. Her neck was too short to be graceful, she was definitely thin—you could see her ribs underneath her fuzzy hair—and she wouldn't look at me. My friend said that was what her donkey sire had done when she first saw him. He turned his head away and wouldn't look at her until days later when he decided she could be his friend.

One of the endearing things I learned about mules was you should treat them more like dogs than horses. They have a strong desire to bond with you, to be your buddy. The more they bonded, the better they would take care of you as you rode the trails. I wanted that. I loved my horses, but I couldn't really swear that any of them were bonded with me enough they would rather spend time with me than eat or be with their horse friends. This could be fun.

The little mule needed a name. Even though she wasn't exactly a classy lady, I'd give her a cool name. Mirabella came to mind. It seemed to suit her somehow, and it would give her something to live up to.

The first night I went out to the barn to see her before going to bed. I offered her a carrot, but she just turned her head away. I dropped it in her feed box, gave her a good scratch on the neck and left. The next morning the carrot was gone and when I offered her another piece, she took it. We were making progress.

Later that morning I got her out, tied her in the barn aisle and gave her a good brushing. Mules love attention, especially scratching their hides.

A few years ago, I'd wormed my way into the heart of a little Black Angus heifer by scratching. She and two Red Angus were to be the foundation of a small beef herd. The Red Angus were quite friendly, but Blackberry was a wild thing. The red ones loved to be scratched under their chins and on their necks. Blackberry watched all this and one day came up behind me with her chin in the air for scratching too. The way to their hearts was through a good rub. Hopefully, it would also work with Mirabella.

She enjoyed all the attention. She had big, twirly hair hanging from her long shaggy mule ears, long whiskers on her chin and muzzle, and a scraggly mane and tail. I didn't think using the electric clippers on her would be the best thing to do right off, so I used the scissors to cut out the twirlies, and cut a spot for her new halter to sit behind her ears. With a new halter she looked much more presentable. I threw her more hay and gave her more carrot pieces, which she now took very daintily from my fingers. A child could have fed them to her. My best show mare would happily take your whole hand along with *her* carrots.

Later that afternoon I took her for a walk along our bridle path. The gentleman I had purchased her from said I could lead her anywhere—or maybe he meant *he* could lead her anywhere. We'd gone a short distance when we came upon my three beef cows standing almost buried in tall grass. Up came Mirabella's head and up went the long ears as tall and stiff as could be. "What on earth are those creatures?" she seemed to say.

I scratched her neck, talked to her and jiggled my rope, all to no avail. She turned tail, dragged the rope out of my hands, and trotted off toward the barn. Well, that was no good. I'd now taught her she could get away from me. She trotted about thirty feet, stopped, and looked at the cows again. This was excellent; maybe I could catch her. She was showing some sense in not bolting to the barn, snorting all the way as a horse most likely would have done.

As I got close, she trotted off another thirty feet, stopped, and again looked at the cows. I was impressed with her thought processes, but wished she'd let me catch her. The cows, ever imbued with a great sense of humor and glee, proceeded to follow us half buried in the long grass, along the fence line. Mirabella decided the barn was the safest place and trotted back.

After I caught her, we went into the arena which also bordered the cow pasture, and where I could close the gate behind us. If she pulled away again at least she wouldn't go far. We walked calmly to the fence where the cows were now eating and paying us no mind. Mirabella hardly looked at them. I patted her, gave her a carrot and called it quits for the day.

The next morning she greeted me with her hee haw whinny, which sounded like a Model T car being started. It was quite unusual if one hadn't heard mules braying, and to me, it was a most endearing sound. We were making great progress in bonding. I didn't turn her out into the pasture with the horses because I wanted her to bond with me, not a herd of equines.

Removing my new mule from her stall, I began a training session. I wasn't paying much attention to Mirabella as I tied up Lady Blue, my Giant Schnauzer. When I turned around, the mule had put her foot on the lead line just inches away from where it attached to the halter. A horse in this situation usually will pull back dramatically, breaking something, or at the very least terrorizing himself. Mirabella calmly lifted her dainty foot off the rope before she put any pressure on it at all. I was surprised. That was notable for sure.

The wheelbarrow was standing in a corner of the arena with a few wisps of hay in it. Before I could collect her, Mirabella walked up to it and stood between the two handles. *Oh dear.* I could see a wreck coming as she tried to extricate herself. I headed toward her to back her out, but before I got there, she calmly picked up her front foot, stepped over the handle and followed it with her hind one with inches to spare.

My horses would never have been so sensible. If I hadn't gotten to them quickly enough they would have stumbled over the handles, turning the wheelbarrow over and frightening themselves in the process. Chalk up another for the mule. Days and months later my amazement and wonder at the thought processes of mules would turn to irritation and worse, but for now I was enthralled.

Mirabella followed me as I wove around the arena, stopped and backed her up. She followed at my back as if she was following another mule. I let her eat some grass. We were becoming great buddies with food, and a lot of scratching. That evening when Erica, my helper and friend, came to do chores, I decided to have her ride Mirabella. They had a successful ride over poles, between poles, and around the arena. For her reward we turned Mirabella out with the horses for the first time.

The following day I just had to tackle those long hairy ears. She would look so much better with the hair trimmed out of the insides. Using the small quiet clippers, I started to cut; she didn't object, and soon had a beautiful pair of clean clipped ears. Her coat was getting shiny from all the brushing, and with her clip job she was transforming into a real Mirabella. After her beautification process, I led her outside to show her another part of the farm, and also to test her.

She followed as docile as a dog. We walked past a pile of rocks and new rolls of fencing—guaranteed to spook my horse. She hardly looked. She followed me over big old fence posts recently pulled out of the ground and into the older small barn and down a narrow aisle with no protest.

I patted her neck and said, "Such a good girl, Mirabella. You get an A Plus and some carrots."

Mirabella had been here a week, doing quite well with her little lessons and bonding, so I asked Erica if she would like to take Mirabella on a trail ride. I would ride Hallelujah, my retired show horse, and leave the young mule to the young rider. It started out well, with the little mule standing still for Erica to mount. It sort of went downhill from there.

First off, she didn't want to go through the back paddock gate that would take us to the trail. I wanted Erica to go first, as a test, but Mirabella was having none of it. She simply would not go through the gate. Rather than make a big fuss right off the bat, I took Hallelujah through first. Eventually Mirabella followed. Next we came to a rather narrow bridge over a dry creek bed and Erica tried to get her to go across. No, NO and NOPE, not going across that scary looking thing. I took my horse across first, but still it was NO! She refused to follow.

Erica got off and tried to lead her across. She did the typical "mule thing"—planted her feet. The mosquitoes were eating me and Hallelujah alive and Mirabella showed no sign of moving. What to do? If we stopped, would that show the mule she had won? Well, no matter, we weren't getting anywhere standing at the bridge, so I opted to leave it and go on. Mirabella was very cooperative with Erica's dismounting and mounting. We continued along the trail with Mirabella leading, going along at a good walk. She was perfect in every other way for the rest of the trip.

I was getting the vibes from Mirabella that she wanted me to take her across the bridge, but at the moment that wasn't feasible. I decided as soon as I could I would lead her down and see if I could get her to cross. We'd been bonding very well; she'd followed me wherever I went ever since the cow episode.

The next day I turned her out with the day group of horses. My show horses go out at night, because I work them during the day so they are accessible to me, plus the dark of night is easier on their hair coats, causing less bleaching. I decided to get Mirabella from the pasture and work with her, but she rebelled.

My opinionated new mule decided she would take baby steps to her stall—I pulled her halter and she resisted every step of the way. When we got to her stall, she wouldn't go in. I'd asked the man I bought her from what we should do to get her to cross the bridge. He said, "Get a whip and hit her butt while you tell her to 'come up.'" I had been going to tackle the bridge that afternoon, but with these goings on, I determined that getting her into her stall would be lesson enough—and probably stressful enough for me. Why was she being so mulish today? This was the worst she had ever been.

I got my buggy whip, which is longer than a riding crop, but shorter than a lunge whip, and tapped her rear end. She went past her stall door, not in. It was interesting, though. She didn't act scared or frantic like a horse might have; she didn't fight me, she just wouldn't go through the stall door. I made her back up several stall lengths, then come forward again. She did it, but went past the door again. It was quiet insubordination that was for sure.

Finally, I got her aimed into the stall, hit her decisively with the whip and in she popped. I told her she was a good girl, rubbed her head, and then we did it again. This time she went in nicely. She had given in easily; a session with a horse could have been more dramatic. Again, I was impressed, but would she remember next time?

The following morning she went into her stall like a perfect lady. Yes, indeed, she had remembered. I figured I should work with her some more in the barn arena before tackling the bridge. It was still hot and I didn't want to get into a fight I couldn't win. I needed more practice getting her to go where I led or pointed her. I dragged out my ten-foot jumping poles and made a bridge by laying two alongside each other. I put plastic feed sacks in the narrow path between them. I led her to it and she followed with no hesitation, even stepping on the plastic. Well, that wasn't hard; I'd make it more difficult. I dragged over a bale of hay and put it at the beginning of my "bridge" so she would have to walk over the hay before she could enter. Stepping gracefully, she picked up each foot and daintily placed it over the bale. "Too easy," she seemed to say.

This little mule impressed me in many ways. Her quiet manner, even while being obstinate, being willing to try new things with no hesitation—at least on the ground and away from the bridge—and remembering each lesson, was grand. I knew all mules weren't like Mirabella was at that moment, but she was giving me a gentle education, one that I could handle.

Mirabella was good for me. She had excited my senses again, got me wanting to train something once more. All my horses were aged and quite well trained. For a season, I thought that was all I wanted; now I was becoming interested in teaching once more. It was fun not to have to repeat every lesson over and over. Mirabella "got it."

After a few days, I got up my nerve to ride her in the inside arena. There was no one else around and I wasn't going to take any unnecessary chances. She stood well for me to mount and walked off when I directed her to go. Steering was a little iffy, and stopping was a lot iffy. She would need more of a handle before I felt brave enough to ride her on the trail. Riding around and around an arena that is only sixty feet wide and 130 feet long is rather boring for any horse or mule. I likened it to doing exercises or homework, but it would make a better animal.

Mirabella had no use for it at all. She didn't know how to stay on the rail (go around the perimeter), and she kept cutting the corners and drifting in to the middle. We practiced turning—I had to pull her head way around. With a well-trained animal, just the squeeze of the reins is enough of a signal. I'd been told that mules pull against you if you just pulled back on the reins to stop. They could set their jaw and stiffen their necks and pull just as hard as you did. One way to stop was to teach them to turn their heads around just a little, or if necessary, if they went too fast or—horrors—bolted or ran away, you would pull them in a small circle to stop. But don't try to out pull them. We worked on this for awhile and then stopped.

In the back of my mind was the thought I really needed to take her to the narrow bridge she had refused to cross, and see if I could lead her over it, but the weather continued hot and humid, and I put it off again.

I had no desire to end up with a stubborn mule on an intolerable July day.

A few days later the weather changed to something more pleasant. Today was the day. Would Mirabella trust me and go across? How long would we be there?

With some trepidation, I dug out my old rope training halter that hadn't been used in quite some time, put it on her and started walking down the lane to the bridge. She followed quietly past new rolls of fencing and new shiny gates. As we got closer to the bridge, she slowed her walk; she remembered the place, all right. I took a firm hold on the rope and walked purposefully towards it.

We got no farther than she had gone when Erica was with her. I told her to "Come up." Nothing happened. I'd taken a small riding crop with me; I decided against the longer driving whip, which would be more confrontational. I popped her butt with the whip and she went around me in a circle. With that momentum, I took a step onto the dirt of the bridge. She skirted it nicely.

We had been doing this dance for fifteen minutes and I was getting aggravated, to say the least. Darn stubborn mule! Again I pulled harder on the halter rope, and *pop*, the halter came untied, and there was Mirabella standing, looking at me with no halter on. "Well, dang," I muttered, "that just tears it. Now she will run to the barn and I will have really taught her that this is a bad place."

I don't know who was more surprised, Mirabella or I, when she just stood there looking at me with those big brown mule eyes. A look of pity seemed to emanate from them. Pity for this poor human who thought she could coerce a mule to go where it didn't desire to go. I was surprised that she was still standing there. I took a handful of grass and offered it to her. As she ate it, I replaced the halter, telling her she was a good mule. A horse would have no doubt spun around and farted as it galloped back to the barn with not a backward glance, as if to say, "Take that!"

But we still had to cross the bridge.

Mirabella was not fighting me in any way, she simply was not moving. I was near tears. This was not what I wanted or had in mind when I got a "broke" mule. The man I had gotten her from had just told me he'd sold the rest of his mules and I was of the mind to go to the house, phone him, and tell him to sell Mirabella too. I was fed up.

I know she read my mind because immediately she took one step closer. My heart almost stopped. I petted her and told her all she had to do was cross the darn bridge. I tugged more, and she took another tenuous step, and then another. Then she backed all the way off. That was okay. I was so happy that she was doing something besides planting her feet in one spot.

It didn't take too much longer before she walked to the middle, step by slow methodical step, and then with no fanfare or horsey type excitement, such as running over the person leading her over an "animal eating bridge," she calmly walked the remainder of the way. I let her eat grass on the other side and then wondered if getting her to go back across would take just as long. It didn't. She simply followed me back over and then back again. One simple lesson and she was good to go.

I was so incredibly happy. It meant some kind of breakthrough for us. She had trusted me and no harm had come to either of us. I led her home with a big smile on my face.

Chapter Five: Mirabella the Trail Mule

By now Mirabella was bored silly with riding in my arena and her heart definitely wasn't in it. She turned, stopped, and more or less stayed on the rail, but she wouldn't go faster than a slow pokey walk and that was no fun for me. I decided the time had come to try her outside, but I didn't want to ride her alone. The next chance Erica had, she took Nugget, my gentle, quiet, older mare, and I rode Mirabella.

Mirabella moved in behind Nugget like a real trail mule, head to tail. She had no desire to pass herd boss Nugget. We walked and talked, enjoying the trail like experienced pairs. When we got a little way from the barn, all of a sudden, Mirabella sped past Nugget at a big bold trot.

"Whoa, whoa!" I yelled none too quietly. It was reflex to pull straight back on the reins, and sure enough, Mirabella totally disregarded the pull and kept going. All this happened in seconds, but it seemed longer to me as thoughts of a mule runaway flashed through my mind. Then my brain began to function and I remembered to pull on one rein and turn her head around. It worked like a charm; she turned her head, took a few steps on a circle and came to a complete stop.

As I was congratulating myself on my expert mule riding, I saw Erica's dog Ginger who had come dashing up behind Mirabella. At the same moment, all of us realized what had happened, and actually Mirabella's actions had been natural and not outlandish at all. Good old Nugget paid absolutely no attention to the happenings, but Mirabella had been intelligent in her response to listen to me and turn around. We went the rest of the ride with Ginger following or trotting along beside us. Mirabella kept her eye on the dog, but otherwise was accepting. We had locked Ginger in the barn, but she was accustomed to joining Erica in her rides, and had figured out a way to escape.

The rest of the ride happened without incident, including crossing the little bridge two times. She never looked twice, in fact seemed to cross with delight. Our ride had been a huge success. One can't count on an animal doing nothing in the face of some startling occurrence, but reacting sanely is a huge accomplishment.

Our next ride, I took alone. My biggest problem was mounting. Mirabella absolutely would not come up to the mounting block for me—and she had been. Finally in exasperation, I decided to outsmart her and get on in the barn aisle, using a milk crate. She is not as big as the other horses, and even with my creaky knees, I thought I could manage. The aisle would keep her from going sideways, but not backward.

The little dickens backed up every time I got ready to put my foot in the stirrup. If I were younger and spryer, it wouldn't be a problem. This was not good; I couldn't let her get away with such bad behavior. I slapped her neck and told her in no uncertain words that she was being very bad.

I had worried about disciplining a mule. I talked to several mule breeders and trainers how to handle some situations. They all assured me you needed to make them mind you, and you could punish them if necessary. The main thing seemed to be that whereas a horse might forgive you if you were not completely fair, or got carried away with your punishment, a mule would not. They have a high degree of what is reasonable and correct chastisement.

After the second set of slaps on the neck, Mirabella stood absolutely still; she didn't even twitch her long ears as I climbed on her back. I got to thinking this was strange, and perhaps her saddle was not comfortable. I promised her I would find a solution.

I rode past Hal, my husband, who was building a fence; she never bobbled. We went back the lane into the hay field with all the hay equipment, which looked like prehistoric monsters. Most horses have some degree of fear of them. She never wavered, just walked in, around and back out. I was getting that silly grin on my face again!

I didn't have time for Mirabella for several days—days during which she decided to become just a little naughty. The horse herd had accepted her, and Sugar Plum, a young mare, had determined that having a special friend more her own age was cool. Now when it was time to go out to pasture, the mule started making a racket in her stall, pawing and hitting the door, and worse, pushing her head and neck out the half door of the stall until I feared the door might break.

By the time I got to her stall to open it, she had worked herself into a state of agitation. I knew if I just opened the door, she would crash out and a bad habit would be formed. I opened it and flicked my hands in her face, saying, "NO!" She backed off and as soon as she stood quietly, I said, "Okay," and stood back. Mirabella was forgetting that *I* was supposed to be herd boss.

Finding a correct saddle fit for the mule was turning into a big quandary. She was young and hadn't finished growing. Her withers were lower than her hips and every saddle slid forward. She definitely needed a crupper or britching to keep it in place, and I didn't have any. This could be her permanent conformation, but I hoped not. Young horses, and I guessed, mules too, grew in stages. First the rump, then later the withers caught up. If I was lucky when Mirabella finished growing, she would be nearly level.

The next saddle I hoped would work on Mirabella didn't. Now I was back to square one and I couldn't ride her knowing that the saddle wouldn't fit right. With owning, showing and training my Tennessee Walking Horses, I had learned quite a lesson on saddle fit. My prized show and breeding stallion, Praise Hallelujah, was extremely talented. One day his show saddle started creaking. Upon investigation, it turned out the tree had broken. This actually had worked to the horse's advantage because it let his shoulders move more freely. He became awesome, not just great.

That set me forth on nearly a year's investigation for proper saddle fit. After much money, frustration and time, I found one that both the horse and I liked, but it never allowed him the extreme freedom of movement that his broken saddle had provided. Golly, I sure didn't want to do an extensive saddle search again for a mule!

By good fortune, the Great Celebration Mule and Donkey Show, was being held in Shelbyville, Tennessee, in a few weekends, and I planned to go. I could investigate mules, mule saddles, and mule people. It sounded like great fun. Maybe I might even get another mule. Mirabella was spoiling me.

During the Celebration, I got more information on saddles for mules, and also realized a lot of the mules at the Celebration wore western saddles like the one I already owned. I bought a mule saddle pad designed with a special insert in the front to make the saddle level. Now when I got home, I was all set to ride Mirabella.

I desired to ride her by myself like I rode my horses, because when others riders had time to ride, I didn't. I asked Bob if he would drive the golf cart around the field as he did when he took his dog Hershey for a walk. He volunteered to walk with me instead. Off we started, Bob and Hershey and Mirabella and I. At first Mirabella followed Bob as she had Nugget, but she walked faster and soon we were ahead with Hershey trotting first in the front and then in the rear. There was one bridge over our stream that I hadn't yet tried to cross with her. It was wide enough for the Kubota tractor to go over, but it was only a hump of dirt, and it had no sides. With the water flowing under it, it was just a little scary. I wanted to try it, but didn't want to get into a big hassle. I kept debating with myself whether to try. When we got to it, Bob said, "Maybe you should try while I am here."

Mirabella had been good with the rest of the trail. She had spooked a couple times, but it was not violent, and she had gone on. Did I want to risk our truly good ride? I decided that I did, and approached it right after Bob and Hershey crossed over. Nope, she wouldn't cross. I tried a couple times and was about to give up and try another day, but Bob said, "Do you want me to lead her across?"

Remembering what a time I had leading her across the other one, I almost said "No," but instead agreed to try. He grasped the left side of her bridle, walked off and she followed with no fuss at all. There came that silly grin again.

When we reached the barn, I gave her a big hug, lots of scratches and several carrots—then I did something special for her—I gave her mane the "mule cut." Her mane was about eight inches long, but it didn't do anything for her appearance. In fact it seemed to accentuate her short neck. I took the scissors and hacked off most of it, leaving only two inches to stand up straight. It wasn't level, sometime I would have to do a better job, but this was sort of like a Girl Scout badge. She had passed a test and I was proud and pleased with her.

Several days later I decided to join two other riders with Mirabella. I wanted to see how she would do in a larger group and I wanted to take her to the neighbor's woods that had a stream meandering through it, giving several chances to cross water. Since one of the other horses was known not to cross water, we opted for the no water route. I rode at the end and Mirabella was perfect. She did a couple mule things that made me smile. One of the little downgrades went into a wet muddy area.

The horse I was following tried to skirt around it, but that way took him into some brambles. When Mirabella got there, she calmly took her little mule steps off to the side that was the driest. In another spot the trail was muddy in the middle. Both horses squished through the mud while Mirabella daintily stepped off to the side. Either way was safe, it was just interesting to me that she assessed the path and realized that she didn't need to break stride, but neither did she need to step in the mud. By now, I was gaining confidence in my mule.

On this ride we would encounter water. Erica was determined to teach the other horse to cross. Our first crossing was the hardest because it was wider and steeper into the flowing water. This was no torrent, or real daunting crossing. Any experienced trail rider would scoff at the degree of difficulty, but to our green mounts, it was enough. The first two were experienced and went right across. Mirabella was next and she went across too, but after fooling me into thinking she was going to calmly walk across, she jumped it. Oh, well, at least we were across and she was calm.

The next day we had three horses and riders. I led the group for a ways because I wanted to see how Mirabella would be if I rode alone. She did fine, twitching her long ears back and forth as Ginger, Erica's dog, went back and forth beside her, in front and behind her. We crossed the bridge with no sides as we were in the lead, and we were off to a great start.

Later I changed positions and rode second. Mirabella immediately began to fuss, turning her head first to the right and then the left, and speeding up into the tail of the first horse. It dawned on me that the last horse was from another pasture, not one of her herd buddies and she did not like him on her tail. Someday I would have to figure that one out, but for today, I moved into first place again where she had a familiar mare on her tail. Oh, Mirabella, you were certainly making this ride interesting. How interesting I had yet to discover.

When we came upon our first and the scariest water crossing, I had to encourage Mirabella to go through it—and she jumped it again, but this time I was prepared and hung onto the saddle horn. There was another water crossing very soon. This one was broad and shallow, but very muddy. I was in the lead and Mirabella balked. She wanted nothing to do with it. She abruptly decided to turn left and go through the trees, knocking my knee in the process. I got her turned back around and headed to the water. Cashmier, the other mare, hesitated just a little, but when she crossed, so did Mirabella.

That was not the end of it, however. Now Mirabella was upset; all she wanted was to go home as fast as possible. She didn't run off, but she wouldn't settle on the bit. Instead she chose to flip her head up as high as she could. In that position I had little control.

I was becoming frustrated. She wasn't dangerous, but I certainly wasn't having any fun. We had one more gentle, easy creek to go over. She crossed safely, but was still in an awful hurry to go home and put the woods and stream behind her. The down slope with the muddy bottom where on the first ride she had been so careful, she charged down, not heeding where she was going. Again, it wasn't dangerous, just annoying. I could see by all this behavior that she was definitely in need of more training.

As we got closer to home, she settled down. None of my current horses were barn sour. In the way distant past I'd owned one and soon sold her. They are a true pain. I'd just watched a DVD on mule training by Steve Edwards where he admonished his viewers to never encourage a mule who loves to hurry home more than being ridden. I had plans for Mirabella when we got back. She sure was not going into the barn and her stall. No carrots for her either!

She was so perfect the rest of the ride, I almost forgave her, but knowing she really needed to learn this "do *not* rush home" lesson, as soon as we reached the barn, I rode her in the inside arena for ten minutes. Next we went outside to the arena and rode. She was a little slow about it and wanted to go out the gate and back to the barn, but she wasn't nasty. Back into the inside arena again and then back to the outside one. After 20 minutes of riding I put her away. No brushing, no carrot and no petting. I didn't allow her to go outside that night with her friends. She stayed in her stall.

I had a theory about her behavior, other than lack of training. Mary Long is an animal communicator, much like the lady on television who talks to animals. Animal communicators have become quite popular and with good reason—many owners wish to understand just what makes their pet tick. My animal communicator friend and I had visited with Mirabella soon after I'd purchased her. I firmly believe people can communicate on another level with their animals. Even as a child, one of my greatest passions was to talk to animals. In my much later adult years and after meeting Mary, I actually had become more adept at "hearing" their silent voices. Mary does it so well, it is an occupation for her.

In our conversation with Mirabella, she told us she was *my* mule. I was looking at other mules to purchase, and she was miffed. She said any other mule could be Bob's mule, but she was mine. Indeed she had bonded very strongly in just a short time. I think possibly because she'd never had an owner who was interested in bonding with her. She'd only had her breeder and the trainer up until I purchased her. People, myself included, talk about how a dog or cat "chose" them. Well, Mirabella had chosen *me*.

While at the Mule Celebration, I eventually found and purchased Samson, another mule. He was older and better trained, and in my mind—magnificent. Mirabella was jealous. My plan now was to take the two mules on the trails and ride with Bob. I was working with her so Bob could ride her and follow the other mule. She was rebelling and sabotaging my plan. She did not want to be "Bob's mule!"

The next few days after our disappointing ride, the weather turned very hot and humid; the mosquitoes took over the woods and riding there was put on hold. Mirabella needed more lessons at any rate, so we stayed in the arenas. I had worked with the farrier to put a heavier shoe on her rear feet and leave the front barefooted. This was to help her swing her hind legs underneath her and start to gait better. I bought Mirabella as a gaited mule, but she really didn't gait.

Sometimes plans just change. It was nobody's fault that Mirabella couldn't gait or match Samson's longer and faster stride except at a trot. Even with the heavier hind shoe, she was simply gaited differently. It might take months, or even years for her to develop a faster gait, if at all. My horse friend Connie, and her good trail riding buddy Alice, came one day to see my new mule. Alice rode a mule named Colonel, and told me after she'd met Mirabella that if I ever wanted to sell her, to be sure and let her know.

I gave much thought to my next step with Mirabella. She was a truly wonderful, sweet little mule, but she wasn't working out for my plans, so I called Alice. In a few days she came with her daughter Lori, and her own mule, Colonel.

I rode Mirabella, Alice rode her, Lori rode her, and then Lori and Alice rode together with Colonel. The two mules seemed to like each other. Mirabella was very particular about her horse trail companions and didn't like several of them. She was happy to ride beside, in front of, or behind Colonel. Thank goodness for that. I had warned Mirabella not to sabotage this opportunity for her to have a great new home. It seemed she had listened.

We tried several saddles, different riders got on and off. This can make an animal grumpy. It is like they'd say, "Well, make up your mind and get on with it. I want to go back to my stall." She took it all with good grace. When Erica went by with the feed cart, her long ears swept forward and she took steps to follow it. When gently reminded she had other things to attend to, she acquiesced. Lori wanted to see if Mirabella would stand still while she put on her raincoat. The mule did. Next Lori, Mirabella, Alice and Colonel all went outside into the rain to ride. Mirabella was simply perfect.

Lori said she'd buy her right then, but the next thing was loading her into the horse trailer; I was just a little worried because she'd not been in one since she arrived several months ago. This one had a ramp to walk up; the one she'd come in was a step up trailer. This was new to her and it was raining hard. She took hesitant steps up, and then backed back down. After a few tries and a handful of hay in front of her nose, she went in. As I went to the front of the trailer to bid her a final "goodbye," she was happily munching hay. The vibe she gave me was that she was looking forward to her new "adventures."

I got secondhand news of Mirabella in her new home by my friend, Connie, who kept me updated on her new life. The first news wasn't real encouraging. The mule had a pasture with an open stall so she could go in and out as she pleased, but she was pacing the fence. Lori remedied that by putting another mule beside her. I was trying a heavy shoe on her rear feet to help her gait, but she was slipping on the wet grass, so Lori wanted to have them removed. Apparently Mirabella was quite uncooperative. I was surprised, as she had been very good for my farrier.

"Don't worry," Connie admonished me. "Lori is an animal person. She will figure it all out. She will spend lots of time with Mirabella and won't rush things."

The next I heard was Mirabella and Lori had been on a short ride with another horse, meeting a car and truck on the road. I never rode near traffic, but that went well also. The little mule was still taking things in stride.

My next email message from Connie made me laugh. It started out with: "Bulletin! Bulletin! Bulletin! Mirabella went on a real trail ride today with five other critters (four horses and Colonel.) We went up and down hills, over logs and even over a tree trunk that was about two feet in diameter and even up off the ground a little. No sweat. We went through trails where you had to go single file, and trails where you could ride side by side. We went thru brambles and along little trails that had steep drop-offs on one side. She was in the back and also in three other positions. She was really good. Lori had a big smile on her face and said, 'I can't fault her on this one.' Mirabella's big ears were flopping and that's the sign of a happy mule. I think she loved the trail ride! At first we were all afraid that the group would be too big and she would freak out but, other than the fact that she really doesn't want any other critter coming up on her butt, she couldn't have cared less. Really a good day. The weather was perfect and there were no bugs at all. We had a great ride. I think we were out about two and a half hours again."

I remembered my Mirabella smiley faces. I was so pleased that Lori was enjoying them too.

About this same time, I had my first trail ride on Samson, my new big mule. On that ride we encountered "Devil's Drop." It was about a very steep down-slope and was probably fifty feet long. It was quite an experience—one I was not really prepared for. I told Connie to let me know when Mirabella did one of those. She reported Mirabella already had. It was in a different area, but the drop was about the same steepness and longer. There had been no hesitation on going down the drop, but she wanted to hurry. This is a place where hurrying can become trouble, but she would learn. She had a wonderful new owner and rider and being her usual calm and reliable self, she would certainly be allowed the opportunities to become a very *special* mule.

Chapter Six: Samson - One Big Mule

Mirabella had taught me some things about mules, but she wasn't completely trained, and she didn't have the smooth gait I was looking for. I had bred Faith, one of my mares, to Lonesome, a gaited jack—or male donkey—in the hopes of raising my own gaited mule. Neither of these mule projects provided me with a gaited mule to ride right now. I wasn't known for patience when presented with a mission, so I planned on buying yet another mule—this time one that I could ride and gait anywhere—my "perfect mule."

The Mule and Donkey Celebration was to be held in Shelbyville, Tennessee, the first part of July, and it just so happened that I and Carolyn, one of my closest horse friends, were able to travel from northern Indiana to the show. I'd been doing a lot of research on the Internet and found some mules that would indeed be at the Celebration. I was going with my horse trailer and the checkbook, not a good combination under different circumstances.

I could hardly contain my enthusiasm as we ate breakfast; I wanted to see mules! We arrived at the show grounds in time to view the barrel races, which were a timed event. I was fairly amazed; I never imagined a mule could run that fast.

The first stable we visited had some very pretty mules, but nothing I wanted to buy. One black john, or gelding mule, had the most exquisite face—just as refined as a horse, only with long ears. The owner was forthright in telling me that he needed a strong rider, as he had a mind of his own. Forget that, I was after the perfect mule.

Next we went to Locust Creek stable, another place on my list. First I rode a molly. She was a trail mule about the size of Mirabella. She had a relatively smooth gait, but she wasn't as well trained as I wanted. I guessed I'd need to jump up to more dollars and look at the show mules. He had two that were for sale, both johns. I really wanted a molly, but decided to start checking out the boys—just in case. One was a beautiful spotted show and trail mule, the other was a huge black mule.

"How tall *is* he, anyway?" I asked.

Bubba was 16'3 hands. Now that *was* a big mule. It didn't matter to me if he was too big to get on, with my back and knees, I couldn't get on a small one either without a step aid, so what the heck, I might just as well try him out.

I decided to ride the spotted one first; he was quite beautiful with white spots on a brown body, and unlike most mules, he had a full-grown mane like a horse. He was a perfect medium size—not as tall as Bubba, but not small like a pony.

One of my requirements was that the mule had to canter; I loved to canter. There was nothing like it—the breeze in your face and a great animal underneath you, as you smoothly cover the ground at a controlled gallop—yes, I wanted my mule to canter. I was finding out not all mules were trained to canter or lope.

The spotted one did everything very well, including canter, but we didn't click. I had already been told he was a mule who did his job, but was not an "in your pocket" type of mule. I could have lived with that—maybe. Perhaps I could have won him over with carrots and lots of scratching, but maybe not. I have a great mare that I love dearly and enjoyed riding in the show ring and on the trail. She was totally dependable and talented—but she wasn't one that wanted close human companionship. She could take me or leave me as long as I took care of her. I wanted a buddy mule. So I crossed this one off the list.

Bubba was next on the list and was saddled and led to the arena where the big black mule sidled over to the fence, and I climbed aboard. He gave me a superb ride, and I felt very safe, but darn, he was *so* huge.

Carolyn and I'd met his owner earlier in the afternoon, and he told me how much enjoyment Bubba had given him and how wonderful he was. I told him I would buy him. After making a momentous decision such as this, I began second-guessing myself. What had I done? Did I really need a very big black john mule in my life? In the evening,

Carolyn and I went to the warm up area to watch for Bubba where he was going to be shown by his owner. All doubts and second thoughts left my mind when I saw the back number on Bubba's rider. It was 500, the same number I used on my Tennessee Walker stallion, Praise Hallelujah, for so many, many wonderful shows and wins. It was a sign from Above—Bubba was surely meant to be mine.

The next morning was Sunday, and we met the trainer at the show grounds. He loaded Bubba into the trailer, we said our "good-byes," and were off to Indiana. Our horse trailer had drop down doors on the side windows for air flow as we moved and slip-down bars that could be opened to allow the animals to stick their heads out whenever we stopped. All the past occupants loved to crane their necks out and around to see what was going on as we filled the truck with gas.

Our first stop was for Carolyn to catch a quick nap. I got out, opened Bubba's window bar, and left for the restroom. When I came out of the building I saw his big head sticking out of the opening, but he was quiet. He, too, was taking a nap while the trailer wasn't moving. I decided to sit on a bench and give Carolyn twenty minutes to sleep before most likely disturbing her as I got back in the truck. I observed Bubba as two different truckers walked past him to their vehicles. As each one got close, he quietly pulled his head back inside. They had no interest in mules and never gave him a look. I wondered what would happen when I walked toward the trailer. Would he pull back for me, too? Or be happy to see me coming?

Time to hit the road north again and I headed to the trailer, watching Bubba as I went. I noted happily that he turned and looked toward me and didn't pull his head away. Oh, goody. Such a small thing, but great. I had high hopes for Bubba and me becoming the best of friends. This was a beginning....

We arrived home at 11:11 p.m. (a lucky number for me) and my life with Bubba had begun. A lot of the way home I had been thinking about a different name for him, but my mind was a blank. He'd had his name for ten years, it seemed a little strange to want a change, but "Bubba" just didn't do it for me.

The next morning I awoke with the name "Samson" flooding my mind and Samson it was. It was entirely fitting. He was much too elegant a mule to be a "Bubba."

Samson looked even bigger in my barn aisle than he had at the show grounds tied in front of his stall. Good grief, what had I done to myself? He was mammoth, bigger than Nugget, my largest Tennessee Walking Horse mare. I groomed, petted and scratched, and then started to clean out his feet where the dirt became packed into the space created by the shoe. Samson had had "thrush," a hoof condition that affected the bottom of the foot. He'd been treated for it and sometimes the treatment caused pain. As soon as I picked his front foot up, he yanked it forward out of my hand and stomped it down millimeters from my own foot. Hmm. I couldn't out-power him but I sure didn't want this big creature to get the better of me either. I tried again, and again he snatched it away. I understood that he was anticipating being hurt, but at this rate, I was the one likely to be harmed.

The next time he pulled away, I turned and looked him in the eye and slapped his neck as hard as I could with my open palm. It was like hitting the side of the barn and was more for effect than any real punishment. I yelled at him loudly, picked his foot up again and it never moved an inch. Along with expecting pain, I'm sure he was also testing me. If I'd given up, he would have filed that away in his mind, and I would have been starting down the wrong path with my new big mule. I knew I could get away with that type of reprimand with my horses, but how would a mule react?

I was a beginner at this business. I remembered hearing that mules would take punishment if it was justified and if the punishment fit the crime. Hitting him with a whip, for instance, would have been too harsh. I didn't think whipping mules had a favorable outcome anyway. I was told by one of the mule trainers I'd met at the mule show, that mules "go numb" if they're beaten. A horse would become frantic. And a mule could hate you for it—waiting until he could get even. It would make discipline by the owner more creative, not reactive.

I did more ground work with Samson before deciding to ride him. He'd been extremely gentle and trustworthy at the mule show with his owner and trainer, but I didn't know him, he didn't really know me, and goodness, was he ever *big*. After three days of grooming, leading him around and letting him eat grass with me holding his lead rope, I decided it was time for the first ride. I was a wee bit nervous, and had Erica stay with me.

The first problem to be presented was that I didn't have a bridle big enough to fit his head. Erica and I squeezed Samson's face into a bridle that was too small, and used a bit in his mouth that I'm sure he didn't like. I'd forgotten to ask what bit he liked when I bought him, and unfortunately the trainer who sold him to me never answered his telephone when I called for help. That was very irritating. I would figure out all these things myself eventually, but I could have succeeded sooner and *much* happier with advice.

My saddle fit him well because his back was more horse-like than Mirabella's—at least it was level. I was only planning to ride him a few minutes in the indoor arena, so the bad-fitting bridle shouldn't cause too big a problem. I'd had to leave off the nosepiece and the throat latch because they wouldn't reach around his nose or chin. The brow band that went across the front of his forehead was too short, but at least the bit would stay in his mouth. On we went to the mounting block—and there I discovered another obstacle—I couldn't get on my mule!

First of all, he didn't like the mount block anymore than any other new horse, and I couldn't get him positioned right for me to step on. I was more than a little disappointed. At the show where I had ridden him, he had sidled over to the arena fence that I could climb on and then step over onto his back. I'd hoped he would cope better with the mount block.

With Erica's help from the ground we eventually got him in the right place—but I still couldn't mount. I couldn't figure out what the heck my problem was. Surely he wasn't that much taller than Nugget. When I put my foot into the stirrup I didn't seem to have a way to pull myself into the saddle. Samson was a big mule, but his back was not broad and his withers were not defined, although he did have some, unlike Mirabella who was like riding a rail. Finally, with Erica holding the saddle in place I hauled my body into place. Samson wasn't the greatest help either. As soon as I got ready to pull myself up and in the saddle, he backed up a step.

I rode him for ten minutes, but that was long enough for Erica to be impressed with his size and his gait under saddle. I didn't have any better luck getting him to the mounting block to get off either.

"Help!" I yelled to Erica.

This was just great. A splendid mule I couldn't get on or off.

I was truly frustrated. *Why* couldn't I get on my mule? Bob offered to come out anytime I wanted to ride and hold the saddle for me, or even make a higher mounting block, and I took him up on the saddle holding job.

It dawned on me while I was studying bridle parts that there was one horse in the barn that had a head as big as Samson's. It was Erica's Percheron gelding, Maximus. I borrowed the bridle and eagerly put it on Samson, then started through my bit collection to find one that he would like.

True to his word, Bob came out to the barn two mornings and helped me mount Samson. I was able to dismount by myself, as Samson was learning to cope with the mounting block. I took easy rides around the barnyard and outside arena. I was approaching this with great care. I didn't know Samson well and I didn't want any surprises.

After a couple rides with Bob's help in mounting, I still couldn't figure out what was the big difference in getting on Nugget and getting on Samson. I saddled Nugget and prepared to mount, paying close attention to exactly how I did it. Position mare, grasp the reins in my right hand, place my left foot in the stirrup and grasp her mane with my left hand to steady and pull myself into the saddle. *That was it! The mane!* Samson had NO MANE! His had been cut off slick to his neck—it was the "mule style." My handle was missing.

After having some chuckles and heaving a big sigh of relief, I knew Samson was going to have to keep some of his mane. I was told that mules didn't usually have pretty manes like a horse. Theirs sort of go straight up for three or so inches, and then fall over the side of the neck, therefore usually they're clipped off.

Just a few days after this discovery, his mane had grown out an inch, but lo and behold, it was enough for me to grasp and steady my descent into the saddle. Finally, we were ready for bigger and better things. The saddle fit, the bridle fit, I could get on and off by myself—and my mule really liked me.

Samson was wonderful to ride. As I ventured out farther and farther on the farm trail by myself, my confidence in my mule grew. He looked at things, but tipping his head and cocking his ears toward the item of his concern was all he did. I was pleased with my big boy.

Chapter Seven: Miss Ellie

After finding the perfect home for Mirabella, I began another search for the next mule. This one would be Bob's. Our goal was still to become well mounted on safe trail mules and ride some of the beautiful parks near and far. I re-contacted folks I'd met when searching for my second mule, but came up empty. One day I was looking at one of the mule magazine classified sections and my eyes fell on an ad that sounded really good. "For Sale: Miss Ellie, five-year-old, 16 hand black Walking Horse molly. Well mannered and gaited. Over 500 trail miles."

I originally wanted a molly mule when I found Samson, so Miss Ellie sounded super. She was big enough to keep up with Samson, if she was gaited well enough. The part about 500 trail miles sounded *real* good. I called, got pictures and a video. Bob said, "When do we leave?" I guess he liked what he saw, plus he'd been smitten with the idea of riding. She was in Missouri, about eight hours away through easy driving country.

With Hal's blessing or maybe resignation, Bob hooked up the trailer and we headed out. We stayed in contact with John and Bonnie as we traveled, and when we pulled into their driveway around 3:00 p.m., two mules and a horse were all saddled ready to ride. Because of the lateness of the day, and our leaving the next morning, there was little time to waste. We trailered about fifteen minutes away to a beautiful park.

John had me lead off on Miss Ellie, he followed on Rosie, and Bob rode a cute little Paso mare. Miss Ellie seemed right at home going up and down, across mud and paved roads, and many more ups and downs. We rode for about an hour and a half, and then headed back to the trailer. Ellie never hesitated long—she looked at rocks and stumps, assessing their danger index, but even went first when John's mule, Rosy, waited too long looking at a weird appearing stump. I was sold on Miss Ellie and bought her on the spot.

Miss Ellie was a pretty molly. She looked a lot like my Samson. She had big kind eyes and long ears. Her back was good, my saddle, which I brought along, fit her just fine. She had a good fast walk but her faster gait was slower than Samson's. It needed to be more consistent and a little faster, but I could tell she was not like Mirabella; she would be able to improve.

The next morning we went to load her in the trailer which was sitting so that its rear was very high off the ground. I asked John if we needed to re-position it so she could get in. "No," he said, "she will jump in just fine."

I took the lead rope, climbed into the trailer and gently tugged on the rope. Up she came and even though she jumped in, it was an easy landing. "Mules jump differently from horses. They land 1-2-3-4, each foot hitting separately," John said.

Miss Ellie traveled well. She had a toe tapping routine that I could have lived without. When we stopped, she would tap, tap, tap the trailer floor. It was a very lady-like pawing habit, and at least she did not bang on the side of the trailer. Nine hours later we arrived home.

One of the nice things about Ellie was she was used to a mounting block. I shouldn't have to spend hours getting her to stand while we got on. When we rode at the park, John tied the mules to his trailer with a neck strap to get their bridles on. This way, he explained, they couldn't stroll off and leave while he was putting it on.

The first time Bob and I decided to ride our mules, we discovered Miss Ellie had a couple of annoying habits. As soon as her halter came off to put on the bridle, she turned around and left. She was too big and strong to stop, but as she was in the barn, she couldn't go far. This would have to be addressed. That same day I ordered two strong nylon bull collar-straps. It would be good to have even for Samson when saddling up away from home on trail rides.

Her other problem that I *did* notice when I bought her was she didn't want the bridle put on over her left ear. She wrapped her head around my body, put it up and down, and turned as far as her collar would allow. In short, it was a struggle. After putting in a phone call to John, I decided to bridle her as he did—with it in pieces. Detaching the bit and putting the head part on first, then putting the bit in her mouth worked quite well; her ears didn't need to be bent over. I added snaps to the side of the bridle so I could just snap the bit in place. John had told me to have her teeth checked and while she was sedated, to have the vet look into her ear. It did seem that something was bothering her.

Expecting her to be easy to mount, and already used to a mounting block, we led her towards it. She wouldn't get closer than three feet and kept walking around and around. Giving that idea up, I held her reins while Bob attempted to mount from the ground. As soon as he tried to put his foot in the stirrup, she moved backward. We got her stopped and tried again, and again she went back. She didn't seem like the sweet mule I'd ridden a few days earlier. Finally, she stood still enough for Bob to more or less clamber into the saddle. As soon as he sat down, she started off—back down the barn aisle and her stall. Bob was not an experienced rider and she certainly took advantage. I grabbed the rein and pulled her back. Not the best beginning.

John acknowledged that he loved to trail ride and he sheepishly admitted as soon as he thought his mules were ready, or maybe even a little before, he took them out. Consequently, some ground work was skipped. We actually should have spent more time working with her ground manners before riding, but the fall days were getting shorter, and Bob had found a new joy. He wanted to enjoy his mule. Once in the saddle, Miss Ellie never let us down. Her 500 trail-mile experiences kept Bob safe even though he was a real novice rider. She never spooked or refused to go anywhere.

Ellie didn't have a very great stop or "whoa" either. She didn't run off, but just took way too many steps before deciding to stand still. We'd been having a problem with Ellie's moving off as soon as Bob got in the saddle. He kept her from going back to her stall, but she wouldn't stand and wait for the command to move off. I wasn't happy with that either.

Deciding I must take charge of Miss Ellie and teach her some manners, I dug around in the old bit box that stored the many bits which had been purchased over many years, and found one that was a little stronger. I hadn't wanted to use a stronger bit at first because Bob wasn't an experienced rider. Some riders have bad hands, meaning they are rough in the animal's mouth and never learn. Bob was a beginner and I didn't want him to accidentally hurt her mouth.

Ellie wasn't very cooperative with my mounting efforts either, but with Erica's help at the mount block, I managed to get in the saddle. Erica went to another part of the barn and I was ready to teach Miss Ellie a thing or two. She started to move off very fast. I pulled back on the stronger bit and she bolted off at a fast trot. She couldn't go anywhere other than the inside arena, but around and around she went, getting faster and faster, bouncing me up and down in the saddle. "Whoa! Help!" I shouted at the top of my voice.

Erica came running, and in a corner of the arena, grabbed the reins. Miss Ellie stopped and I dismounted, a trifle shaken. Something was very wrong; she shouldn't have reacted like that. I decided she hated the bit. That's why almost every horse person has a bit box with many unused bits. This animal won't like that one, and another horse won't like another one. Finding one that works on a particular animal takes some time and luck. Ellie sure didn't like the one I had used. It apparently had hurt her and she bolted off in pain. I was experienced enough to realize that fact. I also made a mental note to call the vet and get those teeth checked.

Horses teeth continue to grow as they use them to grind their food, but they don't always grow straight or level, and sharp edges can occur which may cut their tongues or sides of their cheeks. If young, they can have loose "caps" or baby teeth and some have "wolf teeth" which are two small totally useless teeth that can in some cases interfere with the bit placement. Ellie was young and could have several problems.

After she ran off with me in the barn, I didn't think Bob should be the one to trail ride her next time, so I put in her old gentle bit and got on. She bolted off again and this time we were outside, but luckily in a small paddock. I pulled her into a corner where she stopped. She was anticipating the same pain as before. When she realized it wasn't hurting her, she walked off behind Samson and Bob.

In a couple of days, the vet arrived with his dentistry tools. To the uneducated, they looked like something from a horror movie. In his bag was a large speculum that would be put into the horse's mouth to hold it open. He had an electric grinder to shape and round the rough edges. It could do a better and faster job than a hand one, but care was required to avoid getting the tooth too hot, or take off too much. With Miss Ellie sedated, he inserted the speculum and opened her mouth. Now he could safely insert his hand and feel for sharp edges. She had some sharp points and two little wolf teeth that were growing off to the outside of her mouth.

He easily extracted the wolf teeth—they have hardly any roots, and smoothed all the sharp sides. Before she woke up, he looked into her left ear. Nothing seemed to be wrong, but there was a lot of black gunk coating the inside. He took a rag and cleaned the ear. I crossed my fingers that two problems had been solved, and left Miss Ellie to finish waking up.

I gave her three days to recuperate before putting a bit back into her mouth. When I rode her this time, she was much calmer. She apparently appreciated not having something in her mouth that caused discomfort. Now, the next things were the mounting block and standing still to get on. I called John again, and he suggested tying her up in the barn arena where I could get on and then unsnap her. That was the way he had always mounted because he was usually by himself in the woods and couldn't take the chance his mules would cause an accident. It was a safe and good plan, and apparently she had taken it to heart. *That* was the only way to mount.

I tied her as he suggested, used a big bucket and proceeded to mount. Back she went to the end of the rope. I moved the bucket and tried again. This time she went forward. I moved the mule this time with a slap on the neck and a stern reprimand. She stood and as soon as I sat down, moved forward. The rope stopped her and I let her stand for a few seconds before unsnapping it. After about three lessons with the rope, I could take her to the same spot, but not use the rope. She stood to mount and didn't move until I told her to.

Next, I tried the mount block; after only a few tries, she came close and stood, only moving off after I gave her the signal. Now this was progress! A few days later Bob and I went riding. He was properly impressed with both my training and Ellie. Once she got the concept and habit, she kept it, allowing Bob to mount with ease out in the open. Before it had been a circus with Miss Ellie turning in circles as he put his leg up, only getting seated because of his long legs. Poor Miss Ellie; we had indeed gotten the cart before the mule. We had more or less skipped grammar school and gone on to high school with her. She was being asked to do things she hadn't been trained to do.

Interestingly enough, as time went on, Ellie forgot about the bad left ear, and we could bridle her the normal way, but we still had to use the neck strap or she would leave. For some reason, she liked to stand at the extreme end of her rope. I noticed she had ridden in the horse trailer like that–with her butt up against the rear wall. Tied in the aisle, she backed to the end and stood quietly, but kept the rope taunt. Who knew what was going on in her molly-mule mind?

John admitted Miss Ellie had not much "formal education." Her stops and turns left something to be desired. She was like stopping a cement truck on a downhill slope and turned like a train. She also was starting to spook just a little. Quite by accident, I found a mule trainer only four hours away and decided to send her away for some higher education.

The more I worked with different mules, the more I respected and loved Mirabella. She had come with long shaggy hair all over, and ears that had so much hair in them they sort of took on a life of their own. After only two days, I had experimented with my clippers to see how close I could get to them. She never batted an eye, so I simply clipped the insides of them. It was unusual for horse—or mule alike. Miss Ellie showed me that.

Her mane had been roached, I'm assuming by clippers, but she acted frightened of them, backing to the end of her rope and looking buggy eyed. I could place the clippers in my hand and rub my hand over her neck, but when I tried to actually touch her nose to get the nose whiskers, she pulled back even more. There was no need to push it. I had decided to send her for training. I would just put this on the list. Someone with more mule experience could handle that one.

Chapter Eight: Four-Wheeling on a Mule

I'd owned Samson for two months when I got an invitation to go trail riding with Carolyn, one of my best horse friends, and several other people I didn't know at all. I was having a saddle fitting problem with Samson, and the one he liked best was a small English cut back show saddle. I wasn't real happy going trail riding with it, but I surmised we were only going on gentle paths. I was crazy about my big mule and wanted to show him off. I certainly did that, but not in the way I expected.

He was calm while we were saddling up, and calm while I struggled to get into the saddle. As soon as I got my rear in the saddle and took a hold of the reins, Samson was transformed into a true "jackass." Up went his head and out went his nose. In this position I had little control of his head. He stuck his tongue out the side of his mouth and unlike our rides at home, he wouldn't put it back in. His mouth felt like a slab of concrete. My riding aids to tell him to drop his nose and "get on the bit" were ignored completely.

There were twelve riders in the group and all were ahead of Carolyn and me except two. I followed Carolyn, and the lead horses were already moving at a good fast flat walk. One of the problems with riding in a large group is all the horses want to be together; seldom is an animal content to lag behind the others. The leading rider sets the pace and unless you don't mind being left behind, you go with the others. I had a gut-feeling this was going to be pretty awful—and it was.

Samson not only had his head above the bit, as the saying goes, he was rushing to keep up and he was *trotting*! My smooth gaited mule was trotting big time. It was like he had no brain at all. Where was all this mule wisdom he was supposed to possess? I talked to him. "It's okay, big fella. Easy now." I leaned down and scratched his neck. Ha, that was a joke. He was deaf and unfeeling. Hopefully, he was not blind too. I hoped it was correct that mules can see better than horses, because he sure did *not* appear to be looking where he was going at all.

The trail wound through the woods, through mud and a corn field. All the while I was fighting with Samson to slow down, stop trotting, and watch where he was going. He didn't stumble a step, but I kept expecting him to go splat and take me with him. After about fifteen minutes, which seemed like much more, I was ready to give up. I felt like such a dummy and fool. So much for impressing anyone with my well-trained mule.

"Hey, Carolyn, Samson is being such a butt. Would you mind terribly if we went back to the trailer? I'll wait for you there and you can ride as long as you wish."

I had to ask her to go back with me because I have a terrible sense of direction and was already lost. We had just started on the trail, but it had a few off-shoots; all I needed was the direct path back. Carolyn had considerable talent in knowing just where she was—on the road in a vehicle or in the woods on a horse—at least I hoped so....

She turned around to look and said, "Maybe the halter we left on under the bridle is interfering with the bit. Let me take it off." Everyone had to stop while we made these adjustments and I wished I could crawl into the bushes and hide. Unfortunately, our fix didn't help. He stuck his tongue back out and kept on trotting.

Carolyn sympathetically agreed to head me back to camp. We passed stumps and other things we recognized, and then suddenly, we were no longer on that trail, but on a new one and going deeper into the woods. I had lost my chance to return. About this time, Samson settled down just a little, and when I realized I was continuing on the ride whether I wanted to or not, I decided to just let him trot and stop fighting with him. The ride would not last forever. I would survive it. He was not being dangerous, just exasperating.

After a few more turns in the path, the group stopped, and I heard some exclamations from the head riders. Oh, boy, now what? We were too far in the rear to see what the comments were about, but it soon became apparent. The "what" turned out to be Devil's Drop—a section where the trail simply disappeared from sight—unless you looked down—*way* down!

One by one the horses disappeared from view as they went down the very steep incline. Carolyn was riding a five-year-old gelding that had little trail experience, or even consistent riding. She was an experienced trail rider, but the horse was green. Up to now, he had done everything extremely well. He had put my trail experienced Samson to shame.

One lady on an inexperienced trail horse said she couldn't do it, but her friends assured her she could and as she headed her horse over the edge, I wondered what kind of fool people I had gotten mixed up with. The horses seemed willing to jump or skid into oblivion, I guess just because the others had gone ahead.

Carolyn's young horse couldn't wait to jump over the edge—literally. He wanted to gallop down it. He had no sense of what it was; he just wanted to go with the others. She held him back and he got turned sideways, a very bad thing as they can trip, tumble down and get hurt—or dead. Somehow she got him stopped and when he got his bearings, he went down more or less safely.

Meanwhile, Samson was having a huge snit right at the crest of the precipitous down-drop. He had been on Carolyn's horse's rear the whole ride, and he had no intention of waiting until it reached the bottom. He wanted to go *now*. I turned him in circles. I was too mad at him to be as frightened as I should have been. The two riders behind me assured me I could do it. "Just point his head down and let him go. Don't let him get sideways."

It all happened in a blur. Over the edge we went with Samson's nose still in the air. I don't remember the trip down at all—in my English show-saddle. Carolyn, who was standing at the bottom looking at our decent, told me it actually was quite nice. He did it just like a pro, even if his nose was in the air. I felt like one of the lemmings that follow each other off cliffs and into the sea where they all drown, except that I had made it, was still alive, and actually exhilarated, if the truth were known. What happened next is one of those strange little occurrences that I like to call providential.

When we finished our descent, because Carolyn was standing off the side, we ended up on the trail ahead of her and behind the other horses. Immediately, Samson became quiet. He put his head back down, tucked his tongue back in, and settled down into a sensible walk. I was almost afraid to breathe, expecting him to act like an idiot again. But he did not. For the rest of the ride he was a perfect mule and I had the most superb time.

This little riding episode wasn't shared with Hal. As "in the day," when my sister Linda and I were young and traipsing around the Pennsylvania state forest lands all alone with our wonderful horses, most of our escapades were kept to ourselves. It fell into the category of what "Mom and Dad don't know, they can't worry about—or tell us to stop doing it."

Why Samson acted so badly behind Carolyn's horse and perfect in front, is a mystery I can't answer for sure, but later after owning him for many months, I came to the conclusion it was because he is *very* dominant. He always preferred to be the leader, although, with our own horses and mules, he would acquiesce to follow when asked. In this instance, since he had trailered with Carolyn's horse, Samson felt he had to be the boss on the trail.

Another possible scenario presented itself when I read the April 2010 issue of *Western Mule.* Ben Tennison, the editor, wrote an article about "buddied-up mules."

He wrote that it didn't matter if two mules hated each other in the pasture, they could become inseparably in love on a trail ride, or on a trailer ride, even with a mule they have never seen before. Maybe that is what happened to Samson. He was afraid Carolyn's horse was going to leave him when it went in front, when it was behind, Samson felt secure.

Miss Ellie had entered our life with little fanfare except for the anticipation of great things. Bob had become truly fascinated with trail riding the mules, and as soon as fall weather and time constraints made it possible, we started hauling the mules about forty-five minutes away to different horse parks. Our first trip was one week after Miss Ellie had made the nine-hour trailer trip from Missouri to Indiana. She didn't seem real interested in getting inside the trailer, but after a little coaxing and an apple, she acquiesced and popped in. Samson loaded perfectly.

Russ Forest was absolutely gorgeous. Just a little color to the leaves made it even better. The weather was a wonderful 70 degrees. On the trail were two bridges, one regular size and another quite narrow—more for people. Bob rode Samson because I trusted him to take care of a new trail rider, and I rode Miss Ellie. Bob came to the first wider bridge and Samson put on the brakes and started backing up right into me and Miss Ellie. That was odd, because several weeks before I had been there with Samson and he'd been faultless, never hesitated at the bridge at all. After standing still and looking at it a couple minutes, Samson decided to cross. Miss Ellie wasn't sure at all.

Bob was talking and cheerfully riding away from me, and didn't notice I wasn't right behind him. "Hey, wait!" I yelled. "Come back!"

With Samson waiting on the other side of the bridge, Miss Ellie crossed. When Bob spotted another very narrow bridge, he muttered, "Oh no!"

I said, "Don't slow down or hesitate. Keep going and know Samson will go over."

On my earlier outing I'd ridden Samson over that bridge too. Bob and Samson crossed with no problem. Again Miss Ellie was certain she would not fit and surely should not tempt fate. After some minutes of checking it out and a slight encouragement by my small spurs, she started across, putting her nose to the ground. She took a step, sniffed, took another, sniffed more and in like manner crossed to the other side.

The rest of the ride was uneventful except when we headed back to the trailer. From quite a distance off, we heard children yelling and laughing. As we rounded a bend in the trail, it was clear what the noise was all about. Fifteen or so little pre-schoolers were on an outing in the park, shrieking happily as they swarmed down the middle of the road toward the mules. Bob wondered what we should do. Samson seemed to sense they were not harmful, but Ellie wasn't at all sure.

When the children spotted the mules, they started running to us, flapping their arms in their brightly colored coats and shrieking even louder. Now, that *was* a sight! About the time Ellie decided that it might be a great idea to turn around and leave the vicinity, the teachers and helpers got the little ones under control and along one side of the road.

Back at the trailer, we unsaddled and started to load the mules. Samson was to be first and he refused. What the heck was this? Thinking that he didn't want to leave Miss Ellie who was still tied to the trailer, we loaded her first. We tried again with Samson and got nowhere. It is a bad feeling to be ready to go home and not be able to. Much better to have the animal refuse to load going away from home in my mind. At least you are home.

Samson didn't misbehave; he just stood there, letting me pull his head inside the trailer, but nothing more. Apples had no effect. I had heard you couldn't bribe a mule. Don't know if it is true—Miss Ellie seemed to bribe quite nicely, but Samson was having none of it.

I stood there, all kinds of thoughts rushing through my mind. I knew there was no forcing this big mule into a trailer. It seemed like a long time that I stood there pulling his halter, but it really was only five minutes. Then, without warning, he quietly jumped into the trailer. One of the things that came into my mind as I stood there was the other time Samson and I had ridden in Russ Forest with Carolyn and her horse.

It had been a warmer day and we'd ridden quite a bit at a flat walk—equivalent to a slow trot. Our animals had worked harder and consequently were hotter. He popped right into the trailer that day. When we arrived at our destination which was only fifteen minutes down the road, and opened the trailer door, both animals were dripping with sweat.

They had been warm, but certainly not sweating when we put them inside. I felt really dreadful. I was surprised they hadn't cooled down with the open windows and the air blowing through as we went down the road. Did he remember that incident and not want to repeat the uncomfortable ride? I think so.

Okay, this ride should be fine and hopefully he would forgive me. A person who had worked with mules for fifteen years had recently told me that contrary to the saying that mules will not forgive a bad experience—or the person who caused it—they would if they liked you. I sure hoped that was true.

Our next venture was to the home of the lady who had purchased Mirabella. She lived next to an abandoned gravel pit where wildlife abounded, and mowed trails wove between and over the hills. Both Ellie and Samson loaded without problem. Now, however, I didn't quite trust my big boy. I wondered if we would be coming home as easily.

This ride would turn out to be a fantastic experience on another glorious fall day. Miss Ellie showed her mettle in taking great care of Bob, and proved I had made an excellent purchase. Samson was his usual mellow self. This was our first outing with others since his terrible exhibition when I rode with Carolyn and her friends.

We rode up and down gentle hills, saw wildlife and much beauty. Samson walked fast, being long legged, and no one cared if he was in the lead. He loved it there. He was the scout, looking for anything that might be dangerous and require a stop and look. Miss Ellie, who was on his heels, had her ears flopping off to the side and popping back and forth as she walked. Samson was on alert; she didn't need to be worried.

We had so much fun that when we were asked if we wanted to trailer another hour into Michigan and ride at The Bluff, we quickly agreed. Samson loaded slowly and I apologized.

"Heck," my friend Connie said, "this is nothing. I once had to leave a horse that wouldn't load and go back for him the next day." Not exactly the words I wanted to hear.

Riding at The Bluff was a little more difficult in places. It had been raining off and on for weeks and the ground was quite muddy in certain places, but it was a very beautiful spot. More fall foliage, a lake and a stream with a covered bridge, a mini pine forest and a cliff that made "Dead Man's Drop" look easy. This one was steep and very slippery with mud.

Samson and I were in the lead and before I knew it, we had gone over the edge and were on the way down. Samson was oh-so-careful and very good. This time he was looking where he was headed—which seemed to be straight down in gooey, slimy mud. I knew he was picking his way slowly, but he seemed to gravitate toward the edge where the trees were and it was less slippery, but also no room for my knees. I had to gently guide him back to the greasy mess.

Bob, who was following closely, later told me it was interesting to watch his descent. Samson picked up a foot, placed it in the mire and if it didn't slip, then brought another leg forward. In some places we must have been close to dragging our butts in the mire because his tail looked like it had been soaked in mud. After we completed the slope, I heaved a sigh of relief and accomplishment. My relief was short lived because all too soon, we came upon another muddy slope. Being more or less accomplished "mudders" by now, the second one was easier, but all the same I was glad to hear that was the last of them.

Samson loaded slowly, but after a few tugs, and dire threats, we were on our way back home. When we arrived, Bob remarked the mules looked like ATVs that had been driven through the wilds. With mud streaked flanks from being flicked by muddy tails, and mud to their knees, our trusty mules were a dirty mess.

Samson was the first to come out of the trailer, as he'd been the last in. I walked up to his left side and untied his rope from the trailer ring. Before I could utter the words "back up," Samson had whipped his head to the right yanking the lead from my grasp and nearly spun around to go out head first. Fortunately, Bob was standing right at the door and grabbed him as he exited.

Brother was I mad! I really didn't think it possible for a mule as large as Samson to have the room to turn around and whirl out the door. I snatched the lead rope from Bob and started pulling, yanking and yelling at my mule. How *dare* he?

Despite his size, Samson wasn't normally a belligerent, ornery or obstinate mule. (Later I learned he could be ornery *and* obstinate....) After three minutes, or even less of this berating, he calmly hopped back into the trailer! I was just as surprised at this action as I had been at his unorthodox exit. I shut my mouth, which was hanging open in near shock, led him back to his tie, and then quietly backed him out the proper way.

After the problems with loading him into the trailer the last few times, his polite and easy entrance was another mystery. Had he and I had a breakthrough of some kind? Would he now enter nicely and give me no grief? I wanted to check it out and I planned on having a practice session, or maybe more, as I did my foals and young horses. I really wanted to feel sure he would hop into my trailer whenever I asked.

A few days later, I was talking to another mule friend who had been living with them for many years. I told him what had happened. His words of advice on practice loading were, "Don't do it. He did it once. That is usually all it takes. Just practicing on something a mule has done right only pisses them off!"

Well, I sure didn't want that, so I never did my practicing. Anyway, winter came and the "hauling off to trail ride" days were over. I guess I would see just how long his memory was when it came time to load again in the spring.

Samson and Miss Ellie

Chapter Nine: Samson Goes to a Show

One of our smaller horse shows was coming up and it was only forty-five minutes away. I decided to take one mare for my eight-year-old niece to show, and Samson. Tennessee Walking Horse shows have a division for "Country Pleasure" which allows any gaited breed to enter. It would be our debut into the Walking Horse world.

It promised to be an interesting weekend weather-wise. Heavy rain could be expected—or not. Northern Indiana and southern Michigan can have very strange weather on the eastern side of Lake Michigan. I probably wouldn't have bothered going, but my niece had been taking lessons all summer and for one reason or another, we'd not yet made it to a show.

All went without a hitch. Hal, as usual, stayed home, Cali went with Bob and me with the mule and her horse. She was pretty subdued, not like her usual talkative self, but helped get the animals settled in their show stalls. We went to McDonalds for breakfast, which she didn't eat.

"Aren't you hungry, Cali?" I asked.

"No, I still have my stomach ache from the flu," she said quietly. She had been plagued with it the previous week, but if she'd still been sick, I was sure her mother wouldn't have allowed her to come with us.

At home we'd had no rain; getting to Cassopolis, Michigan, we found they had been deluged with at least an inch. The ring was a quagmire. The show was postponed for two hours while the show committee decided what to do. Because Walking Horses do not trot, but rather do a smooth gliding gait, going through deep mud would be very hard on them, if not disastrous, possibly causing lameness. The show committee decided to hold the halter classes and the 11-year-and-under saddle class in the small indoor arena. That would be a good thing for the young riders. They would all be contained in a smaller and safer area.

We got Nugget out for Cali to practice with, and that was when Samson began to make his presence at the fairgrounds known to everyone within any degree of proximity. *Hee haw, heeee haaaaw,* punctuated by serious striking of his front feet on the stall sides. What a racket. Tying him up was no good, he just made more noise with his front feet. Throwing him hay had no affect either, it just got tromped underfoot.

He was doing a great job of again embarrassing me, as folks stopped by to see what all the noise was about. Several grinned as they peered into Samson's stall. I had planned on impressing my friends and other exhibitors with Samson, but not in this fashion. I hoped this outing wouldn't be a repeat of our first trail ride!

There was some confusion as to whether Cali's class would be held in the small ring, or in another big outside one. I thought we should have her practice ride in the big one just in case they used it. What to do with Samson when we went?

In the interest of keeping the barn in one piece, I decided to lead him along with us, putting a stud lead on him, running the chain part over his nose so I would have more control. He was as placid as a puppy dog as he followed Nugget to the riding area, but as soon as Cali mounted and started to leave, one really big mule got very upset.

Fortunately for all involved, he settled down when he figured out she was only going in a circle and not heading completely away. I wondered what he was going to do when I tried to show him in *my* class, leaving Nugget in the barn. Big gulp...maybe I should think about this some more.

Finally, it was time for Nugget and Cali to enter their class. There were four little eleven-year-and-under riders. They were just darling, all dressed up in their riding suits, hair pinned back, gloves and with a touch of make-up. I mentioned to her mother that Cali had said she might still have the stomach flu.

Her mom laughed and said, "She has been fine. I think she has butterflies and doesn't know the difference between a sick tummy and a nervous one!"

As Cali entered the ring, I was now the one with the butterflies. No matter how wonderful and how well trained a horse is, you never really know what will happen, especially with a new and relatively inexperienced eight-year-old rider.

Nugget and Cali before the class: "We can do this!"

All went off without a hitch, and Samson was quiet, thanks to Bob who stood in his stall the whole time feeding him hay, one stem at a time to keep him occupied. Cali received her second place ribbon, exited the arena and found she had a tremendous appetite for everything her mom had packed for her to eat. I still wondered about Samson's and my class....

Hours later in the afternoon, the main arena had dried out enough that the rest of the show was held in it. It was still muddy and I was very glad that Nugget's class had been in the dry arena. With her arthritis, she could never have shown in the mud, and one little girl would have been very heartbroken.

In due course, Samson's class was called. He would be inspected by the DQP, (a steward) to certify he was sound and not "sored," a practice used by some owners that puts a blistering agent on the front ankles to make Tennessee Walking Horses step higher and fancier. I had practiced picking up his feet and palpating around the ankles to get him used to the idea.

I was worried because his thrush and necessary treatment of his front feet had made him reticent to pick them up, thinking something was going to hurt. I'd already been embarrassed enough by my big mule today, I surely didn't need to be "turned down" by the inspector because of an unruly animal.

We saddled up, and headed to the inspection area. Samson was his normal quiet and wonderful self. Apparently leaving Nugget *behind* was not traumatic. I got lots of looks and smiles as I walked my mule down the path. Many friends and family members were already sitting on the bleachers waiting for our debut.

Bob came with me, carrying the big muck bucket that I would turn upside down and stand on to mount. We had practiced at home. Samson was still quiet and his inspection went without a hitch. In fact, Samson picked up his front feet before the DQP even touched them. The inspector was duly impressed with everything about Samson, his size, his attitude and his beauty.

There would be three of us in the class— a Fox Trotter, a Rocky Mountain Horse and Samson. This would be fun. It didn't matter what placing we got because this was just for pure pleasure. I had nothing to prove, nothing to promote, nothing to sell, just enjoy myself.

We entered the ring; Samson went first. He never missed a beat. The first gait was a walk, and the second was "favorite gait"—whatever smooth trail riding gait your animal performed. After so many years of perfecting the Walking Horse gait for the show ring, it was nice to just let Samson do his thing, which was a nice Walking Horse-type running walk. We did our gaits both directions in the ring and then went into the center to line up and wait for our placings.

"First place is Samson," the announcer said. What a hoot! My friends were cheering and I was beaming. I felt as great as when I had won a big class on my stallion at a very prestigious Tennessee show. Our debut had been a huge success. I wished Hal had been there. He would have gotten a kick out of the whole thing, but as with the horse shows, he would have been bored to tears waiting until our classes. I would never ask that of him.

Samson and Rose

Chapter Ten: Mirabella Comes Home

It is said, "All things happen for a reason," but I am still asking myself the reason for this one. When Lori bought Mirabella, everything was going along at a fine rate. They were bonding and life was relatively good with the exceptions of a few minor ups and downs. The evening they arrived home, Mirabella decided she didn't want to unload from the trailer. It had poured rain all the way there and rain was pounding the trailer, the ground, and anything outside of it. I don't think it was the rain that bothered her so much as I doubt that she ever backed out of a trailer before. When she came to me, she was allowed to turn around and come out head first, and she had never been inside one since.

Lori's other horse and mule weren't happy to see another animal arrive to share Lori's attention, but eventually they worked out their differences. Her first encounter with the electric fence was acceptable. Lori made sure not to be beside it or Mirabella when she touched it. No point in having Mirabella blame Lori for a nasty shock. The hind shoes I had put on Mirabella were not what Lori wanted for trail riding, so she had them removed. I was unhappy and surprised to hear that she was not a good mule for the farrier. She had been perfect for mine. It turned out this was not the man Lori usually used, and her regular farrier ended up having no problems with her. Maybe it was too much too soon after being uprooted from a home where I know she was extremely happy.

Lori rode her alone and with her mom and mom's mule Colonel. She rode successfully with larger groups, but Mirabella continued to have her own ideas about who should be following on her tail. Her stopping needed work, but all these things were just the regular getting acquainted situations that happen with all new animals.

Lori rode with her husband, "a once a year rider," going to a beautiful private riding area in Michigan. They went at the beginning of hunting season and hunters were moving into the cabins and setting up deer stands. None of these things bothered Mirabella. At one point they were almost up to the animal's knees in mud, but Mirabella kept her head and kept on truckin'. All in all, life was normal and good—until that day in November.

Lori and her mom Alice, along with their two mules, headed out to the Pit. The Pit is an old gravel area with several very deep holes and plenty of very nice riding amid interesting terrain, as well as deer, wild turkeys, rabbits and other small animals.

It was the day before Thanksgiving; the trees had lost their leaves, but the sky was blue and the sun was shining. Just perfect for riding. Mirabella and Lori were in the lead with Alice and Colonel in the rear. Suddenly a large red Pit Bull dog came zooming over the top of a high bank through the tall weeds—at the level of Mirabella's head. Everyone was taken quite by surprise and Mirabella spun around to the left and started running. As Lori told me the story that she and her mom had pieced together, it sounded like the "Perfect Storm" of trail riding and with tragic results.

After Mirabella spun around, Lori's saddle started to slip off to the left. Lori admitted that the saddle never had fit Mirabella just right, and she planned on getting a new one "sometime." Lori was trying to get the saddle righted and use the one-hand stop at the same time, but Mirabella wasn't stopping. Mirabella was running, dodging trees and a water hole, and finally Lori came off.

Lori recounted, "It wasn't pretty and I was mad at myself for falling off. I heard Mom yelling at something, but all I knew was that I couldn't get up. I looked up and Mirabella was walking back towards me, and then she stopped, and put her head down and touched mine, and just stood there."

Alice moved Mirabella so Lori had room to turn, but she still couldn't get up. Lori worked for a Rescue and Ambulance Service, and the good thing about their mishap was that Lori had taken her cell phone, which she said was the first time she ever had. After getting Lori loaded into the ambulance, Alice mounted Colonel and led Mirabella home. Mirabella didn't seem upset by the episode, nor a big grain truck and a rattling gravity wagon pulled by a pickup truck they met on the way home.

Later in piecing together the facts as Alice had seen them unfold, the big red Pit Bull had taken chase after Mirabella. Alice started shouting at the dog and waving her arms after Lori fell off, afraid that the dog would attack her as she lay on the ground.

The dog turned and came charging back to Alice and her mule, circled around and then took off away from them. Colonel hates dogs and has done damage to some; perhaps the dog sensed that this was *not* the mule to be reckoned with. Possibly it would have ended differently if Colonel had been the lead. Certainly it would have been different if the saddle hadn't slipped and Lori had more chance to stop her mule.

The day Alice told me the story over the phone, she also asked me if I would take Mirabella back, as I had said I would. My heart skipped a beat and my mind went into a whirl as I tried to remember exactly just what I *had* said when they bought her.

I never offer to take back animals when I sell them. I know some sellers do, and my hat is off to them. My reasoning is if I make that offer, I'm not sure just what condition the horse—or mule would be in. Things could have happened to change the animal. I am neither a dealer nor a professional trainer, so what would I want with a damaged animal?

Taking Mirabella back under normal circumstances would be one thing, but now she'd had a bad experience, and mules being mules—would that incident ruin her? Would she run off again? Be afraid of dogs? I got real quiet as Alice talked, my mind spinning.

I asked what she wanted for her and she wanted the full price they had paid. She said to think about it and let them know. After I hung up I did think about it, and was mad at myself for making the offer, which I eventually remembered I had. Alice had been buyer savvy and had asked me if I would take her back, if needed. I really liked the little mule and didn't want anything to happen to her, so if they had to sell, I guessed it would be good to be in the loop. We had not talked about price or how long the offer would be good, or under what circumstances.

I stewed about it that day and had a sleepless night, but when I awoke, I knew Mirabella was returning. I called to tell Alice and she then told me about Mirabella's coming back to Lori lying on the ground, and putting her nose on Lori's head. That brought tears to my eyes and I knew I had made the right decision. Not only because I had given my word, but I had to do it for Mirabella. Three days later she came home.

I put her in a stall where I and other visitors to the barn would pass by frequently. She could put her head over the stall door as in the past, but she was a little different. Her other living arrangements with Lori had been very nice, but dissimilar. Her stall door was always open and she could go in and out at will. When not ridden, she could be on her own.

I like my stall accommodations because the horses all are handled each day as they get put in and let out. They have their friends to eat and play with, but at least part of the day, they realize they are owned by humans. Mirabella had gotten a little independent and pushy. Her first lesson was to remember that when her stall door was opened to let her out to pasture, she was not to run over the human.

The next day, I got her out and attached her to the cross ties in the barn aisle. She moved back and forth, side to side. She wasn't at all pleased. Lesson number two was to accept confinement whether in a stall or being tied in the barn. After awhile she settled down and I put her back in the stall.

The following day, I tied her up and started to brush her. Goodness, what carrying on! Swish, swish went her tail while she moved all four feet at the same time—back and forth, side to side, everything but up and down, ears flat back against her head. She had always loved being brushed; what was wrong? I felt along her back muscles and that made everything a lot worse. It was an easy diagnosis. Her back was sore, not just a little, but really, really sore.

Two usual ways to cause back soreness such as this was a bad fall, or a bad saddle. Between Mirabella's saddle not fitting right to begin with and then her accident with the saddle and rider off to the left side, it was no wonder she hurt. One of the things I loved and appreciated about my mules was their stoicism when it came to discomfort.

They ignored a lot that would have made wimps out of my horses, but this was beyond ignoring. I'm glad I discovered it before putting on a saddle and starting to ride. I hoped she would not have done something such as buck or run off from the hurt, but I guess I couldn't have blamed her.

Her mule physical therapy consisted of massage, liniment and my cold laser, used for treating muscle ailments in both man and beast. I now knew riding would be put off until later, but ground work would begin with her wearing my mule pad and my saddle. I didn't want to hurt her, but did want her to realize my saddle was not going to cause pain.

One of the following days, I happened to look out my window and saw her tearing like mad around the pasture across the creek. She was all alone, it was chore time, and it appeared all the rest of the horses had come in and she was left behind.

I called Erica who was doing the chores, and she said that Mirabella had gotten spooked by the neighbor's dog that loved to lie in wait for the horses to cross the creek. This dog had his own sense of humor, which none of us appreciated. He was not mean, but the situation could be dangerous. Because of the brush and trees along the fence, which made it difficult for the horses to see that all the rustling they heard was caused by the dog, he took them by surprise. If he had run up to the fence barking, they would have paid no heed. The problem was they didn't know the noise was a dog. Riding by this same area could be unpleasant for the same reason.

Oh, that is just great, I thought. *Another dog situation and she is running again.*

Erica walked back to get her, and found her in the middle of my three-cow beef herd. When she saw Erica coming, she trotted toward her. "Save me, save me," she seemed to say.

With a lead rope, gentle words and ear scratching, they eventually made their way past the frightening spot and on to the barn. I had called the neighbor lady and she kindly put the dog in the house. That incident was a major breakthrough. First, Mirabella had trusted and allowed Erica to help her, and second, had walked calmly and quietly all the way home, not frantic or silly because of another unpleasant dog experience. I was pleased. Perhaps this was going to work out after all.

It was clear in my mind when I took Mirabella back that she was only here to be resold. To that end, I had Erica and a couple other girls who helped out with the horses, be the ones to work with her. After the dog and the culvert crossing situation, I felt confident that Mirabella would trust and be happy with Erica. The girls could let her trot along and enjoy that gait; I couldn't ride a trot with my back problem.

I wanted to be a part of her "reconditioning" though, and when I rode my mules, I put Mirabella into a bitting rig, which was just a strap around her belly with rings attached to the side of it, and I attached the reins to those rings. In this way, she could walk around in her small paddock and teach herself to "give to the bit" and flex at the poll instead of sticking her nose out when she was ridden. I used a plain snaffle for this purpose, and soon she was walking around in her pen with a beautiful head set.

In a couple of days, I saw Erica ride her. She stood still as could be at the mounting block, and walked off when instructed. I still was not exceedingly happy with the saddle fit; I used my special mule pad and a Western saddle, but it appeared to run down hill because her back was still higher in the rear. Mirabella didn't object in any way and I was very impressed as the two of them walked then trotted around the arena like it was an everyday occurrence.

I remembered my first rides in the arena on Mirabella as she dove off the track to wander into the middle of the area. She now had her neck flexed and her nose held in as they trotted around, making circles and crossing the diagonal. Man, was I impressed! Mirabella was living up to her past quickness in learning.

Mirabella and friend

Erica laughed happily. "Maybe we should do dressage with her!"

Mirabella had an opinion on everything and in one case it almost had tragic consequences. Kathryn, one of my farm gals, called one afternoon at chore time. "Rose, you better come to the barn, Mirabella almost killed your calf!"

My heart beat faster and I squeezed my eyes shut. *What next?* I couldn't believe my ears. I rushed to the barn and heard the story.

My Red Angus beef cow had her calf two weeks previously and the cows were religiously kept from the horses. When Kathryn started feeding she noticed the cow and calf were in the wrong area, but thought to get them later. Unfortunately, Mirabella happened upon the scene beforehand. Grabbing the little calf, which probably weighed 100 pounds, she proceeded to shake, drag and toss it around. Kathryn had an extremely hard time getting the mule away from the besieged calf.

The baby calf had bite marks on his body and acted in shock. The poor momma cow stood by bawling and bewildered by these dreadful events. I gave the calf some pain medication and in an hour he was back to nursing. Cows are tough.

What had caused this awful incident? At first I wanted kill Mirabella. I had heard of mules ravaging dogs, cats and other young animals. Mirabella seemed so sweet and never acted a renegade. Then it came to me in a flash. The calf was the same color and roughly same size as the red Pit Bull dog that had attacked her. Was she was after revenge?

The utmost caution was used by all of us to keep Mirabella away from the cows and their babies until the calves were large enough to look like *cows*!

Chapter Eleven: Samson Makes His Presence Known

Samson and Hallelujah, my retired and gelded Tennessee Walking Horse stallion, shared a pasture by themselves. I boarded a young horse that had been injured and was on stall rest in Hallelujah and Samson's part of the barn. We conjectured that the youngster had gotten himself into trouble by thinking he was the protector of another horse, his buddy, and had picked a fight with the wrong opponent. Receiving a solid kick in the shoulder, the bone chipped, necessitating surgery.

Our stall doors are open at the top so the horses may stick their heads out. Every day as I led Hallelujah and Samson by on their way out to pasture, the colt would flatten his ears and charge the gate, giving a nip or bite if he could reach the horse walking by. One day he got a solid bite on Samson's back. I watched for retaliation, but saw none. Samson kept walking as though nothing had happened. He went by the colt's stall on his way both in and out of the barn for several days; I did, however, endeavor to keep a safe distance away to avoid further confrontations.

Samson bided his time. One day as I was bringing him in from the pasture all the right conditions were there for payback. I was on Samson's left, the horse's stall was on his right; I had made mental notes to stay away from that stall, but this day I was in a hurry and forgot. Samson made his move. With no advance warning of any kind, quick as a rattlesnake's strike, Samson reached out and grabbed the colt's nose in his mouth. Making no sound or movement of any kind, Samson just held on while the colt squealed in anger and pain.

I was taken totally by surprise and while I was thinking how to make him stop, Samson let go and resumed his walk to his stall as though nothing out of the ordinary had occurred. I locked Samson in his stall and hurried to look at the colt's nose. I couldn't see a bite mark of any description.

The next day there was no swelling and I wondered if Samson had actually held the young horse's nose between his teeth. Another mystery in the realm of horse and mule ownership. The colt was much better after that disciplinary action and while he sometimes would reach out toward the other horses, when Samson walked by, he turned his head to the side, or pulled in a bit. He was not about to risk the big mule's ire again.

Early that winter, the weather was mild and the horses enjoyed their outside time, but there was little grass left to eat. Because of this, the male horses—and mule—made up games and some of it was rough. Praise Hallelujah had lived by himself as a stallion for eighteen years. When gelded, he reveled in the larger pasture with *grass*. His stud pen had very little. He was happy to keep up his search for any blade of green that he had missed the previous days. Samson, on the other hand, was a different matter. He was full of hay and mischief.

One morning I turned out the horses as usual with Samson and Hallelujah in their separate pasture from the mares, and started feeding the calves. Out of the corner of my eye, I saw something that registered on my brain as odd, and turned around to look. There on the ground was Hallelujah with Samson over him. I couldn't tell whether Samson was tearing at Hallelujah's blanket, or doing something worse.

All in a flash, thoughts of a friend's miniature donkey gelding and her horses flooded my mind. Gus was the cutest little thing. About the size of a very large dog, he was trained to pull a cart, but my friend Patty had him just to add to her menagerie of livestock. It wasn't long before she realized she had a big problem with Gus.

Her horse herd was comprised of an older gelding, a young gelding that had been one of my breeding stallions at one time, a Lipizzaner mare, and a young Walking Horse filly. Because the older gelding and mare would take none of Gus's aggressive attempts to get the better of them, he left them alone. The young filly was the recipient of his many neck bites, but since she never fought him, he didn't attack her. Vision, the younger ex-stallion-gelding, got the brunt of Gus's dominating show of force.

Gus came to Vision and jumped up at his withers, grabbed onto his neck or mane and held on. If Vision ran, Gus just held on and was carried along with him. When Vision turned his head to bite the little donkey, Gus went for the jugular, and taking hold with his teeth, brought Vision to the ground.

Both Erica and Patty on two different occasions watched in disbelief. Each time the ladies got a whip and drove Gus away from the downed horse. Obviously, Gus had to go. I could hardly fathom Samson treating Hallelujah like that, but there was my prized horse on the ground.

I yelled at Samson, but if he heard me he paid no heed. I prepared to rush into the pasture and separate them, but Hallelujah got up, shook himself and walked off, his blanket still intact. What had been going on? Some rough boy play that ended up with one on the ground? I decided to separate them the next day. I didn't want Samson to harm Hallelujah. He outweighed the horse by at least 200 pounds and could throw his weight around.

Up to now, Hallelujah had actually enjoyed playing with Samson. When I put them out they reared and waved their front legs in the air like two battling wild stallions, but it only lasted a couple of minutes and then they were off searching for that elusive grass. Now they were playing rougher and longer.

The following day, I put those two in different but adjoining pastures. The next thing I heard from Erica was that Hallelujah had kicked through the fence as in the old days when he was a stallion and had objected to having any of the geldings within his immediate proximity, even if they were separated by a ten-foot buffer. Well, okay, guess that wouldn't work either. So far he and Samson hadn't hurt each other, but by trying to get through the fence, Hallelujah scraped his leg. Back together they went. I was getting fed up. One can only do so much, I thought.

Several days later Bob was taking the dogs for a walk along their pasture and called me on his cell phone. "Rose, I just wanted to let you know that Samson is chasing Hallelujah all over the pasture. Up and down the fence line, and around and around. He has his ears flat back and is just inches away from Hallelujah's rear end."

"Oh, that's all right," I replied. "They are just playing. They play pretty rough."

"Well, okay, but it doesn't look like play to me. Wow, Samson just bit Hallelujah's blanket. I saw it tear."

I looked out the dining room window and could see part of the pasture. Samson was indeed running Hallelujah and it didn't look like fun to me either. Plus a hunk out of a winter blanket wasn't a good thing for my pocketbook.

"Oh, my gosh! Hallelujah just kicked Samson in the head! I *heard* it!" Bob exclaimed.

I'd seen him kick at Samson before when they were playing more gently, and crossed my fingers and prayed that he would never connect with a part of Samson that would injure easily—like an eye. I certainly didn't blame Hallelujah. He needed to put old Samson in his place, but I hoped it wasn't going to become a big vet bill or a deformed mule. I was counting on the fact that a mule would be too smart to have his head so close to flying hooves.

After getting kicked, Samson just stood there. Bob said that he didn't seem to be injured, but it did take the wind out of his sails. In a short time, he went back to trying to conjure up grass to nibble, probably in his macho mule manner, pretending nothing had happened.

Erica said she didn't see anything wrong with him at chore time, and I didn't either. If it had happened to one of my horses, at the very least, their neck would be out of whack and need the horse chiropractor. After that episode, Samson pretty much left Hallelujah alone. When I put them in the pasture and Hallelujah tried to start some roughhousing, Samson just turned his head or walked away. It seemed that Samson could take discipline as well as mete it out.

Samson was ten years old and well trained and didn't require the riding during the winter that the younger horses and mules needed—or so I figured. The horse stalls had open tops so the animals could stick out their heads and look around. They loved it and that made their stall time much more acceptable.

I tied my horses and now my mules in the aisle with two ropes, one on each side, called cross ties. One of the tie areas was right outside of Samson's stall, and with his open door he could reach out and bite the animal I was grooming. After several days of this behavior, I began shutting his door so he couldn't reach out.

If I thought I had a cranky mule before, I found out it could be worse. Now Samson "stall walked," a nasty habit where the animal walks along the side of his stall, turns quickly and walks in the other direction. He was getting himself all riled up, his ears were back and I think his eyes turned into red coals of anger. Yikes! Back to the drawing board. What to do, and *why* was he acting this way?

I wondered if he was getting too much high protein feed. At my boarding and breeding farm I raised good quality grass and alfalfa hay. Perhaps it was too rich for mules. I had already cut back on their meager ration of grain, giving apples and carrots instead. Samson looked like a volcano ready to explode—riding him could be a bad deal if he acted like this when I got on him.

He was only turned out with Hallelujah, and their play had become much more subdued. Perhaps he had too much energy to burn off. I thought about turning him out in the other field with the twenty geldings that I boarded. But I dropped that idea because I couldn't take the chance that he would roar into their group and cause mayhem. I always hated to add new horses to the established herd of horses. They had their "pecking" order already settled. Who was the top dog, the middle-men and who were the loners.

One day, several years ago, I had been standing at the barn door observing the horseplay that was going on. There were two very dominant geldings that I hoped were just playing. If not, then some kind of battle was going on. As I watched, one horse grabbed the mane of the other one. No big deal, usually after a playful tug, the other horse would let go, but not this time. As the horse continued to hold on to the mane, the other one finally decided that enough was enough and reared up and struck the mane-holder in the jaw with his front foot. I heard that thwack and saw the horse shake his head several times, then drop it and just stand there.

I ran out to check the damages. It appeared that the cheek bone had been broken, and I brought him inside. The vet concurred it had been broken, but would heal on its own, given time. If I had not seen it happen, I would never have guessed just what had made that strange injury. Who knew what kind of damage a boisterous mule could hand out? This was making me remember why I had wanted a molly mule and not a gelding or john in the first place. The mollies that I had were happy to eat and "hang out" with the other mares. John mules have the reputation for creating trouble when bored. Another thought was to put Samson and Max together. Max was Erica's big Percheron gelding. He would surely hold his ground with Samson, but maybe *Samson* would get hurt. Besides, Max was the herd boss of the geldings, removing him would anger him, I was sure, and the herd would have to resettle and find another top banana, causing more possible injuries. Best to leave it alone, I decided. But what the heck was wrong with Samson?

The next day while I was getting ready to ride a younger mule, Samson talked to me in a quick picture and a thought. He was jealous! He didn't want me spending all my time with the other animals. Even though it might be work, he wanted his riding time too. He wasn't too well fed, or bored, he was simply envious of my time spent with the others. Like my retired show stallion, Hallelujah, he was unhappy.

When Hallelujah retired from the show ring, I knew it wasn't going to make him content. Since there are only so many days in the week, I had to spend more time training his daughters to carry on the show banner, and Hallelujah was left to his own devices. Having pasture time and breeding mares was not the same as the one-on-one time spent with me in training, and eventually that caused all kinds of havoc in our lives. Samson was not going to take my neglect of his needs quietly either.

It turned out easy to fix. I had two young horses that I crosstied in the aisle to get them accustomed to being controlled. I simply brought Samson out and crosstied him too. He was beside my tack room, so every time I walked in or out, I could pet him and now and then give him a carrot slice. *And* I made sure to ride him.

Lady Blue, my Giant Schnauzer, was sure she was a herd dog; after all, her ancestors had been bred to herd and protect. Her idea of helping turn the horses out of their stalls was to grab and hang on to their tails as they started out the door. Somehow, she had never been kicked by any of them, but was a habit I tried and tried to break – and failed. Her Schnauzer hard-headedness was in full swing. She only held on for about five seconds, but I shuddered to think of her grabbing onto Samson's tail. She was a nosy dog and loved investigating a stall, and eating horse poop, a delectable doggy treat. It didn't matter if the stall was empty or occupied. Of course, Samson's stall was on the list.

    I watched her like a hawk each time she went in while I was filling Samson's water bucket. He was always busy eating his hay and seemed to pay her no heed. She was usually only interested in sniffing here and there, but this particular morning she was sniffing too close to his hind feet. About the same time I told her to scram, Samson picked up his left hind foot and made a very slow cow kick off to the side. Blue saw the movement and skedaddled. Samson never lifted his head or stopped chewing his hay. It was a "shot across the bow" so to speak. He had not meant to kick her, just warned her to get away. If he'd wanted to actually kick her, I know it would have happened and it would not have been pleasant. Lady Blue decided to leave Samson's stall alone after that.

Chapter Twelve: Sugar n' Spice

I admit, I don't know what was happening with me and mules, but for sure, they were accumulating. Mirabella had just come home and now I had three mules. Mirabella would be for sale again—to the right home, so I guess I could say she really didn't count. Miss Ellie was doing better with her lessons, and Bob and I had enjoyed several great rides in the fall.

I reasoned I needed three gaited mules so one of my daughters could and hopefully *would* go riding with Bob and me. Daughter Michal had a great ride on Samson with me on Ellie, admitting that riding mules was a lot of fun, a lot like four-wheeling. But truthfully, the real reason was, I was in love with mules. I was getting another one for me.

I kept looking at the magazine ads and checking out any of the gaited mules for sale. I met some very nice folks, but my criteria that the mule had to gait at seven miles per hour to keep up with Samson, struck all of them down. Fortunately, the sellers were honest and said that finding a mule that gaited at that speed was going to be hard. I was beginning to believe it. It did make Samson look even more a prize in my eyes.

In an issue of a mule magazine, I spotted an ad for mule hauling. That was the first one I had seen, and had been wondering if I did find a mule that sounded too great to pass up, but it was in the south or west, how I would get it? Driving far might be out of the question for me. I called the gentleman, had an informative chat with him, and broached the question about gaited mules. Did he know of any?

He gave me several names, and added that he had a friend who had a gaited molly that he thought of very highly. His name was Loyd, and I recognized him immediately. He ran beautiful colored ads of exceptional mules in the mule magazine. Usually they were not gaited mules, but they were so nice looking and had such great write ups, that I wished I was able to ride one that trotted. I called him immediately.

Mules, Mules and More Mules

There were several things I was looking for in another mule. First, it had to be safe. Second, it had to gait, and third, I was looking for one that was over 15 hands. I was simply used to riding my taller Walking Horses, Samson was 16'3 hands and I liked tall, or at least not short. Sugar was only 14'3. I was turned off by that, but Loyd had many impressive things to say about her, most importantly, he was sure she could keep up with Samson. She was going to be nine in the spring, she was a seasoned trail mule in some pretty harsh country, she was well trained, pretty and sweet to boot. Man, it definitely sounded enticing. I told him I'd sure think about her.

The next day, I got out all the smaller horses in the barn and measured them. They were all 15 hands or taller. This wasn't so good. Loyd had said she was out of a Quarter Horse mare and a gaited jack, and her physique was like the mother, so she had some real substance to her. I looked at a Quarter Horse mare I was boarding and tried to imagine riding her, but she was also 15 hands. 14'3 hands is *only* one inch shorter, but for some reason it seemed more than that. I was having quite a time with this issue. I slept another night trying to resolve my dilemma.

The next morning, I called Loyd again, talked some more and was even more sold on Sugar. He said she just suited him in every way, and if he wasn't in the business of selling mules, he would keep her for himself. She'd been ridden by many people, so she wasn't fussy. She wasn't extremely attached to any one person either, like Ruth Ann, the molly I had considered purchasing when I bought Samson. Loyd said he had some business in Ohio and if everything worked out just right, he could bring her up to me and then go on his way. I was always looking for "signs," like Samson's show number of 500, and having her delivered to my door was a good omen.

I got up the next morning and realized that if I didn't buy her, I was going to regret it. It was a lot of money to spend on a mule that I had not seen, but somehow it felt right. God was smiling, I fervently hoped, so I called Loyd and said I would take her. He said that he had two others interested in her, so I wired the money and Sugar was mine, but I must admit I still had a qualm or two. Her size was one, and I had just sent quite a sum of money to a man I didn't know, and without seeing or most importantly, riding the mule. I was such a nut about gait, what was I thinking?

A few days later, Loyd called saying he was leaving the next day, and would arrive around noon the following day. I was on pins and needles, like knowing a really large birthday present was sitting in a closet and I was dying to see it! In due time, they arrived. I remembered when poor Mirabella arrived, all shaggy and on the thin side—certainly no beauty.

Sugar was definitely a different mule. Stocky and actually taller than I was guessing, she was well groomed, ears clipped, and her shaggy winter hair appeared to have been judiciously trimmed. I had seen her picture and knew she was fine looking. In person, I was not disappointed in the least. I was the happiest about her size. She might be 14' 3, but since she was stout, she didn't look small.

Hawleywoods Sugar photo by Loyd Hawley

Loyd led her into the barn; she did a double take when she saw my big mounting block that promised to eat mule and horse alike—the one that took every mule I had gotten so far, days to come up to its side, stand still, and let me on. Miss Ellie had been trained to a mount block, her owner had used one all the time, yet when she saw mine, she forgot all about how to do it. Samson in all his wonderfulness was not good at it either.

Loyd told me Sugar would get up to the side of a picnic table for one to mount. *I'll see,* I thought.

We put her in a stall and I showed Loyd where I planned to keep her until we got acquainted. It was a pen with other horses on two sides; the third side faced the pasture where the rest of the mares would go. "Well," he said, "she may worry the gate a little—I don't think she will jump it."

Say what? Jump it? "You don't really think she will jump it, do you? Has she ever jumped anything before?"

"No," he admitted, "not that I know of."

He seemed somewhat seriously concerned. Super. I'd never even thought about my mules jumping my fences, even though some are trained to "coon" jump. Mules can jump like a deer. Unlike a horse that gets a running start, a mule can jump from standstill and bound over a fence. This is handy when someone is coon hunting (hence the word), comes upon a fence with no gate, and needs to get his mule to the other side. Some throw a tarp or blanket over the fence, some do not cover it. Mule shows include competitions in coon jumping.

Lord have mercy, surely Sugar was not one of those! I locked her in her stall for the night. Tomorrow we'd see about this jumping thing.

I really wanted to have Loyd ride her, show me how she operated with someone she knew instead of my starting from scratch, but somehow it didn't seem fair to Sugar. She'd been in the trailer for hours on two consecutive days, and Loyd was not yet at his journey's end for the day, so I just asked some questions about how my two saddles fit on her. Discovering that both worked fine, and I had a bit in my special bit box which was just like the one she was accustomed to, I was all set to ride, but I wanted to get to know her more. I figured the "three day rule" should suffice. It seemed to take three days to wean young horses and calves and to get a new dog used to his home. I'd do some ground work with her for those days, and keep her separated from the herd of mares.

The next day, while I tied Sugar so she could watch, Erica and I worked on "de-spooking" Miss Ellie by flapping a blue tarp around her. I didn't suppose Sugar was spooky, but any de-sensitizing to stimuli is always good. Later I took Mirabella into the arena. She was always curious and loved investigation just for the sake of sticking her nose into something. She traipsed back and forth over the tarp, making crackling noises as she walked. I picked it up and placed it over the mount block. Mirabella pawed at it with her front foot, and then tried to pick it up in her teeth. Obviously, she wasn't scared of it in any way.

I took Sugar into the arena and showed her the tarp. She wasn't spooked by it, but neither would she set a foot upon it. Even Samson had walked over it when I asked him. What was her problem? After doing a dance around and around it, I had one of the girls put it on the ground in front of the aisle into her part of the barn. When I led her up to it, she never looked at it, but walked over it as though it wasn't there. Maybe she just wasn't into fun and games.

Later that morning, we turned her out in her private pen, turned the other mares out to the pasture, and crossed our fingers. She did nothing but stand under the tree by the gate, looking wistfully at the others. She had two horses close-by on the other side of the fence, but she seemed to have no use for them; in fact she was quite spiteful towards them. She probably knew that someday soon she would be galloping in the field with the mares.

Friday I had more time to play with my four-hooved critters. I tied Sugar up in the barn aisle and rode Miss Ellie. Sugar had to adjust to being left. She danced around some, and then settled down. Then I started to work with her. I put my blue tarp and some poles on the ground; somehow I wanted to get her to walk over it no matter where it was, "just because I said so." I walked up to my contraption, stepped over it, and Sugar followed with no hesitation.

We went outside where the young cows were, and did more groundwork. I led her forward, backed her up, and turned her around; she was faultless. The cows were at the fence watching the proceedings, so I walked up to them. This time, I was smarter than with Mirabella. We were in the arena and the gate was closed. I didn't want her to pull away and leave if the cows spooked her. Loyd had said she was used to passing them as she went down the road, but nose to nose was unknown. The cows came closer to the fence and Sugar held her ground, looking not the least perturbed. One stuck its nose through the boards and Sugar nipped at it. She passed the cow test. Months later when she decided to practice being a Quarter Horse and chase my cows around the pasture, I realized that *not* being frightened of cows could be a problem also.

Finally the day arrived to ride her for the first time. Bob kindly put in his presence so I would have "backup." I saddled Sugar, led her to the arena, and tried to get her up to the mounting block, but she did the mounting block dance all the others had already perfected. It didn't matter, she was short enough I knew I could use a small milk crate. I had to make sure she didn't move off just as I put my foot in the stirrup, because my old bones and muscles couldn't keep up with a walk-away mule, so with Bob holding her by the mounting block, I climbed on board.

She "blew her nose" at some of the objects in the arena such as the wheelbarrow, the dogs playing, a partly open door to the outside, but she didn't stop walking. She thought the mule in the mirrors that lined the arena would surely like to be her best friend, and kept trying to touch her with her nose. Soon she was walking around in a fairly business-like manner. I clucked to her and squeezed lightly with my legs to push her into a faster gait. I was both nervous and excited to see how fast she would go. The big question still was: could she keep up with Samson?

She wasn't very speedy, but she was still feeling her way around the arena. She had a great stop on her, and turned very nicely. Those were really good things I truly appreciated, especially after Miss Ellie, whose training definitely needed to be continued. All in all I was pleased, and since Bob was waiting in the cold arena for me to finish, I quit on a good note. I couldn't get her to go up to the block at the right angle so I could dismount, but since she was shorter, I could slide to the ground without it. Perhaps having a shorter mule was going to work out fine.

I had promised her I would turn her out with the mares, and after our little ride, I did. She was the last to go, and so had to enter the herd milling around the back door. I probably should have done it differently. When the mares saw a new face, they had to chase after her, putting her in the bottom of the herd spot. She neatly scooted her butt around, dodging open mouths and didn't seem unduly alarmed. Soon they went through the gate into the pasture.

The mares continued chasing her at intervals, but I had noticed from watching Mirabella that the mules didn't run all around as my horses would, they just ran off or in a small circle around the dominating mare, staying just out of reach, but not expending any more energy than absolutely necessary to stay safe. Sugar did the same thing except she let fly with those hind feet many times. *Oh, boy*, I thought, *she is not going to take kindly to the bottom placement in the herd.*

The next day I rode in the outside arena. She snorted and gawked at some things, looked but didn't snort at the cows. I noticed there was one thing she didn't like to do—stand still. Figuring she was likely nervous at being in a strange place, I wasn't too worried. She also wanted to follow another horse. It took some time before she would stand in the arena and let the other horses work around her and not want to follow.

She had spunk and spark, but if she and I could work it out together it would be fine. A horse or mule that fidgets and dances around when other horses leave wouldn't be to my liking. At the end of this ride, she sidled up to the mounting block and with just a word or two, stood still for me to dismount. We were making progress in several ways.

I rode her again the following day and we got more speed. I was beginning to hope that she really would keep up with my big boy. This day I placed a plastic tarp on the ground along with some shiny plastic bags. I checked out her spook reflexes in the safety of the enclosed arena. She was cautious, unlike Mirabella who knew she could have some fun with them, but walked over and around everything I asked. I was feeling more adventurous, and that evening Bob and I took her and Samson outside on a short trail. Now I would really get to check out her gait.

Because it was so muddy, we just went down to the creek, crossed it and rode around the garden center, which stored many trees, bushes, vehicles and big rocks used for my brother-in-law's landscaping business. I was impressed at how slowly she went behind Samson into the creek, turned and climbed up the hill. So far so good; I was getting that silly mule smile on my face again. Again, she looked at things, but never spooked, *and* she kept up with Samson.

Bob was not holding Big Sam in at all; in fact, I think he was having a blast. I had chosen Samson to go with Sugar because I was sure he wouldn't spook. Miss Ellie had shown that she was capable of some interesting twirls and I didn't want to show them to Sugar. Bob seemed a little disappointed when I asked him to ride Samson, but now I thought he was loving it. I didn't need to urge Sugar on; she just matched Samson's speed at a nice rack. I glanced at Samson a couple of times and the expression on his face was one of worry. "How fast is that little upstart going to go, anyway?" he seemed to say.

We came home the way we went, going back down the hill and into the creek. Sugar was cautious and didn't rush after Samson who had gone ahead. This was a short and easy ride, but she had done superbly. I was more than pleased and feeling ever more confident with her.

Sugar in the pasture was a different story. Watching her the very first day run along the fence beside a gelding in the next paddock, I had the feeling that she wasn't going to be Miss Nicey Nice in the pasture. She had her ears flat back, kicked in the air close to the fence, and squealed. Miss Ellie and Mirabella had never done that during their adjustment period. They were content to have a friend close by and go stand under the tree.

When I turned Sugar out with the herd, she stayed away from the others, but only so far. If they had pushed her, they might have felt those flying hooves. The first night, I asked Erica what happened at feeding time when they all came in the barn. That night she was one of the last ones, staying back away from the pushy bossy mares. The next night, she was among the first. Erica said she didn't make a fuss; the other horses just parted away and let her through. I wondered what Sugar said to them.

After Sugar had been here about a week, I had her in the cross ties after riding her. As I walked past, I heard her say to me in a mind communication, "I want my name changed to Susie Q." By now I was getting used to my animals and those entrusted into my care, putting thoughts into my head. I did a quick double take, stopped and looked at her. "Well, why not, I have changed almost every other mule's name, why not yours?" And that day she became Susie Q.

I'd barely gotten Susie Q and enjoyed a couple of rides on her, when winter came with a vengeance to northern Indiana. Early winter had been mild and had spoiled me; now with near zero and some sub-zero nights and very cold, snowy, windy days, I was staying in the house. Going out to feed and turn out my animals was exercise enough.

Susie and the rest were in for hibernation. Two months later the weather broke enough for more mule riding. So far I hadn't ridden Susie by herself, although I had been assured she would be fine.

Turning Susie out with the mare herd had helped her a lot. She seemed to feel sure where "home" was. She knew she belonged, this was her place. She no longer fretted when another horse rode with her in the arena. She would stand and watch, no longer wanting to "keep up" even in the barn. About this time I discovered a new piece of horse equipment – the bitless bridle. As its name implies, it has no bit, but control is given by straps around the head and across the nose. The information stated that horses loved it; it cured many vices such as head tossing and even fretfulness on the trails, the idea being that if the horse was comfortable, he would act better. It sounded fine to me, so I got one.

Susie was out of a Quarter Horse mare, and was quicker moving and more responsive to all the riding aids than the other mules. I decided I would try her in the bitless bridle first. She had a great "whoa," so I was confident she would stop. Riding in the inside arena was the best way to start, but we soon went to the outside one. Susie was perfect; she seemed more relaxed, her smooth gait was faster, her head shook and her ears flopped, just like they should, but usually that happens after several miles on the trail.

My next ride was outside. The weather was crazy this year. First mild, then darn awful, now a spring-like day in the 60s. I took to the trail around the farm, which was muddy as all get out, but Susie maneuvered it well. I didn't quite trust her to be good with the mares already turned into the pasture, so I rode before letting them out. Susie did want to keep an eye out for her friends—why tempt fate? She was good, no spooks, even going by the partially hidden swing set that belonged to the neighbor. Hearing the swing move with a squeak, and the children talk and laugh without seeing them always made the horses nervous.

Her dainty feet didn't slip in the mud; she crossed all the bridges with only a few gentle snorts and a tilt to her head. Coming home she got her speed up, and it took some strong aids to remind her to gait slowly. Her only flaw I could see was her very mild "wanting to be with her friends" attitude. After three little circles to slow her down, she decided she really could just walk the rest of the way home. My confidence grew in the little sorrel molly. Someone can tell you all kinds of great things about a new animal, but until you experience it for yourself, you just are not totally convinced. Susie Q was giving me that good old "mule smile."

A couple years later Susie had become a most steady and favorite mount. One peaceful late spring morning I was riding in the neighbor's woods along the fence line beside a cornfield, and I came upon a very distressing sight. Caught in the fence was a small, spotted, baby fawn. It had tried to jump after its mother and became entangled in the top barb wire. Susie was quiet when she spotted the baby who was lying on the other side, strung up with his foot held up high and tight. I dismounted and tied her to the fence a little way to the side. I hoped I could set the fawn free, but the leg was twisted around the wire and nothing short of wire cutters would work. The baby lay as though dead, but I could see his ribs move ever so slightly.

I led Susie to a log, and had her put her front feet over it and stand while I got back into the saddle. Then we hustled back home at her fast racking gait for Bob and the golf cart with tools. Bob and I returned and cut the fawn out of his predicament while the mother stood about sixty feet away, watching intently. The deer herd had become quite used to horse and mule visitors, even the golf cart which Bob used to walk the dogs, and we could ride very close to them. We quietly left after our good deed. The fawn was gone later in the day and I am sure I saw him and his mother months later. Susie had been perfect.

Sometime later, Susie was much less than perfect.

It was evening and when I turned out the horses, I noticed that all the cows hadn't gone into their back pasture: three of them were in a horse pasture, and one was the month old Red Angus calf.

I was disturbed because I knew Susie had a fondness for chasing the cows. I didn't think my problem through well enough, and headed out to the pasture where Susie was grazing with the cows who were in a far corner. I should have taken a rope and brought Susie back to the barn first. I would pay dearly for that oversight.

I headed for the cows and thought I could quietly herd them along the fence line back to the gate. The problem was we had to pass by Susie. The older steers decided to run, buck and play, and Susie took chase. Four pastures joined together like spokes on a wheel at one point by the barn, and all the gates were open. When the cows and Susie ran, the other seven mules and horses joined in, including Nugget, my older arthritic mare, whom I loved dearly, but who should never gallop about like a maniac.

Susie spotted the little calf and soon had him cut from the rest of the cattle. She galloped madly after the frantic baby who ran into the wire mesh field fence and bounced off like he was spring loaded. Susie never missed a beat as she lengthened her stride, opened her mouth, and flattened her ears flat back on her head. Round and round they went, and into another pasture where the poor calf again bounced off the fence.

I was screaming at the top of my lungs, but of course, it did no good. Nugget was tearing around neighing to someone; I never figured out why she was so upset. Nugget loved foals. Did she think this was a horse baby in danger? It certainly *was* in danger. There was no doubt in my mind if Susie caught the calf she would kill it.

Bob was gone, so I had no help. All I could do was stand and contemplate a horrible disaster. When I ran out of the barn to separate the horses, mules and cows, I had left the back door open, an error that probably turned out to save the day.

On one of the many gallops through the several gates, and into different pastures, the horses, mules and one lone, very frightened to-the-point-of-losing-his-mind calf, peeled into the barn, down the aisle and into the inside riding arena.

At this point, I had no idea how this incident was going to end. As I stood there watching this horror film continue, Bob walked into the barn, the frightened calf ran up onto one of the big piles of sawdust that we stored in the arena corners, and the horses and mules milled around the arena. Susie still had her eye on the prize, but fortunately, didn't climb the pile after it.

Somehow, we got the horses headed back down the aisle and out the door. The calf was even more terrified because now Bob was chasing him. When he ran into a corner, Bob got a rope on him, but the calf had no idea how to get out the barn. Both Bob and I decided that cow ponies had a definite place in a cow herd. Those beef calves are strong! The calf reared, bucked, lay down, struggled to his feet, then reared and bucked some more as he ran as fast as his stubby little legs would go. Somehow Bob got him out the door with his momma, who was having a hysterical mother meltdown.

The calf was not the same for months after that event. Our four beef cows are tame so I can handle them for breeding, feeding and doctoring. I didn't try to tame the calf because he was going to end up in the freezer, but usually because momma is tame, the steer calves gentle down. Not poor little Sonny. It took Sonny a long time to again trust a human.

Chapter Thirteen: Miss Ellie Goes to Boot Camp

I found a mule trainer in Ohio who was close enough for me to consider for Miss Ellie. After talking to Bryan, I thought he sounded knowledgeable and also gentle enough for Miss Ellie. I had experience with horse trainers and not all are created equal. Some are harsher in their training methods; I wanted Miss Ellie to learn, but not be handled roughly. She had several issues I wanted Bryan to work on, but the most important was stopping.

It was winter by now, and I did my own training in our inside arena. She did quite well in there, but when I rode her out on the path again, she was back to running through the bit, as the saying goes. She had no "whoa." I was following Bob on Samson down a short but slippery side of a creek. I wanted her to stop and wait until Bob was down before plunging over the edge. The bit might as well been a ribbon in her mouth for all she cared; she was going right then. It was at that moment I made the decision to send her for sure. That was pretty awful mule behavior and could be dangerous.

My wish list had several behavior modifications for Ellie. First and foremost, she had to learn to stop. Turning wasn't real great either and she had been getting spooky. When she spooked, she twirled around and headed in the other direction. I couldn't get the clippers near her head, and although she loaded into the trailer okay, she wouldn't get in the last slot of the three-horse slant load. I wanted her to ride in that space when Bob and I traveled with Samson and her to faraway places, and I needed to take hay and mule supplies. The provisions would be loaded in the front, not behind the mules. She refused, and I could understand it; the last space seemed smaller because of the angle of entrance. I knew she could fit; she wasn't sure.

I was impressed with Bryan when we met. He obviously knew about mules; there were a lot of them on the farm. Many were tied, some with hobbles on their front feet, to teach patience in standing. Miss Ellie loved to paw the ground with her left foot. It was annoying and hard on mule feet with or without shoes. I mentioned to Bryan he could do that to Miss Ellie too. No mule looked hungry, but many were deep in mud. The weather had been very wet in his area; Miss Ellie would be kept in a stall, he told me. He said he liked her; she was a pretty mule, and gentle. He was sure she would be very trainable. My plan was to leave her for one month, and then I would pick up where he left off, hopefully with a good foundation.

The first week she was gone, I called for an Ellie update. "Goodness," Bryan said, "I see what you mean about stopping. She doesn't have one!" Too true.

Next week he said they were making progress. "But I'm not at all sure if you rode her up to a busy highway right now, and told her to whoa, that she would, but she's getting more supple. I can turn her head around better in both directions." Miss Ellie was very stiff in both directions—like a board. She would need to limber up before she could accomplish much.

The following week I heard, "She's better, but not as far along as I thought she'd be. She's still stiff, but she is learning to back up some." That was good; I hadn't been able to get her to back one single step while on her back. "And she lopes some, actually pretty good for being out of a Walking Horse mare." (Gaited horses sometimes do not canter or lope well). I had asked him to lope her a little because if something scared her and she took off, at least she would have had some experience being stopped while loping. Bryan agreed that was a good idea.

He also told me her running walk gait was getting a lot better and faster. That was something I hadn't asked for. Gait training was a whole different ball of wax. She had gotten faster at her gait while I had her, so I figured over time, I could improve that part. I was elated. She had trouble keeping steady in it, and she didn't go fast enough to stay with Samson without breaking into a trot. She was Bob's mule and he wasn't very proficient at keeping her going. A lot of trotting occurred.

I asked about the clippers. He said he had spent an hour one day just having them running and rubbing them around her head. Wow, that was patience. I knew I had chosen the right person. My patience seemed to evaporate the older I became. And then winter came with a vengeance. Both Bryan and I agreed it was too cold to ride. It was zero or some above during the day and below at night. I sure didn't want to ride anything. He said he wouldn't charge me training and Ellie had a rest.

Two weeks later, the weather broke and it was back to work. Now she made faster progress and while Bryan wished she was better, I was sure I would be happy. I hadn't expected a "thirty day wonder," just hoped for improvement. It was still rather cold and dreary at home, so I decided to leave her another two weeks so when she did come home, I'd feel like working with her. I didn't want her to settle in back at her home with her friends, pasture turnout and no working. I was afraid she might forget, or rather think she only worked at Bryan's.

When we arrived to pick her up, Bryan showed us our new and improved mule. She had a nice slow lope on a loose rein, and my gracious, her walking gait had improved immensely. I could hardly believe my eyes or take them off her. He told me I could show her at the mule shows and she could do well with more work. "And," he added, "not every mule lopes as well as she does." I glanced at Bob; he didn't seem elated with the idea of showing his mule. Oh, well.

Miss Ellie's ears had been clipped, but I asked him to show me how to do it. It took just a few minutes for her to remember clippers were okay. Bryan pulled her head down towards the ground with a rope halter and then rubbed her ears. He told me to do that if she acted startled having her ears clipped.

I had one more thing I wanted to see—loading her into the back slot of our trailer. She wouldn't ride home there; the load balances better if the weight is farther forward, but I wanted him to do it while she was there. Part of her training had been to teach her to move away from a swinging rope: back, sideways or forward. He held the lead rope in his left hand, positioning Miss Ellie at the doorway and twirled the other end of the rope at her butt. After just a tiny hesitation, she popped the front half of herself inside; then she backed out.

That was all right; the animals need to learn how to back out also. At the next twirl of the rope, all of Miss Ellie entered the trailer and stayed there while Bryan entered and petted her and then he told her to back out. He loaded her three more times and she was perfect. He mentioned that the space was too small for a person to enter and try and lead the mule in. That was what I had been doing. He said she would need to hop in by herself. We loaded her into the front slot and headed for home.

Her stall at home has a door which opens out to a small paddock. When she first came from Missouri, she was not at all used to being stalled. She spent her time outside, standing under the tree, even sleeping outside at night. When the weather got colder I had to start shutting her door. After being at the trainer for six weeks in a stall, she was happy to be out again even though the weather was rather chilly.

The next day, I turned her out with the mare herd. There was no jostling for position; she seemed to slip right in where she left off. That night when Bob did the bedtime stall check, he told me she hadn't eaten all her hay. "Don't worry," I said, "mules eat slower and maybe she found some grass in the back field and wasn't real hungry." Her grain was gone and that was good. It was a little strange, however. I hadn't given her much hay. Surely she wasn't sick.

The next two days I couldn't ride, but on Saturday, I kept her in with a couple other mules and let the other horses outside. Many times the ones left inside are very upset. Miss Ellie handled it fine. Again I noticed that she hadn't cleaned up her morning hay, but her grain was gone. She was thinner than when I sent her away, nothing to be alarmed about; I figured with hard work, she had gotten very fit, and there wasn't any fat. *I* should be so lucky.

I got her out of the stall and cross tied her. She just stood there with her head hanging down like she had been ridden down the Grand Canyon and back. She looked depressed and dejected. The saddle didn't fit quite as before because her back was thinner. Not to worry, I can really make my animals fatter, perhaps too easily. I knew you were not to over feed grain to mules; they didn't need the energy or calories. I had gotten mules because they weren't supposed to be spooky; I surely didn't want to *make* mine that way.

One mule trainer told me a story about a fellow sending him a bad mule. The mule was purely awful. He kicked, couldn't be tied, couldn't be ridden—and he was a young mule. The trainer said he wondered if *he* would be able to get anywhere with the animal. After the young obstreperous mule had been at the trainer's barn and on his feeding schedule, he noticed that each day the mule mellowed more and more. It turned out the gentleman who owned the mule had been feeding him too much rich grain. The story hasn't the best ending because after the mule returned home, quiet and well trained, his owner again fed him too much and he was right back where he had started.

My mules got grain because the horses did, and they would be upset if others got some and they didn't. Their amount was (as Erica liked to joke) twelve pellets with an apple or carrot. A horse, on the other hand, would frequently receive four cups. My mules were pleasingly plump and happy. Spring was right around the corner, and Miss Ellie would soon be grass fat again.

Grass fat is a nice kind of plumpness for pleasure mules and horses, but those same animals in competition, or as work animals pulling wagons and plows, for instance, need more than grass to give energy. When I was fifteen years old, my very first horse was a medium size draft horse. He had been used for farm work and skidding out logs. He was tough, but certainly not pleasingly plump. After I had him fat and pretty on our grass pasture, I proudly showed him off to his former owner.

"Yeah, he is pretty, but if he was working, he would lose it all. He is soft."

Well, that was the farthest thing from my or Smokey's mind. Grass fat is pretty, but doesn't give the explosive energy that pleasure animals do not need. At least at this point in my mule ownership, that is what I thought!

After saddling her and finding a bit similar to the one Bryan had used, I began to lead her out to the inside arena. She wasn't coming: all four feet were planted firmly. Now this wasn't good; it seemed she didn't wish to be ridden. I had a rack of riding crops along the wall, and I reached for one to encourage her rear to move forward, but as soon as she saw the crop in my hand, she went into reverse, rather quickly, I might add.

She had been taught to back up out of the trainer's space, and respect his position. Did she think going backwards was what I wanted, or was she over-reacting, big time? She had her head up high and didn't look exactly relaxed. I rethought my plan. I had better do a little ground work with her before I got on her back—to remind her that I was in charge, but first I had to get her out into the arena. Also in the whip rack was a buggy whip which is longer by about four feet. Using that, I could stand by her shoulder, lead her with the reins and tap her on the rear end at the same time. After the first tap, she moved forward, but she still wasn't pleased.

Under her chin, where the curb chain of the bit rests, she had gotten a sore. It wasn't bad, horses have gotten as bad or worse by a halter rub if it was adjusted too tightly, but I adjusted the chain so it would lie below her sore. I don't think Bryan lowered it for her, in fact, it likely had the result of making her back off the bit more and stop better, which in her case wasn't bad either. I knew I had to be firm with her; certainly, we were going for a ride.

Before getting on, I "shooed" her rear over in both directions, as Bryan had done. Then I told her to back up by shaking the reins just a little. We ended up backing half way down a 100-foot aisle and it wasn't my idea either. Next, we headed for the hated mounting block. It is rather pyramid in shape, with the top part level. I think they can't judge exactly where it is. A tree stump or something square didn't elicit that problem, but she had perfected the task before she left. Now, Miss Ellie hung back and wouldn't come up to it. Here I stood, perched on the top, pulling my mule with the reins and she had again planted her feet and stuck her head up in the air. Dang.

I got off and got the crop, tapped her rear end a little and finally got her in the right place. She stood well as I clambered on, and stood until I got ready to move. She had to wait until I said go. It wasn't to be her decision; one of her lessons had been to stand until told to move. I practiced stopping, which she did, and turning, which she did. I enjoyed her faster running walk gait. At one point, I must have unintentionally given her the signal to lope, because she lifted off nice and easy. We loped around on a loose rein, and when I told her to stop, she did. Great, great, great. I was very pleased!

Our next chance to ride was the following day, this time with a friend. First I let out the other horses and mules. I think I would have been fine with Ellie staying in with the other mule that was to be ridden, but she had gone outside in her adjoining paddock and saw all the other mares running out to the field. Now she was pissed and I had to go out and fetch her. She thought about running away from me, but when she walked into the corner of her pen, she turned and saw the apple I had in my hand. Leading her toward the barn, she did a quick stop and pull back, but gave in when I yelled at her to stop it. She was having a battle within herself whether to be good or not.

As soon as I tied her up, I knew she was not in a submissive mood. She had her mind on leaving. I told Ann, my riding buddy, that before we rode I'd better take her into the arena and work with Miss Ellie remembering just who the boss was. I did very gentle movements with her rear quarters going over, and then gave her an apple slice. I'm sure Bryan would have a few words to say against that, but Miss Ellie was different from before. I appreciated her training, but she expressed unhappiness as well. I wanted to sweeten the training pot.

I moved her rear quarters the other direction, gave an apple slice, had her back up just a few steps, then encouraged her to return to me and gave another treat. Now she seemed quiet, her head hanging in submission, and she was happy. *Now* we could ride.

I knew Miss Ellie's mouth was likely tender and certainly her chin was. What would happen if I used the bitless bridle? I do know before I sent her to Bryan, I would never have thought of riding her with no bit. I decided to give it a try. I was with another rider, that would be a safety factor and I wasn't going to go off galloping across the fields. I should be safe.

Our ride was superb. Miss Ellie couldn't have been better; her gaiting was wonderful and she responded to the one hand stop in the new bridle with just a firm squeeze of my fingers to tip her head to one side. She slowed from a running walk to a trail walk with a firm squeeze with both hands. Before we left the confines of the barn arena, I had pulled her head to the side, showing her how it felt. How much of Miss Ellie's reticence to leave the barn aisle was related to her thinking her mouth was going to hurt? After that painless ride, would she walk out happily? Time would tell.

Sadly, time would also convince me using a bitless bridle wasn't the safest thing to use on the trails. I decided I would rather have something to give me an edge in stopping in an emergency. It still hangs in my tack room. Maybe someday I will try again, but what I discovered about myself in those early mule ownership days, was I wanted to *ride* on the trail. I had trained my show horses for thirty years and they were splendid. Now I wanted something different—a steady quiet animal for trail and I was tired of training. But what I later learned was that steady and quiet also required continuing training. Total retirement was out of the question!

Chapter Fourteen: Maybellene

I now was the proud owner of four mules: Mirabella, who was in the process of finding a new home, Samson, the new love of my life, Miss Ellie who was Bob's mule and Susie Q, Little Miss Perfect. My mules had the knack of giving me serenity, which my body and soul so craved. Just brushing, giving carrots, and stroking their faces as they hung them over their stall doors, gave me peace. As much as I loved and appreciated my Tennessee Walking show-horses and their talents, I wouldn't say they made me feel tranquil. They had, however, made me happy, somewhat famous, and fulfilled my dreams for that time in my life. My mules were different.

They were multiplying quickly too. My dear, long time friend, Ann, watched my growing fascination with the mules, their multiplication, and remarked one day, "I think I want a mule too." That was all it took to get me on the telephone to Loyd and John, two men from whom I had purchased good mules, asking them to keep their eyes peeled for another good gaited, gentle and well trained mule.

By the time a good mule is advertised in a mule magazine, it could be gone already. That happened with Susie Q. I bought her before her full page ad appeared in *Mules and More*, by hearing about her beforehand. Two months later Loyd said he was still getting calls on her. One lady wondered how much money it would take for me to part with her. When John called in late February to tell me about a new mule he had just purchased, I was all ears.

He said Maybellene was a sorrel molly about 15 hands, around nine years, and was well gaited. Samson and Miss Ellie were registered, but many are not. Buying from a reputable person is really the key, because without the papers, you don't know how old they actually are or anything about their breeding. I knew that both Samson and Ellie were out of Tennessee Walking Horse mothers; Susie Q was out of a Quarter Horse mare, but that was known only because Loyd had known the mule all her life. Any more about Maybellene was a guess, as John had picked her up at a mule sale.

John kept in touch with me as he spent the days with Maybellene; he knew I loved gaited mules, and he thought she was an exceptional one. I told him to give me first dibs when he put a price on her and was ready to sell.

Shortly after that conversation, the phone rang. It was John. "Well, I've had my last ride on this mule," he said. "She just does everything I ask of her. There isn't any more I can do. Today the wind was blustery, stuff was being blown around, and she just kept on going, never looked sideways at anything. I even rode her by a busy road, and although she didn't like it, she kept her head. She gaited up a storm doing a flat walk and when I told her to go on, she speeded up into her foxtrot. She's ready to go."

I knew John had been thinking of taking her to Eminence, Missouri, on one of the spring trail rides, so I was surprised he was letting her go already, the ride was only a few months away. I asked, "Why now?"

"Well," he said, "I am really loving this mule and I need to move her on."

"Why don't you just keep her? I can tell you really like her."

"The problem is, she doesn't have a job here. I have one mule I will keep, but being in the business, I need to sell them when they are ready. It will be hard for me; this one is going to be more like an adoption."

I knew exactly what he meant. I had sold some horses when I was breeding and raising them, and it was the same way. Not every animal pulls your heart strings, but now and then one really gets to you. If you can't keep it, at least knowing it is going somewhere good helps a lot. I knew John was happy I would get Maybellene.

"If you *ever* don't want her, you let me know, whether it is next month, or twenty years from now, and I'll take her back. There has been only one other mule I ever said that about in fifteen or so years of mule trading. Maybellene is the second."

Mules, Mules and More Mules

What more hearty recommendation could I ask?

"There is one thing, though. She has an issue about her ears...."

That was too bad, but I wasn't going to pass up on a darn near perfect mule because of touchy ears. I figured I could live with that. "And," he added, "she isn't real good with her hind feet. She doesn't kick, but she leans real bad. My farrier put shoes on her and he got along with her okay." That didn't please me a great deal either, but if she didn't kick....

I decided I could trust John, he was fussy about to whom he sold his mules, trying to match up mule and rider. After meeting me when Bob and I got Miss Ellie, he was sure I would get along with Maybellene. He did comment, "She is all business. She has a job to do and places to go. I love that." That was one reason he had wanted to take her to the Eminence ride. He wanted to show her off.

He further said, "She is rather standoffish. Not a 'mule in your pocket' kind of mule. It took me about two weeks to get her to be friendlier. Food helps—she *loves* to eat!"

These things didn't please me a great deal either. I was spoiled with my friendly mules. I asked John what he knew about Maybellene's past.

"All I know is that she was run through the sale by an outfitter. He was selling a bunch of mules. I liked the looks of her and thought she was gaited, even though no one said she was. I don't think they knew what they had." An outfitter. Hmm; that probably explained why "she had a job to do" and wasn't super friendly—and maybe why she liked to eat.

"Who named her?" I asked John.

"I did. She reminded me of the song 'Maybellene' by Chuck Berry. Have you ever heard it?"

Well, no I hadn't. "Why did she remind you of the song?"

"Berry sings about chasing Maybellene in his V8 Ford and some of the words, such as 'As I was motorvatin' over the hill, I saw Maybellene in a Coupe de Ville Cadillac rollin' on the open road' reminded me of this mule. Like I said, she has places to go."

Cute. This was one mule's name I would want to keep.

I called Patco Transportation and arranged to have Maybellene picked up rather than going to see her. That was fine with John. He said he had used them a couple times to ship mules and he liked the hauler. The bad thing about it was that John wouldn't get to see my face when I rode her. I promised to tell him all about it.

Two weeks later, Pati, the driver, called to leave me a message saying, "I have picked up your pretty mule."—oh, boy, I liked that part—"She was real good at getting into the trailer with the wind blowing." It was a ramp load trailer, and I knew John's was a step-up, so it was different. "She just looked at it for a minute and then hopped on in." That was great. So far so good! On April Fool Day, Maybellene arrived at the farm. She was home.

Maybellene *was* standoffish; she stood toward the back of her stall, and while all the other horses and mules had their heads hung out of their stall doors, hers was nowhere to be seen. When I walked past or to her, she wouldn't come to say "hello." When I walked into her stall, she took two steps away, but she didn't turn completely around and she did let me stroke her neck. If I tried to entice her with a carrot or apple, she swiftly snatched a bite and then quickly turned her head away again. Goodness, she acted like a wild deer.

Grain got her more excited and she would come and dip her dainty muzzle into the pan I was holding. John had suggested I feed her by hand and let her realize I had real goodies for her. Eating grain was no delicate matter. She shoved her nose into it and practically inhaled her small amount, chewing fast and diving in for more. I was making a little progress. It seemed slowly over the week she had been here her eyes were getting softer; she didn't look as alarmed as the first few days.

I doubt she was quite 15 hands tall, she was a nondescript brown and she looked like she was pregnant, which of course was nearly impossible. (There are records of rare mule birthings). I wasn't sure just what that big tummy was. Her neck was one of her good assets, being of moderate length with no "donkey" dip and upright like a horse.

Her head was the most interesting thing about her. It was small for a mule—at least in my barn. She had an Arabian dished face with a small muzzle and her eyes were dark and lovely, especially when she was relaxed. She had the shortest tail I'd seen on a mule, her feet were strong looking, and her legs were straight as they should be.

Each morning I got her out and did something with her, even if it was just to brush her coat. She liked being brushed, not so much the feet cleaning. John had been right about that, too.

As I brushed her, I noticed that her coat was coarse and pretty shaggy. Susie Q's soft coat had been slick and shiny when she arrived. My other mules had nice coats too, so it wasn't a mule trait. Then I saw a strange indentation in her rear; at first I thought it was a fat pad. One of my friends had an older mule that actually looked deformed; when I asked him why, he laughed and replied, "It's just fat. She loves to eat and is older so I don't ride her anymore." It sure wasn't pretty. I wasn't going to like it if Maybellene had the start of a fat pad.

The more I studied it, I saw very short, bristly hair below it on both sides. It dawned on me that those could be britching rubs. There was no question that Maybellene had been well used by her outfitter. How I wished I could get her history. I bet she would have some tales to tell—if she would talk. I had called my animal communicator, Mary, while the mule was still at John's farm. I couldn't wait to talk to her and see what she was like, what she thought about becoming my mule and anything about her past. The conversation didn't go real well.

"She's being pretty quiet," Mary said. "Usually your mules have a lot to say." Mary had been getting a real kick out of talking to the mules. She admitted they were different from the horses she usually conversed with. She called them "serene," and I agreed. She said their thought processes were different too, they were real thinkers. Well, we all knew that about mules already. Sometimes what they thought wasn't what *we* wanted them to think, though.

Every time I called her to chat with my animals, Mary would say, "Guess who wants to talk first?" It would be Samson and nearly always the first thing Mary would tell me was that Samson really loved me. Of course that really warmed my heart. I loved the big lug too; he *insisted* on it!

Finally Mary got Maybellene to warm up a little, but most of her communication was in feelings not words, but one phrase I think I will always remember. Maybellene said that she had heard that I "had a good heart." Were those tears I felt pricking in my eyes? And that was about all of the conversation. She was willing to come to my farm. She was a work mule and likely didn't have any idea what "the good life" could be. She didn't complain, she just didn't know much. She'd never "fallen in love" with a human, so that was yet to happen—I hoped.

In talking to Mary over the years, I learned that animals talk to each other. I used that communication system to have Hallelujah, my stallion, talk to some of his offspring on different matters. It was no surprise to me my mules knew I was planning on another purchase, and had sought out the new one, perhaps telling Maybellene about her possible new home. Susie Q already felt in competition with Maybellene because either she or Maybellene was to belong to my friend Ann. I just didn't know which one yet. Being the mule with all the self confidence in the world, Susie was sure I would want to keep her. I assured her that no matter who actually owned her, she would stay here and I would care for her. Poor Maybellene had no particular hopes.

The way Maybellene gobbled her food was very different from the eating habits of my other mules. I had read that mules ate slower, and would stop eating when comfortably full, not stuffing themselves just because it was "there." I'd seen Samson and Ellie pick up their hay almost stem by stem, munching with a look of sublime happiness. Not Maybellene; she stuffed hay into her mouth like a cow, by the wads, and it looked like she barely chewed it. The cows cram it in, barely chewing, but they raise it back up later and leisurely chew their "cuds." What was with her?

John told me she had gained quite a lot of weight while with him those two months, so I'm fairly sure Maybellene had had some hungry days and learned to eat while the food was there and as fast as she could; probably an outfitter's mule didn't have a lot of leisure time.

Every time I stroked her face and talked quietly to her, for some reason, I felt the tears well up again. Was she telling me about her past life in feelings, or was she telling me how happy she was to be here? I promised myself I would call Mary again. Maybe Maybellene would be more talkative now.

She'd been here a week and the weather had turned "April nasty" with snow, cold and wind. Not my kind of riding weather, which was probably good for Maybellene; she needed to settle in more. I was reading a book by Mark Rashid entitled "Horses Never Lie." It was about passive leadership with one's horses—or mules. Contrary to a lot of the new horse training methods which used round pen training to put one's self in the alpha horse position, Mark's idea was to become the horse that the animals trusted and would follow willingly, usually one of the horses in the middle of the herd, not the animal that always drank first, was first to eat, and scattered the herd just by walking into it.

I am not against round penning, and we have one, but I have only used it once or twice. On one of my first experiences, I put Nugget, my very talented show mare, in the round pen. I had just purchased her and wanted her to "join up" with me, have her understand I was the alpha mare, and then follow me around in the pen. There were two problems to my plan. The first was Nugget had been a stalled show horse since she was eighteen months old, and she was now eight. The second was she had bad arthritis in her knees and that was the only reason her former owner sold her to me to become a brood mare. Nugget wasn't extremely personable. She did her show job and asked only to be fed and cared for. In the videos and live demonstrations of round penning, horses eventually came up to the trainer and followed him about with no halter or rope. I thought this might help Nugget become attached to me.

I took her into the round pen, removed her halter and gently shook the rope at her; no yelling, no whip flailing, and no chasing. To my horror, Nugget exploded into a frantic gallop; she instantly tuned me out, her mind gone blank in her haste to flee. If she had been a younger horse with no physical ailments, I would have probably just let her run and see if she would at some point drop her head, lick and chew, the signs she was ready to let me be boss. To my considerable dismay, I *couldn't stop her!* Round and round she went; I did all that I had seen; getting her to change directions, backing away and not looking at her, but still she wouldn't stop. I was nearly in tears. All I could think of was I was going to kill or lame my expensive, talented and gentle show horse.

I left the round pen, hoping if I wasn't standing in the middle, she would stop, which is what eventually happened. She stood with her sides heaving and sweat dripping from her body. I would never round pen her again.

I never had much success with the round pen theory, although I know others do, and I am not saying it shouldn't be used, but reading about the passive leadership of horses seemed more to my liking. I wasn't far enough into the book to learn everything, but I could see that might be the better way for Maybellene. I also liked the ideas of some natural horsemen and women who taught using a long rope and rope halter, teaching the animals to move their feet and learn their space. Bryan had done a lot of this with Miss Ellie and it was certainly needed, but Maybellene was different from my other mules; she acted like she really wanted to please if she could figure it out, but any kind of reprimanding, even gentle, seemed as though it could upset her and that would be counterproductive in getting her to bond with me.

Mark Rashid said in his book that he noticed when the horses were made to understand that the trainer was alpha, they acted a little like horses he'd noticed in his herd. They did indeed recognize the alpha presence, but it was with resignation, not love. That made sense to me too. I'd seen the alpha horses in my herds scatter the animals, and it wasn't out of loving respect that they moved off; it was one of obedience but dislike.

Maybellene was feeling more at home; she had begun sticking her head over her door partition and snatching a quick bite from an apple. She wasn't comfortable leaving it there and finishing her treat, but it was a start. There were several differences between her and the other mules. First was her pretty head with the big eyes and dished face and smaller muzzle. I had begun my horse farm with Arabian horses and although they were very beautiful, mine were also more reactive to their surroundings. Maybellene reminded me of them. She loved being brushed, but picking up her feet was still a struggle. She didn't fight; she seemed scared to pick them up. Still, she was making progress.

She'd been here two weeks when I decided to ride her and in my customary careful way, was only going to ride her in the inside arena, so I asked Bob to be there. She saddled and bridled fine, and let me mount from a bucket. She didn't like the mounting block any more than the other mules, but she was short enough that a bucket was just fine. She was a tad antsy, but listened okay; when I rode her around the perimeter of the arena, she hurried off. After the first several rounds, she slowed and walked. After some turning and stopping I got off.

Since I had finally ridden her, I decided to turn her out with the mares. She ran and ran; bucked and snorted, galloping out to the back pasture with the herd. She was surely ready for some more room to run. I expressly came out that evening at chore time to put her in the barn.

I couldn't catch her, but she trotted up to the barn where I was able to entice her to me with some grain and gently took her halter. The next day she was worse coming in the barn. I didn't go out, which might have been a mistake, but rather had the girl who was feeding, try to get her. She didn't have any luck, but Shelby, another young teenager who helped chore and would have lived at the barn if possible, went out and just spent as much time as was needed to coax Maybellene to her. My mule definitely had issues in that department.

The next ride was with Bob and Miss Ellie; I wanted to try her on the trails around the farm. Put simply, it was not an enjoyable ride for either the mule or me. She seemed nervous about something—not the trail or the objects along it; it seemed to be something internal. If I tried to whisper or speak very quietly to calm her, it set her jumping ahead, not dangerously, just irritatingly. I couldn't rub her neck: the same thing happened. She didn't want to walk, and I couldn't slow her down. We tried going in front of Miss Ellie, which was better, but she went fast enough that Bob and Ellie were left far behind. We headed to the barn, and it was the first time in my short mule ownership that I came home crying instead of that big old smile. This would never do.

It was an interesting dilemma. John had loved riding her to the point that he was "adopting" her out to me. I know my expectations were that my mules would allow me to feel relaxed, find serenity, sit back in the saddle and enjoy the scenery. Riding Maybellene was like riding some of my younger horses back when I had raised Arabians. They were a little more "up," sometimes nervous, and had a lot of energy; they make great endurance horses. I thought I could retrain her to suit me, but that wasn't a goal I wished upon myself. I was getting lazy and had retired from training show horses; I didn't want to work that hard.

After sleeping on it, I called John and told him I didn't think Maybellene and I were a good match. Truthfully, I was quite embarrassed to make that call. In my defense, since I was berating myself for not going and looking at her, I don't think I would have been able to tell all these things about her in one day's visit and a ride. It was truly wonderful of John to allow me to return her. True to his word, he really did wish to match up the right rider with the right mule.

Maybellene was feeling more relaxed and knew where her next meal was coming from, and that she wouldn't need to fight for it. She began to pick up smaller bites and chew more slowly. Finally, she appeared to be enjoying her food instead of simply cramming it down.

I kept her in the small paddock, since she was going back to John. There was no need to take the chance she might get hurt with the other mules, and she was hard to catch in a larger area. I just didn't have tolerance for those shenanigans. We had Izzy, a yearling filly, in residence that didn't have a horse friend. She was too small to turn out with the horses, she didn't really care for the cows, and living alone she had developed some very nasty habits.

Unfortunately, she had a stifle problem which made it impossible to either lunge or round pen her. She was darn cocky and had no respect for me as a human.

One morning when I opened Izzy's gate to reach for her halter, she plowed out and knocked me down. In the evenings after she had a chance to play all day, she was quieter for the girls doing chores. They didn't see what I saw. She needed company, but company that would teach her to mind her place in life. Maybellene seemed perfect to fill that role.

The first day, the filly ran up to the mule expecting to body slam her, but a stern look with both of those long ears plastered flat back on Maybellene's head put a quick stop to that. Izzy was a smart filly and soon all the mule had to do was give her "the look" or a tail swish and the filly minded her manners. There was not a mark on her and she was not chased around, but she discovered how to behave. It transferred somewhat to me as a person; Izzy wasn't quite as pushy. The filly was not mine, the owner didn't work with her, and Erica didn't have time to do free training. This was not my problem, short of staying unhurt, as I cared for her.

Maybellene was here for about a month before the horse transport could pick her up. In that time she had some lovely "R and R" time, trained a young filly and taught me that even though I loved mules, not all mules were the same, just as not all horses were the same. What one rider desires in a mount another does not. I wanted mules to be pets—as much as one can expect an equine to be, an "in your pocket" kind of mule. I needed *mellow, serene* and above all to be safe. These were not the same qualities I searched for in my show horses, but now things had changed. I was "Grammy" and had other things to look forward to.

I felt I had let Maybellene down; I was embarrassed I wasn't a skilled enough rider to handle her, and had to call John and tell him so. I was sorry I no longer had the ability to work through problems with an animal such as Maybellene. I reminded myself that over the years of selling my own horses, I knew not every horse (or mule) was right for every owner.

Months later, John told me that Maybellene had found a new home with an owner who rode competitive trail and loved the little dish-faced molly. Her willingness and ability to go and go was a plus for him. Maybellene had finally found her special person with "a kind heart."

Chapter Fifteen: Adventure in Utah

After our fantastic Grand Canyon vacation, I came home and bought mules; Bob started looking for the next summer's exciting adventure. We decided to visit Utah and Bryce National Park, taking the mule ride through the canyon. We also made reservations for a private company to take us on a seven-plus-hour ride through the Dixie National Forest and to the summit of Mount Dutton.

So it was that the middle of June 2007, found us driving north from the Las Vegas airport through Cedar City and some beautiful scenery, but as with the Grand Canyon trip, we were too tired to really appreciate it. At least this time I didn't nearly fall asleep during my dinner, but bed sure looked inviting. We stayed in cabins, which I noticed had no air conditioning. At first I was somewhat alarmed, but as it got dark, it got cooler and then actually a little chilly. I appreciated the blankets and closed the windows sometime during the night.

We woke to a simply gorgeous morning with birds singing, the sun shining and temperatures probably in the high fifties. Our first day's private ride was to begin at 8:30, and it would take us out of the park and last about seven hours. I hoped I was up to that long in the saddle. There was no way I could practice at home. The Grand Canyon ride was about five hours down and another five back up. I had survived that.

At Ruby's Inn we found the corral with horses and mules tied to the side, and two trailers with animals still inside. Bob had requested mules for each of our rides. As it turned out, Bob and I were the only paying riders. The wrangler, whom I will call Dave, and his girl friend filled out the party.

It took about twenty minutes to drive to the trailhead, which was fifteen miles north of Bryce Park and went into Dixie National Forest. Cattle grazed here and there on the government property. Being from Indiana, I thought the grass, if one would call it that, was pretty darn scarce and dry looking. Dave said the cows were range cows—tough

Mules, Mules and More Mules

and could eat almost anything. I thought my cows would have a stroke if they saw what was being offered.

Soon Dave stopped the trailer, unloaded the horses for himself and his friend. Next came my mule Casey, who was twenty years old, and Bob's mule Floyd, who was younger. It was a cool morning, but I knew it would get hot before we returned, so I wore a summer shirt and slathered on the sunscreen. After donning sunglasses and my "Grand Canyon hat," I was ready to ride. Bob had on a long sleeved shirt and his trusty vest with all the great pockets for Advil, lip gloss, more sunscreen and other odds and ends. Before the ride was over, he was hot.

The animals had been saddled before loading into the trailer, so they were ready to go when they were unloaded. I went up to Casey and gave him a pat, which he seemed not to notice, and felt under the front of his saddle to check how it fit him. Since I'd had so much trouble getting a saddle to fit Mirabella, and being a saddle-fit-nut, I was curious. My hand slipped under easily, and I figured that was good for Casey; it should be comfortable with no pinching or binding. I asked my stirrups be made longer to accommodate knees which didn't bend well anymore. Hopefully, we both would have a stress-free ride.

The ride had been advertised "for the wildlife enthusiast," and we were to travel through many different landscapes from black rock, lakes and streams, to lush forest. Maybe we would see elk, deer, bald eagles, and an occasional bear or mountain lion. Perhaps those animals lived there, but they certainly kept themselves hidden from our view. Dave mentioned that mountain lions are afraid of mules and when they smell them, will disappear. The only wildlife we saw were two mule deer, some wild turkeys, many jackrabbits, and after we had loaded up the animals and had headed back to the main road, we spotted a mother antelope and her two half grown babies grazing beside the road.

The land was pretty level, but Dave pointed up to Mount Dutton in the distance and said, "That is where we are headed." It sure looked far away, and rough, the peak being around 9,500 feet high. We would ride about 1,700 feet up to the summit, most of it on a road. About two hours into our ride, we arrived in a grove of beautiful aspens with their quaking leaves and white bark. I have always loved aspens, perhaps because of seeing them in my favorite John Wayne western movies.

Rose and Casey with Mt. Dutton in the background

Aspens are a strange tree, growing in large colonies derived from a single seedling and spreading by means of root suckers. Each tree only lives for forty to 150 years above ground, but the root system of the colony is long-lived, in some cases for many thousands of years, sending up new trunks as the older trunks die off above ground. For this reason it is considered to be an indicator of ancient woodlands.

Aspen trees thrive in altitudes between 6,800 and 9,300 feet, and this was our riding elevation. The trees can survive low temperatures of *minus* 78 degrees! They do not like it hot. Dave asked us if we wanted to add our names to the ones carved into the beautiful white bark of some of the trees. We both declined. Actually, I was saddened to see "graffiti" in the wilderness. A short distance farther and we came to a small clearing with a hitch post to tie the animals for a short rest, picture taking, and bug swatting. Nearby was a small pond of stagnant

Mules, Mules and More Mules

water, caught and held during the spring flows. Animals used it for drinking, but it also attracted flies and other insects.

We remounted and went through a special gate that was designed to allow a horse and rider, but no four-wheel vehicles. It was narrow at the bottom and wider at the top. Quite ingenious, I thought. We also left the bugs behind. Still climbing gently, we went through more aspen trees. It was shady and absolutely beautiful until we came to a tree about two feet in circumference and two feet off the ground lying across the path.

Dave stopped. "It must have just fallen, because someone's been here recently to clear the path." Well, it was over or around; Bob and I were sure the animals could get over it if we got off and Dave led them over. Dave thought we should go around, so we started blazing our own path. Unfortunately, a quick go around found no easy way back to the path.

Next we did a hill climb—up and up to the top of the ridge. This turned out to be the top of Mount Dutton but was off the usual path because of the downed tree. The vista was glorious: you can see for a hundred miles on a clear day—and this day was—distant mountain ranges, more valleys, rock formations of red and black, spoiled only by old burned trees from a forest fire. Answering my question, Dave said, "It either was a lightning strike, or a controlled burn."

It looked ugly with dark charred stumps and tree trunks sticking up like broken toothpicks in the blackened area. In one place beauty abounded where the ground was covered with yellow flowers. It was as though they had been planted. I guess having the ground burned off gave them a chance to flourish, but the charred remains of the once beautiful trees was depressing to me.

We hadn't found our way around the downed tree, but it had turned out well from a scenic standpoint. The mules and horses got a strenuous workout going up and back down. It was very rocky and while not exactly steep, they had to be careful. I was glad I was on a mule. I had come to trust them, and felt quite comfortable with all the climbing and rough terrain. The two horses did just fine also, but I was grateful for Casey.

When we arrived at the tree-lined path again, we had to hunt for our exit point. Finally spotting it, Dave decided the animals would have to get over it on their own, which they all did handily. Remounting, we were off again. As with the ride down the Grand Canyon, the part I loved the best was in the inner canyon with the stream, the cottonwood trees and the blooming flowers. Green, green, green. Here, it was the quaking aspen grove. It was cool and I loved those trees.

Still we were climbing, but more gently than our climb earlier up the side of the mountain. Dave pointed to some wild turkeys just feet in front of us. At the top was an opening between a tall rock formation that allowed us to look far away at the mountains. Then we started our descent.

It wasn't real steep, but bad enough and with turns in the path and tree branches to dodge, I asked Dave, "Do people who don't ride often have problems riding down this trail?"

He turned and started to reply, "No…" when all of a sudden Casey stopped dead in his tracks, like he was glued to the trail.

I looked down at where I was sitting and it was pretty much on Casey's neck. The saddle had slid forward over his shoulders and part of it was on the mule's neck. It wasn't going to slide off because the girth still held it, but it was loose enough and without the britching that can be used around the mule's rump to hold the saddle from going forward, I definitely was not in the proper space on Casey's back.

Truly, I wasn't greatly alarmed; Casey had stopped frozen in time and space. Good old mule. Dave quickly dismounted, tied his horse to a tree limb, and scrambled up the rocky path to us, asking me if I was okay. I was, and most of it was because I knew Casey was not going to budge.

On an inexperienced animal, the saddle slipping could have been a complete disaster, scaring it and perhaps making it run down the hill with the saddle tipping to the side, depositing its rider on the ground or dragging the person in a mad scramble to who knows where. I thought I heard a sigh from Dave—I hoped not an exasperated one, thinking about this crazy lady who insisted upon riding with long stirrups.

Mules, Mules and More Mules

I really didn't think I had caused this incident—but I felt guilty anyway. I ride a lot and know what works for my body, but I don't ride in terrain such as this. Maybe I had created the problem by protecting my knees.

Dave helped me off, fixed the saddle while I was saying that I probably should have mentioned I thought the saddle was a little loose the last time I mounted. By now he was probably hoping to be preserved from taking riders who were *not* "dudes." Wishing for ones who just ride, bounce, cling or whatever, going along for the ride and don't make suggestions, comments on the animals or make requests. I felt pretty subdued at this point and promised myself I would keep my mouth shut. Alas, that was not to be.

We descended the mountain with no more difficulties and soon were back into the wonderful aspen forest. This part of the descent was lovely. The trail crossed and sometimes followed the East Fork of the Siever River, a stream now, but a river when rain or snow melt filled it. The animals were given chances to drink as we crossed. Eventually the trail leveled out and I rather timidly asked if we were through descending and if I could have my stirrups lowered another notch. Dave didn't think I should, and I was beginning to feel pain in my knees. It wasn't only that the stirrups were at least a notch short, but some western saddles twist your legs because of the way the stirrup hangs. I tried taking my feet out and letting them hang, but that was worse for the rest of my body.

Around 3:00 p.m., the hottest part of the day, when we had left all our shade covering trees, Casey took a few quick stumbly steps, rather like he was stepping on something hot. On we went, and soon he stumbled more and more. Now surely, I have to tell Dave that my mule is stumbling. Dave turned in his saddle, looked, but saw no stumbles, and said, "He doesn't have a rock in his foot, he's stepping level."

Bob saw him stumble and also remarked to Dave that it appeared to be his left front foot. I wondered what Dave was thinking about his riders at this point. Finally, he turned at the right moment to see Casey stumble, but he kept on going. A little farther down the road Casey almost fell to his knees, and this time I exclaimed, "Oh my, he almost fell!"

But still we went on and by now I was almost in tears, not for myself, although I did have a vision of the poor mule stumbling to the ground and my falling off and hitting my head on a rock, but for poor Casey.

Samson, my big mule, stumbled now and then, and sadly, I am rather used to it. Samson has great recovery and even though he once slipped with both back feet on some wet grass and almost sat on his behind, he recovered himself. I felt the strength in him, and trusted him to right himself more than any of my horses, but Casey's stumbles were coming much too often. I remembered the mule was twenty years old. I wasn't able to keep my mouth closed, and I asked Dave as we stumbled along, if mules got arthritis like horses did, knowing full well they did. I hoped my comment would elicit some help for Casey at a later time. Dave had no comment.

This was a situation that could befall any rider. Any horse or mule could go lame on a ride. You always hoped it wouldn't happen, and tried to take all precautions that are possible. We had to get back, I couldn't walk, but it did fleetingly cross my mind. I felt so awful riding an animal that was obviously having a lameness issue. More tears welled in my eyes and I kept repeating to myself, "I will not cry, I will not cry, I *will not* cry."

Finally the ride was over, with Casey stumbling along for the last hour and a half. That was the worst part of the trip for all of us. Bob and Floyd kept dropping farther behind Casey, and Dave's friend's horse was even farther behind Bob. At the beginning of the ride when Dave got ahead, with Casey on his heels, the others would trot to catch up. Now, everyone, man and beast alike were asking, "Where's the trailer?"

When we dismounted, I could not keep my thoughts to myself and commented perhaps Casey at twenty years of age would be better off doing the shorter rides. I could tell Dave was disturbed with Casey's situation. He said, "This is the first time that mule has not kept up with my horse."

As the animals loaded into the trailer, I said a silent prayer Casey would get the treatment he needed and deserved. He had proved a trusty and dependable mount with guts to get me back to the trailer. I wanted to give him a pat, but he turned his head away as he had when I offered him the apple from my lunch. Casey did his job and asked for no favors.

After that experience, I came to the conclusion that seven hours in the saddle was too many at a time for me. I rode at home for at least an hour a day, but sitting in a saddle that wasn't my own, and for that long a time, was not enjoyment. Bob and I had choices of shorter rides of one to three hours, but we were ignorant of our limitations had chosen the long one. I looked forward to the next day's ride which would be by the same company that did the Grand Canyon rides, and this one would be for only three and a half hours. The Bryce Canyon ride promised much beauty and would be easier and shorter than the Grand Canyon ride had been.

Chapter Sixteen: Bryce Canyon and the Hoodoos

The next morning was cool and clear, and somehow both Bob and I had recovered from our seven-hour jaunt the day before. After a quick breakfast, we headed to the corral. While driving the five minutes to it, we saw the mule train kicking up a cloud of dust as it crossed the road in front of us from the barns to the pen; there must have been at least thirty of them. I walked around the pen, looking at the animals. The horses looked back with interest; the mules could've cared less.

The head wrangler stood beside the gate as we walked in and sized each of us up for our animal. Again, Bob had requested mules, but both horses and mules were available. As I walked through the gate and looked at the long-mustached, well-tanned cowboy with the big hat, I decided to tell him about my Charlie mule experience at the Grand Canyon ride.

"I rode the Grand Canyon last May and had Charlie, the slowest mule. Please, *please* don't do that to me again!"

He grinned, thought for a minute and then said, "Well, since you begged so nicely, you can have Jake."

Bob was next and he asked Bob if he also rode. Bob answered in the affirmative. Last year he couldn't have said so, but a lot of "mule miles" had been put on Bob's behind since then.

"Okay, you can have Tool Time."

That brought a chuckle from Bob. "That's sure appropriate, that is what I do all the time."

We entered the big corral and when the wrangler who would get us to and on our mule came to us, we were to tell him the mule's name. Bob told me later when I told the cowboy I had Jake, he looked mildly astonished. As he led me over to my mule, he said, "So you get to ride Jake? We never put inexperienced riders on him. You will have a great ride, he is like a Cadillac." The wrangler adjusted my stirrups to my requested length, the saddle was comfortable, and I was set to go.

I am five feet four and Jake was a Percheron draft-horse-cross mule, which made him enormous. I could now understand the cowboy's astonished look. I got hoisted up into the saddle and received the instructions on guiding him. Pull right for going that way and left for that direction. He was half of a driving team of Percheron mules, but unlike his female harness mate, Jake was more people orientated, so he was also good at being a dude mule.

**Big Jake and Rose with the Bryce Hoodoos
and a very old scraggly bristlecone pine**

Jake stood quietly, and I wondered why they wouldn't put inexperienced riders on him—aside from the fact he was huge. I looked at the far end of the pen and Bob was sitting on Tool Time, looking relaxed and confident—a far cry from the Grand Canyon trip on Sleepy. When we were all up in the saddles, our names were called and we fell into line. Jake and I were second after Steve our wrangler, with

Bob behind me. Jake moved off smartly with Tool Time right on our heels, and we were off on a stunning adventure.

We had barely gotten started down the trail when a cowboy with a camera snapped everyone's picture as we passed. When the ride was finished we had the opportunity to buy the beautiful 8 x 10 photos. This descent was fairly gradual, not a strenuous ride at all. First we saw the bristlecone pine trees, which are a mystery in themselves. From Wikipedia, I discovered that bristlecone pines are some of the oldest living organisms. One such pine named "Methuselah," after the longest lived person in the Bible, is located in the Ancient Bristlecone Pine Forest in the White Mountains of eastern California, and measured by core samples, is said to be about 4,700 years old.

To preserve Methuselah from suffering the fate of an even older bristlecone pine named Prometheus, which was cut down in 1964, the exact location of the old pine is kept secret.

Bristlecone pines grow in isolated groves at and just below the tree line in these areas. Because of cold temperatures, dry soils, high winds and short growing seasons, the trees grow very slowly. The wood is dense and is resistant to insect invasion as well as fungi and other pests. As the tree ages, much of its bark may die and in very old specimens often leaves only a narrow strip of living tissue to connect the roots to the handful of live branches. This makes some of them look like they belong in a horror movie. Another interesting bristlecone pine fact is that their needles stay on the limb for forty years, unlike most other pines which lose needles every few years!

As we went farther down, the landscape became bushier. A lot of manzanita was evident; also at this level, we saw ponderosa pine. When we went around one corner, a whole forest vista opened up, with the pines seemingly growing from the bottom to the rim in a carpet of the deepest green. The ponderosa is the southwest's tallest tree, growing to one hundred and twenty feet with trunks in three to four foot widths. It grows on dry mountain slopes, which is probably why we saw them in Bryce Canyon. That sight is one of several that I know I will never forget. The reds and pinks of the hoodoos and surrounding rock formations were lovely, but the dark green of those magnificent trees just set the landscape off like an artist's pallet.

Bryce Canyon ponderosa pine and hoodoos

Jake was doing wonderfully well, and I was having a super time. He kept right up on the next horse's tail, in fact a little too much. He walked right along and would have been willing to pass the other animal. I knew this was forbidden, and I asked Steve if I was allowed to pull him back.

"Yes, he is part of a team, and they are used to feeling the pull in their mouths. They work up into the bit." That explained perhaps one of the reasons why a total novice wouldn't be riding Jake. It was easy for me, second nature in fact. He checked back fine, and after awhile stopped trying to pull ahead of the other horse.

Jake had one other little habit that was slightly disconcerting. As we were going down the path and came to the rather sharp turns, instead of paying complete attention to his path ahead, he gawked in the other direction. I would rather he watched where he was placing his big feet! After a few of these turns, I decided to steer him. As we came to a turn, I gently tugged his head in that direction. Steve later mentioned that Jake had recently been purchased so I guess he hadn't seen all of the trail that he wanted to. After many more trips up and down, he would likely not care what was in the other direction.

The rest of the time Jake was "in the zone," just plopping along, kind of in a mule trance. I was enjoying the scenery, but I did notice a lady hiker who had stopped still so the mules could pass. I felt sorry for her as she was being covered with our dust. Jake, however, hadn't seen her at all, and as his big head pulled along beside her, he startled and stepped three steps to his left.

"What was that?" Bob asked.

"Oh, Jake wasn't paying attention, no big deal," I answered.

We both remembered Sleepy's interesting reactions to hikers on the Grand Canyon ride. After being poked by two hikers' walking sticks, Sleepy was convinced hikers were out to get him and began to seriously distrust any he saw.

Bob's mule, Tool Time, was a trifle disconcerting at times, too. We were warned at the beginning of our ride, just as we had at the Grand Canyon, that some of the mules liked to "walk the edge." At the Grand Canyon ride, the lady in front of me had one that did. I tell you, it was scary to see from behind, let alone be sitting on that mule. A few times she turned around to look at me and I think her face got several shades paler each time. There were only *inches* to spare. I was looking!

"Maybe you can encourage him to stop it?" I suggested.

"I can't," Bob said, "my hands are too full, holding the camera and taking pictures." Which could explain how he ended up dropping the camera requiring Steve to stop, get off, retrieve it, and then remount. Between the two of us, we certainly made our "dude" rides interesting for our wranglers.

I was more concerned about Tool Time's edge walking after I saw the horse in front of Jake step close the edge with a hind foot—and the ground crumbled and slid way, way down the side of the path. The dirt in Bryce was softer in places than the rocky paths of the Grand Canyon. The horse seemed not to notice, and his rider was completely oblivious, but then she was a dude and there is something to be said for total ignorance.

Still descending, the next level of trees was the pinyon pine. The closer to the bottom we got, more pinyons happily existed in the dry hot rocky area. The pinyon also grows slowly—a ten foot tree can be eighty to one hundred years old. Pinyon pine nuts are edible and have been on man's diet since 4,000 BC.

The other tree sharing this middle elevation area of the canyon was the juniper. Juniper trees have fleshy cones, which look like blueberries. Steve told us the berries are used in making gin. The Piaute Indians, who lived in that area long ago, used the tree for medicine, the berries to make beaded jewelry and the wood for their hogans, firewood and fence posts.

Hoodoos—how can one describe or explain them? I had one personal comment, and it was: simply overwhelming. The total ride was one breathtaking view of pink-colored strange-shaped rocks after another. Bryce Canyon hoodoos are unique. I discovered there are other hoodoos—one in Kansas, which collapsed in 1998, and some interesting ones in southern Alberta, Canada—but none have the color or cover such a large area as the Bryce Hoodoos.

Bryce Canyon is not really a canyon, but a three by two mile bowl-shaped amphitheater cut into the edge of a plateau and is about one thousand feet deep. When I got home, I had to research the "how" of Bryce.

Hal had remained home, but I regaled him with history when I returned.

"Did you know Bryce's story begins about 144 million years ago with a shallow sea covering that area of Utah?" I asked him. Getting a smile, I continued, "Over those millions of years, layers of mud and silt collected on the bottom of the sea in varying thickness and composition. This dull brown material makes up the canyon floor.

"During the next period of 66 million years ago, the highlands to the west eroded and that dirt which flowed into the sea was rich in iron ore. Millions of years later when exposed to erosion, the iron would rust and give the rocks pinkish and reddish hues. These layers would be known as the Clarion Formation and would make up Bryce's fantastic formations and brilliant colors."

I was getting sort of a glazed look from my husband by now, but I continued, because I had found it fascinating, and I had a captive audience.

"The conditions along the rim of the plateau were ideal for erosion. The water from melting snow and rain raced down the slopes and found natural fault lines in the rocks. These eventually were widened by several forces of nature. The water in the rock cracks froze (frost wedging) then thawed, making them larger, and the wind constantly worked its magic."

I showed Hal pictures we had taken of the hoodoos in the canyon, and even he was impressed. Hal wasn't a hiker or mule rider, so he wasn't likely to ever see them in person, but how they had been formed caught his interest.

"Over time, many fins or finger looking rock formations protruded from the plateau sides as erosion carved away parts of the walls." I continued, "Next, part of the erosion cut windows here and there out of the fins. Finally, some of these windows became large enough to separate parts from the solid fin and a hoodoo was born—a large portion of rich iron colored rock standing alone, or connected by sharp ridges, now not as protected from the ongoing wind and moisture erosion. Because the hoodoos are formed from four different rock types—limestone, sandstone, dolomite and mudstone—they eroded at different speeds, helping to give the fantastic shapes and forms."

My little geology lesson left Hal somewhat dazed, but he readily admitted the hoodoos were a true national treasure.

Many of the strange shapes and formations have been given names. Thor's Hammer—a small rock perched upon a larger, longer rock formation, Fairy Castle, Queen's Castle, Queen's Garden, and a hoodoo that is said to look like Queen Victoria, a resemblance I failed to see, but perhaps I was simply too overwhelmed at that point.

Our guide wrangler, Steve, was quite interesting, but again as with the Grand Canyon ride, the only people who could hear him were the closest. This time I was one of them, not bringing up the far rear on Charlie.

Steve had jokes to tell as well as history and sometimes it was hard to separate the two. Looking at one rock formation, he pointed out that it looked like a lady playing an organ with a preacher standing behind her, reading the Bible.

"Ladies," he said, looking at me and the other female rider right behind him, "What kind of music do you think she is playing?"

We were silent and then the other lady said, "Beethoven's Fifth?"

My mind was still working trying to be smart and creative, but failing.

"Oh, come on girls," he said. "It has to be hard rock!"

Silly us.

We crossed the Bryce Canyon River bed several times, which was now dry and I envisioned it raging down the canyon. Steve said one could be caught in sudden storms that would make it flow and could be extremely dangerous.

At one curve in the path, Steve turned to Lady Number One—I never did get her name—and said, "Follow the horse in front of you," which was with the first group just ahead of us, and without further words, dashed up a short steep hill, turned a corner, and disappeared from view. Now, that was interesting. What was he up to?

We were now at Peek a Boo Trail, a hiking/mule trail, and passed several foot travelers. Soon we turned another corner and reached a rest area. We were all aided in dismounting, and Steve gave us water to drink. He had rushed around a path on his mule and had beaten us to the rest stop to prepare the cool and refreshing water.

We put the mules and horses into a small corral, saddles and bridles still on, and allowed them to drink. This brought about a lot of mule/horse discussion as the equines decided just who would get to drink first, second, third, and so on down the line. The dominant animals drank first and there decidedly was frequent squabbling as they reminded their peers who was above them in rank. As they jockeyed for position at the water tank, I noticed Jake. He didn't seem to want water, and stood under a tree with his head hanging, resting. Right beside him was another mule who looked distressed.

His ears were back, not flat back as in anger, but in unease. He kept picking up his left front foot, setting it back down, and then up again, never letting his heel touch the ground. No one had noticed him, he wasn't in Steve's "string" and I was still feeling weird about my ride the day before on poor Casey with his lameness. What to do? Speak out or be silent? Mind my own business?

Gathering my courage, I spoke to Steve, "Do you have a lame mule in there?"

"I hope so," he replied. There was that dry humor again.

"No, seriously."

"Which one?"

"The one with the red saddle pad," I said.

He looked and quietly called the mule's wrangler to check the animal. As the mule limped toward the center of the corral, I could see a large rock stuck in his shoe. Just hitting it with another rock did not dislodge it. Steve went to his saddle bag and got a tool, which did the trick.

I felt great. This was the obvious and easy to fix lameness Dave had been looking for with Casey, but Casey's problem was something worse—something hopefully to be determined back at his corral.

Soon we mounted and began the climb back up. When we reached the bristlecone pines again, we knew we were nearly at the end of our ride. When we had almost reached the top, Steve stopped his mule Blondie, and told us a story. I imagine this one was true.

He said he and his son were gathering cattle out of some rough country. Steve had trained and then bought a nice working cow horse. He let his son ride it for this roundup. Steve said the little horse was game, had a big heart, and his son had run him from one point to the next, seldom giving the horse a breather. When they stopped to rest at the bottom of the canyon, Steve told his son to give him the reins of his horse. When his son did, Steve led the horse up and out of the canyon, while riding his own horse, and made his son walk up.

Steve said his son was still mad at him to this day about that. I ventured an observation that I bet that made his son a better horseman.

"Nope," he replied, "he now rides motorcycles."

We hadn't gone more than ten feet before I mentioned to the lady in front of me that I felt sorry for the animals climbing up and up with their riders.

"Oh," she said airily, "that is what they are supposed to do." I guess the story about our guide's son had gone over her head. True, these were work animals, doing their jobs, but a kind word, a pat and a sincere mental thank you would not be out of line. By this time, she had started listing off to the side of her saddle, either by intent to rest a weary part of her bottom, or simply because she didn't know she was off balance. Her horse trudged on, never complaining.

It seemed to me that Blondie, Steve's mule, was walking faster and faster. Jake had no problem keeping up, but we now had laggers behind me. Steve would stop now and then. I said something about Blondie being in a hurry.

"Yep, she is homesick. She likes those mules back at the barn. It makes her go home faster."

I chuckled. We called it "barn sour" at home, meaning not wanting to leave the barn and in a hurry to get back. "Homesick" sounded much nicer.

We soon reached the top and the road that went by our exit point. I saw Steve hurry up to the roadway, stop, and turn Blondie sideways so the rest of us had to halt also; we couldn't get out onto the road. Steve talked to a young couple walking past, telling them where they could get information about the mule ride into the canyon. Then he said to me, "The animals hate child strollers and umbrellas."

He had gotten there first to be sure none of those monsters would be at the top to frighten ours. And here I thought these horses and mules were impervious to everything. Come to think of it—strollers and umbrellas would not be seen on the paths up and down Bryce Canyon! Rabbits, rocks, trees, hikers and the like, they would get used to. Avoidance of strollers and umbrellas (and big black garbage bags) sounded good to me.

Delving back into Bryce history, I found that the canyon had been named after a Mormon pioneer, Ebenezer Bryce. He and his wife Mary had located their farm below the "canyon." It was reported that Bryce said of the area, "It would be a terrible place to lose a cow." Indeed, it would. Neighbors began to call the area Bryce's canyon and the name stuck. In 1928 the area was made into a National Monument and later into a National Park.

It had been an incredible experience. I would do it again and soon. It was a ride I would heartily recommend to all my friends and family. Not nearly as strenuous as the Grand Canyon, but rewarding, oh so beautiful—and weird. There are few words to describe or explain the hoodoos. In fact, according to G. K. Chester, who wrote a pictorial book on Bryce, *hoodoo* is a true geological term meaning "we don't know what else to call them."

A legend of the Paiute Indians, who inhabited the area for a hundred years before the arrival of the European Americans, claims the hoodoos are ancient "Legend People" who were turned to stone as punishment for bad deeds. Another definition of a hoodoo is "to bewitch." Regardless of why they are called "hoodoos," they are a stunning part of our wonderful country that is not duplicated anywhere else on our planet.

The wind and rain, freezing and thawing continue to erode about the thickness of a sheet of paper from them each year. In millions of years they may be gone. But that still leaves plenty of time for many more visitors to become enchanted with Bryce's hoodoos!

Chapter Seventeen: Mirabella Is Sold

I thought I had a buyer for Mirabella, and we stopped working with her. Perhaps because we had been pretty much ignoring her, she became very dominate and pushy. She was terribly bossy with her pasture mates, insisting upon being let inside the barn first and running me over in the process. Her next act of domination was to appoint herself the "stallion" of the small herd, actually mounting a mare that was in season. When she was in heat, she was moody and didn't want to be led or moved. Her ground manners were disintegrating before my eyes.

I told the girls to ride "the pants off the mule." Not all at one time, that would be abusive, but to try and ride her every day, either in the arenas or on the trails. Being put back to work did wonders for her disposition. The girls all loved her and I really enjoyed watching them ride her at her lovely trot around the big outside arena. I told Erica, "I sure wish I could find someone who would enjoy these talents. She is too lovely and fun to just be an old trail mule." But I found no one.

A day in May, I was visiting an old horse friend. Eli was an "ex-Amish" young man, having left the faith years ago. He had done wonders with Lordy, an abused gelding sired by my stallion, which was being trained by a man in Tennessee. Lordy, the stricken gelding, had been a rescue horse. My friend Carolyn called me one day saying, "Would you buy Lordy for $500? Otherwise he is going to the killer sale." Apparently, Lordy had retaliated against the trainer's abuse by kicking him, and now was on the big "Shit List" for horses.

"Of course," I answered, thinking I must have a big hole in my head even contemplating this deal. I didn't need a damaged animal to live with, and Lordy was ugly to boot. He got his name upon the owner's first sight of him after birth when she exclaimed, "Oh my Lordy!" Both sire and dam were quite beautiful horses—what happened to the poor colt?

Carolyn did her part by bringing the horse from Tennessee to Indiana at no charge. I don't know what I would have done without Eli. He came to the barn and started over with one scared and mentally scarred animal. Before he was finished, Lordy had turned into a creature that at least one could ride, but he still was ugly. Lordy's story has a good ending. One of my other boarders bought him; he more or less grew into his big ugly head and gawky frame, developed a sweet disposition, showed he had talent, and became one of her show horses.

Eli had just finished telling me about riding his horse along the road, sixteen miles round trip, and leading another horse who was spooky. It was good education for the nervous one. *Aha*, I thought. *I wonder if he would take Mirabella and put a good road "finish" on her*. I was too scared to road ride and ours were too dangerous anyway. She wasn't particularly frightened of anything, but it seemed a good education. So Mirabella went to live with Eli for three weeks.

Unfortunately, she left my barn with a sore on the inside of her front leg that wouldn't heal. I kept putting a healing powder on it, and while it held its own, it didn't go away. I wasn't too worried about it and asked Eli to keep powdering it for me.

While she was with Eli, Erica put an ad on the internet for her. Almost the next day I got a call. The man came with his trailer to Eli's farm, looked at her, rode her, wanted to buy her, but was concerned about the sore on the leg, which now Mirabella was biting. He wanted to know if I would take her back if it became a problem.

"No," I said. I wasn't going to do that again. It was too hard on me and the mule. "What I will do is bring her home, have it looked at, treated, and we can go from there." That was satisfactory, so Mirabella returned to the farm. My first look at the leg made me look a second, longer time. Indeed, it did not look good. It had a big bump and she continued to irritate it by biting it. It definitely needed a vet's look.

After determining the bump was an injury-caused sarcoid, he surgically excised it. After a week, it appeared to be coming back, which was not surprising, he told me. Next he treated it with a product called Xxterra which stimulates the body's immune system to fight the problem. It has good success especially on an area such as a leg where it can be bandaged. Dr. Hammond was sure it would heal completely.

The gentleman interested in Mirabella called to check on her progress, called Dr Hammond, and then called me back saying, "Dr Hammond is sure she will heal completely, but I should wait until treatment is completed, unless you sell her to someone else...."

"No, I don't think I will do that. The only other person I would sell her to would be someone who would continue her in the "English" riding style she has been ridden in. I would love for one of the girls to have her, but I don't see that happening. Why don't you call the end of August?"

He agreed and hung up the phone. I knew from earlier talks that he wanted a "using" mule. He would ride the Eminence, Missouri, and other big trail rides. I remember feeling a little sad that she would be kept in a pasture with shed type shelter with other horses, not her stall. I had asked him, "She won't just be a work mule, will she?"

Sometimes those long trail rides can be strenuous as well as hazardous. He had told me he had to sell an older mule because he wasn't up to the rides anymore. In other words, she *would* just be a mule. I didn't see long brushing and mane combing, ear clipping and carrots in her future—still it was a sale and Eli, who had met him, assured me he was a nice enough man.

One afternoon, Shelby, my young boarder, was all excited. "Rose, you should have seen Erica ride Mirabella yesterday! It was a hoot. We had come back from a nice trail ride with Mirabella on her best behavior. When we reached the barn lot where the two big 'chewing logs' are, she had Mirabella jump them!"

Erica Reid was my second Erica. My first, Erica Yoder, had come as a green fifteen-year old-girl who loved horses and after ten years with me, had become a horsewoman in her own right. She had married Mike, the wedding was on the farm, and her horse, Kit, had been included. Now they were moving to Springfield, Missouri, so he could do post-grad work. I would miss her sorely. She had been like a granddaughter to me and I had grown to love her very much. Wondering how I would carry on with the farm activities without her, the Higher Power that works in our lives provided not just another young lady to assist me, but another *Erica*!

Erica R. was twenty-two, had lived in New Hampshire, and relocated here with her folks—and Joe. Joe was a handsome16'2 hand chestnut Thoroughbred, and she was very involved in Three Day Eventing. In this horse discipline, horse and rider compete in dressage, cross country jumping where the obstacles can be rather strenuous and difficult, and stadium jumping. She showed me a taped Three Day Event competition and all I can say is that my appreciation of her riding skills certainly increased. The same could be said of Joe.

Joe was one of the nicest horses, and surely the nicest Thoroughbred I had ever seen. He was sleek, trim and beautiful and ate a *lot*. He was sensible and easy to care for. After seeing Erica show him, I thought even more of him. Since Erica Yoder, who had ridden Mirabella for me, was leaving the farm, I hoped I would find someone else to ride her. The younger girls who had horses at the farm were willing, but I really wanted someone who had more experience to keep Mirabella in line if needed. Anyone who could ride Joe in Three Day Eventing had more than enough ability.

"Gee, Erica," I said, "I heard you jumped Mirabella over the logs. I sure would love to see that."

The next day I got a demonstration and was quite impressed with the little mule. She cantered up and floated over, or she trotted up and jumped gently. Eli had free-jumped her over some large logs on his farm, but not ridden her over anything. Her canter was controlled and pleasant. Earlier, I had asked Erica Yoder to start her canter for me, but at that time Mirabella either didn't want to go into a canter, or didn't care to stop. Somehow, now she had her act together. Erica R. just had no thoughts that Mirabella wouldn't go over a log, and after seeing her riding Joe over much more frightening objects, I knew Mirabella could feel Erica's confidence.

Out of the blue the next day, Erica said, "So, Mirabella really is sold?"

"Yes, at the end of the month he will pick her up if her leg is healed, I would rather sell her to someone like you, but I guess that's not going to happen."

A few days after that conversation, Erica called me on the phone, and said she would really like to buy Mirabella, but her folks weren't nearly as enthusiastic. "I worked on them all weekend, even cried tears, and told them that she doesn't even need shoes." Joe needed costly specialized farrier care.

"Really?" I asked. "If there is anything I can do to help, let me know. Her board could be less—she doesn't eat like Joe!" My heart quickened. How great would that be? It was a dream come true for me. Someone to keep her doing what I thought she looked great doing, and she could stay here. I crossed my fingers, but I also knew from a purely practical sense, Erica's parents couldn't fathom her desiring a *mule*.

Two days later, I was mowing a pasture with the tractor and mower when my cell phone rang. "Hello," a familiar voice said. And then cell phones being what they are, I heard some fragmented words that sounded like, "I am going to buy Mirabella."

"Say that again," I replied, "You sort of broke up."

"I am going to buy Mirabella," Erica repeated. "I just really like her and can't imagine her living anywhere else. When I realized she was really leaving, I had a meltdown. I told my mom, 'I can't believe she is going away.' I haven't felt like that about any animal except Joe."

I knew she had had lots and lots of horse experiences in her young life, so this was no small matter.

What an incredible phone call that was. I think Mirabella and I had been waiting for that call ever since I sold her the first time. What a life she would lead. A terrific young person to love, trust and please, and the adventures they would be destined to enjoy, I could only guess.

Now I had a slight predicament on my hands. What to tell the gentleman who had said he would buy Mirabella at the end of August? I have had it happen more than once—I'd have a horse for sale for a long time and no one is interested. Suddenly I'd have two buyers for the same animal and one of them was sure to be unhappy. I pondered what to say to him.

"Erica, are you *sure* you want Mirabella? What if I move or you move? Are you willing to work out any situation?"

"Yes, yes, I am. I am committed."

Okay, I thought. I wanted to be sure before I called the other prospective buyer. No sense in ending up with no one to buy the mule.

I called the first gentleman on Monday morning and said, "Remember when I mentioned that I'd really like one of the girls who had been riding Mirabella to buy her? Well, one of them wants to. Can you live with that?"

"Sure," he said, "if that is what you want to do." And luckily, he sounded as though he meant it.

I gave him the name and number of a mule person I trusted. He thanked me and that was the end of it. Finally, Mirabella had found a new and very special person to give her heart to.

Chapter Eighteen: Ornery Samson

July was very un-Indiana-like. Bob and I had just returned from our Bryce Canyon vacation in Utah, and our present weather seemed more like that of the southwest. Indiana is corn growing country with humid, hot days and nights. In such weather it seemed you could see and hear the green corn stalks getting taller inch by inch. This summer we were in a drought.

If you didn't need to worry about farm crops—hay, corn, or pastures staying green and growing—the weather was actually wonderful. The sunny days with low humidity and cool evenings were delightful; it was the perfect horse or mule riding weather. One of the times I rode Samson past Linda, my sister, I mentioned I was doing my yoga. She does yoga for real, but I preferred my version.

I claim the early mornings for myself. At 7:30 all is tranquil, still cool, and since I am a "morning person," my energy level is high. I disliked Indiana's finally joining most of the rest of the country in changing to daylight saving time. Before last year, we stayed on the same time all year around. However, it *had* been confusing trying to remember that just fifteen minutes away from home into Michigan, my friends were an hour ahead of me. I didn't want to go to bed and have it still daylight. But finally Indiana joined the rest of the eastern United States. The one very good thing it provided for me was one extra hour of morning coolness. 7:30 was really 6:30 in sun time. It was a splendid time to ride.

We had lost forty acres of our land by eminent domain in 2003. Thirty acres was woodland and ten acres was a hayfield. It was akin to losing a friend. Our once peaceful, idyllic, and secluded one hundred and fifteen acres had become seventy-five very unsecluded acres. Now a busy four lane highway rumbled at the end of the property. No longer could we look out the back of the barn or our house and see the peaceful hay field melting into dark green woodland. Neighbors commiserated with one another.

One man who had experienced the law of eminent domain on his property for another, even busier four-lane road, told us, "You can look forward to hearing trucks, sirens and the noise of traffic all day and even at night." Our peace was shattered.

Bob had made trails through the woodland and it was a serene and cool place to enjoy nature. Now it was gone. Jake, our neighbor to the south, lost part of his woodland, but part remained on this side of the big road. He graciously allowed me and my boarders to ride on that property. Bob again made trails that wound around trees, crisscrossed each other, up and down slight inclines and across the meandering little stream that although it only flowed after rains, made the terrain interesting. This was my meditation place—where I found my peace to start the new day.

Because of the exceptional summer weather, my morning riding was even more treasured. Hal had insisted that I get a cell phone and actually remember to take it with me when I went riding. Horseback riding is a contact sport. If you are lucky, the contact will be with your behind on your horse's back, if not, then some part of your anatomy will contact the ground, and likely none too gently. Over the last few years, I'd had more than my share of falls off my horses. The first improvement I made was to get and wear a riding helmet, buy stirrups that allowed your foot to quickly spill out if you fell off. One of a horseman's biggest fears is being dragged to death. Next, I bought an Australian saddle with "poleys," a kind of thigh support that is supposed to keep you in the saddle better. The fourth was to buy mules.

For my early private morning rides, I had two horses and two mules to choose from. Nugget was fourteen, a great show mare and just as great trail horse. She enjoyed a fast gait, and that ride was more like driving a Ferrari. She was not spooky. Sunday was another younger show mare, and she also was splendid on the trails. Sunday was built like a "full figured woman." Not fat, but lots of body. She tended to be a tad spooky, but she was built close to the ground. I think perhaps her center of gravity made it more difficult for her to spook and spin. It is the spins that are the worst. Her little spooks didn't frighten me.

Susie Q, the little Quarter Horse mule that gaited up a storm, was very safe. She only "startled"—jumped a heartbeat to the side or stopped an instant, then she was on her way again. Little Miss Perfect was my pet name for her.

Then there was Samson, my favorite buddy, the new equine love of my life, my true and trusted friend. I loved riding Samson on these early morning jaunts more than any other animal. I had to make myself take the others. I enjoyed them all, but Samson was special. We seemed to be on the same wave length. Mary Long, my communicator friend, had said of Samson when she first talked to him, "He is so serene." And that was what I took pleasure in—Samson's tranquility.

Soon after I had purchased him—and was reveling in the safe feeling that riding a mule was giving me—I heard him tell me in my mind, "I will take care of you, Missus." I was nearly giddy with happiness. Finally, in the golden years of my life, I had an equine that I could trust not to dump me as we rode.

"Give Samson some hay at chore time tonight, I am going to take him out for an early evening ride," I told Erica. The second year I owned him, my mule had begun doing some naughty horse-like acts, such as spooking. Some extra riding would be good for him. Bob was on a trip, so tonight I would be riding alone.

The week before Bob left, he and I had been coming back toward the barn after a perfectly delightful ride in Jake's woods and the fields. I was in the lead; we were gaiting, the speed of a slow trot, not just a slow walk. Unexpectedly, Samson put on the brakes, dug his front toes in the ground, spun quickly around, and ran in the other direction.

Earlier, during another of his little tantrums when he decided he didn't want Miss Ellie to go first, and determined that if he couldn't be in the lead, he would just go sideways down a hill, I realized that my mule was getting naughty.

When I got Samson under control and returned to Bob and Miss Ellie, still standing in the same spot, I tried again to get him to move forward, and the second time he spun around, but this time didn't run.

"The cows are lying close to the fence. I think that is what has him spooked," Bob remarked.

Contented Red Angus

Okay, the darn cows again. I hadn't seen them, or I would have approached more carefully. Well, it made sense, but I sure hated it. According to my research on mules before buying one, I was told: "Mules, taking after their donkey side of the family, stop and assess the situation, deciding whether to stay, fight or run. There had been no time to assess anything. Samson had reacted—a horse trait.

Another symptom of his growing lack of calmness and concern for me occurred one morning when I was putting him and Praise Hallelujah in the barn. As I opened the pasture gate, Hallelujah let out a big "woof" alarm sound. I have only heard it from my horses when they are frightened of something—real or imagined. It is the monstrous snort that tells the rest of the herd to flee, danger is here. The horse snorted three more times looking toward the creek. I could see nothing. By now Samson was upset. He reacted by refusing to move his feet. Eventually,

I got him into the first stall right inside the barn door, where he acted like he might jump over the side.

Samson didn't like cows, but over the year of living in a pasture beside them, he had become quite accepting, which made this encore of naughty behavior very odd. Another time, I was taking him from the pasture into the barn and a cow was standing in the general area. The cow didn't move a muscle, but Samson turned and ran away, pulling the lead rope through my hands and giving me a rope burn. I was flabbergasted. What was happening to my Sammy Boy?

I talked to two mule trainers, asking if Samson was getting too much grass to eat; I knew he wasn't getting too much grain; he got a few grains a day with his daily wormer. They both said it was possible. Loyd told me a story about a mule he had sold. The new owner called him back about a year later and said, "I want you to take this mule back and sell him. I can't ride him, he bucks me off."

Upon investigation, it was determined that the owner had been feeding the mule a gallon of sweet grain each day. Goodness, that was enough to make a horse crazy, let alone a mule that neither needs nor can handle all those carbs. For the mule's retraining, Loyd told me he put him in a dry lot—no green grass and fed him only a small amount of hay. "Then I tied him up for hours a day," he continued.

Loyd explained, "Tying up a mule is like a child's "time out." It gives them time to think about the fact they are a *mule*. I'd suggest you tie yours up and leave him there."

I called Mary Long. The first thing she said was, "Gracious, he is very tense. He's acting like a *horse*." She had hit the nail on the head. Yes, indeed, he was acting just like Praise Hallelujah, his pasture mate! We explained to Samson that he was not to act like a horse, he was a mule. Neither Mary nor I thought we had really gotten through to Samson.

My next ride alone was in the morning and it was a pleasant, uneventful, and relaxing outing. My surprise came when I had finished untacking Samson and started to lead him back into his stall. He wouldn't budge. It made sense not to want to leave his stall to be ridden, but not to refuse to re-enter it. Then I had an illumination. He was "tying himself up." My mule was asking for his "time out."

"All right, we will give you that time, but in your stall," I said to him.

Four hours later he was still standing contentedly in his corner. I turned him loose. Next day, I again tied him again for several hours and again he was tranquil. Great, I thought, I've got the solution to my naughty mule's conduct.

Monday evening, as I saddled Samson, I was looking forward to another ride like we'd had the day before. He had been absolutely perfect. Starting into the neighbor's woods, Samson stopped gently and gazed off to his right. Standing only ten feet from me was a big doe. Her dark luminous eyes stared back at us. She twitched an ear, flicked her white tail and stamped a foot. Giving her the idea that she had frightened us off, I turned and took another path. I loved these deer meetings. It was Mother Nature at her best.

As we rode home in the dry creek bed, one of a neighbor's peacocks squawked at us as we walked by. The creek bed was deep, so the peacock was almost at head level. Samson barely looked. A few steps further, I felt his hind foot snag something. Stopping and looking down, I saw his foot caught in an old wild grape vine. He hadn't reacted in the slightest. Backing him up a couple steps untangled his foot, and we continued home. It was idyllic—just the perfect ride for my old bones.

Up to a point, my next evening ride was going just as well. Bob had made several sloping paths into the dry creek bed. Close to home I turned Samson into one. I was in my "zone," relaxing and thinking about nothing in particular, just enjoying the evening; I held the reins loosely in my hands. As I leaned slightly back to go down the rather steep but very short bank, Samson stopped like he had hit a brick wall and spun around to the right. I knew I was going to fall. As I lost my balance and crashed to the ground I kept repeating, "No, no, *noooo*."

This was a hard fall; it was a long way down. My sacrum hit the ground first, then my shoulders and finally, my head. Thank goodness for the helmet.

Mules, Mules and More Mules

I rolled over in somewhat of an angry daze, and discovered I could stand, but my lower back and left hamstring muscle hurt like blazes. My head didn't hurt at all, no double vision or dizziness. Those ugly looking riding helmets are worth their weight in gold. I looked for Samson, and saw him moseying slowly toward home, snatching a bite of grass now and then, leaving me alone. How *dare* he?

I could see Erica riding Joe, with her current boyfriend standing close by. I called her on my cell phone, but it went to voice mail. When she rides Joe, she understandably doesn't answer the phone. I was hoping for a ride home on the golf cart. Rats. I would have to get back under my own steam.

It was torture, but I could walk. I was almost glad Samson had left. There was no way I could remount and ride, I hurt too much. He had to go the long way around on the path. I could cut across the pasture after climbing over a gate, in excruciating pain. Walking uphill was hard on my hamstring muscle, the large muscle group that lay between my knee and seat bone. Every time I lifted my leg, I thought I'd be sick. It was agony.

Erica saw Samson coming toward the barn, and went to get him. Then she saw me struggling up the pasture hill toward her. Her friend got the golf cart and came to me, but by then I had made it back. I decided to ride the last few yards to the barn, and that's when I discovered that I couldn't walk without pain—and I couldn't sit either. The pressure on the injured hamstring muscle was agonizing. Going to the potty was going to be heck.

The physical pain was nothing compared to the emotional pain I felt at the betrayal by my favorite mule. *That* was hell. I went over and over the scenario in my mind, trying to find a bona fide reason for his action. Again, that was horse, not mule behavior. I could have positively understood it if Praise Hallelujah had dumped me.

As I hauled myself out of the golf cart, I said to Erica, who was holding Samson, "Please unsaddle him for me"—an unneeded request, she was going to do that anyway—"and then tie him up and leave him tied all night." He had already eaten his supper, and a long timeout would be a fitting punishment.

I almost hoped he had faulty vision and saw a "hole" in the ground where there was none, but Dr. Hammond shot down that idea. "His eyes look fine to me. I don't think you can blame his actions on his eyesight."

I went back in the golf cart several days later and at the same time of evening to see if a spot of bright sunlight shining through the trees had made him think the footing was unsafe. I do think that had been the issue, but now I had two problems: what to do with Samson and how was I going to be able to feel safe riding him again—at least alone—my favorite way of enjoying him?

I emailed Mary Long a SOS. Many thoughts jumbled through my mind about my big mule. What he had done was exceptionally dangerous because it was so unexpected. How can you trust a mule that is absolutely perfect virtually all the time, and then unexpectedly does something like dumping me off his back?

When Mary called she said Samson was too full of himself. "He is cocky. He thinks he is the head honcho in the barn area, and unfortunately, that includes you." Clearly, my mule had forgotten that I was "his missus."

Sadly, tying him up hadn't solved the problem after all. My new plan was to separate him from Hallelujah. They were sharing a small pasture, and on the surface it seemed idyllic. They had their squabbles, and some rough play, but if push came to shove, Samson won by sheer size. Perhaps that had given him a swelled head and a superior attitude.

When I gelded Hallelujah eighteen months ago, my plan was to turn him out with his group of mares, but with Samson's arrival, I had changed my mind. Now, I again decided to put Hallelujah with the mares and keep Samson alone. I knew I couldn't turn them all together. Talking to other mule men had satisfied me that the big mule was too pushy and dominate to put with a herd. Someone was sure to get hurt. I once more recollected why I had wanted molly mules—they get along in a herd situation better, and as a rule are not always trying to be boss. At least with a couple of exceptions, that had been my thirty year experiences with my mares.

Samson was given a one acre pasture with a run-in-and-out stall in the barn. He could see the horses, but if they went to the far end of their pasture, they were some distance away. He stood at his fence looking forlorn, and occasionally giving a sad sounding "heee heee haaaaw." It was true, he was not happy. But then, neither was I.

Still trying to figure out why Samson had become spooky and reactive, I wondered if he didn't run enough in his other pasture to burn off energy I didn't use in riding him.

"Erica, how would you like to canter Samson for me? Perhaps you can make him work harder than I have been."

She was more than up for it; I knew she would take no attitude from him. I was so sore and somewhat fearful from my fall that it would be awhile before I felt mentally and physically like riding again. There was no way he should enjoy a vacation while I recuperated. It was going to take me some time to forgive him. I really didn't want anything to do with him.

I think the feeling was mutual. He didn't want anything to do with me either. When I went down the barn aisle where my horses and mules stood with their heads hanging over their doors, he pulled his in and turned away when I went by him. Moreover, I didn't care much for the look in his eye—it was anything but adoring. I emailed Mary Long again.

"Help, I think my mule hates me."

Chapter Nineteen: Reclamation

After getting my latest SOS about Samson, Mary called back and assured me Samson did not hate me, but agreed we had problems. I guessed Samson and I needed "mule/person therapy," and I knew just who to call.

Horse—and mule—training has evolved over time from whipping, spurring, cussing and worse, to a more gentle approach. The term "Horse Whisperer" has become almost an equine word. Steve Edwards, John Lyons, Clinton Anderson, Brad Cameron, Pat Parelli and many more have become famous and likely rich from their horse knowledge which they impart by books, videos and clinics. Their methods are not all the same, but the approach is similar—teach the horse to allow you to be master in a way that does not require beating the animal and "breaking its spirit." A horse "broke" in this way was indeed broken, not trained.

Now-days folks want more from their animals. A lot of new horse owners tried to make pets out of the large creatures and in doing so, created dangerous horses (and mules)—animals that would run over their owners to get to anything they wanted, run away from what they did *not* want, and learn a whole host of bad habits, sure to get their loving, kind, but misguided people in trouble. Horses and other equines are *not* large dogs! Enter the Horse Whisperers.

The principle is to teach the horse to respect the person's space. No pulling to get away, no stepping on toes (yes, on purpose,) but to become a *willing* partner, not crushed, but still allowing the human to be in charge—the head horse of the two, three or more personal "herd." Someone will be boss. It is one of Nature's rules. Does this sound like something my Samson needed?

I met Eli because of Lordy, the abused, crazy and frightened colt sired by my stallion, Praise Hallelujah. It was fortuitous that I asked just the right horse friend if he knew of a trainer I could use for this dangerous, rescued colt. Gordon, who was working with a donkey stallion, or jack, had given me Eli's number. It took Eli days just to gain enough trust from Lordy to touch him, but soon he was leading the colt around the farm. Into creeks they went, over logs, up and down the riding paths. Lordy was frightened of his own shadow and anything else that moved. Before Eli ever rode the colt, he had him conditioned to stand while he swung a big blue plastic tarp over and under him. I was more than impressed.

Eli had been raised Amish, and as a young seven-year-old child he had practiced training one of his dad's unbroken two-year-old driving horses—without dad's knowledge. Eli had hitched the young mare to a buggy and drove her down the driveway, whereupon she ran off and ended up in a ditch. His mom absolutely forbade her young son to ever work with horses again.

I asked Eli how long that had lasted.

"Two days," he replied with a grin.

He had the knack of working with horses. He was a born "whisperer." Even as a child he could not be away from them anymore than stop breathing. Eli exuded peace and self confidence around the horses. He was never in a hurry. "I have all day," he would say. What he knew when he worked with Lordy had been by intuition and practice. Now he had taken training in the Parelli method and learned more.

This time, however, I asked him to come to the farm instead of sending Samson away, for two reasons: I wanted to observe and learn and I knew Samson would be a disruption in Eli's horse herd. It wasn't worth the aggravation. Eli agreed and the next night appeared on the scene with his horse whisper equipment.

When I met Eli seven years ago he was a darn good looking young man. The lady boarders and I tried to guess his age. He told us he was twenty-seven, but he looked like a teenager. He was quiet, almost shy, but had a ready laugh and spoke softly. From then to now I never heard him raise his voice. I wanted to adopt him. He was slender, over six feet tall and emanated strength. He had a remnant of a beard—left over from Amish days, I surmised, but it gave him a slightly roguish look. Everyone loved Eli.

This night he was the same old Eli, hardly looking much older. We said hellos, he wandered into Samson's stall, and Samson wandered out the open back door of the stall.

"I wondered where I stood with him," he chuckled softly. "Now I know."

Eli stood in Samson's stall with his back turned to the door and in about a minute, Samson stuck his head back in. Eli didn't move or look at him and in another minute the mule came back inside and stood beside him. Eli put the special rope halter on Samson's head and we three walked to the arena.

A second important reason for choosing Eli over just sending Samson away to another trainer, was that Eli had gone through a human fear situation as I had just experienced, although his was much more frightening. Eli had been riding Alex, his Paint stallion, along a country road when the stallion spotted an Amish horse pulling a buggy. Alex bolted off toward the Amish horse and Eli couldn't stop him by pulling on the reins. He finally managed a stop by striking Alex on one side of his head and pulling him up to a fence along the side of the road. Eli jumped off and as he put it, "I was shaking in my boots."

After the buggy horse had gone much farther down the road, Eli remounted and rode back home. The more he thought about what had happened, the more he realized how fortunate he was that no one had gotten seriously hurt, and the more alarmed he became with Alex's actions.

"I realized I couldn't control the stallion, and it was very frightening. It was a very tense ride back home. The next day I had him gelded, but knew that I didn't trust him anymore."

Yes, that trust issue—same as Samson and me. Also like Samson's actions, Alex had not shown dangerous behavior before. I had boarded Alex several months one winter so Eli could ride in the inside arena. We often noted how gentle Alex was. He didn't "talk" or behave like a stud. Eli had even bred him to a few mares at his farm.

"Didn't you realize he was getting bad?" I asked.

"Nope, he just got up one morning and it was like something had changed in his mind. All of a sudden he knew he was a powerful stallion with a mind of his own." Sounded a lot like my Samson.

Eli realized at that moment he and Alex were not "joined." Even horse whisperers can get busy with every day jobs and neglect some important issues with their own horses. Now, Eli not only had to retrain Alex, but get over *his* fear of riding the horse again. Eli heard about the Parelli training method and began working with his horse in an entirely different way.

The Parelli system (and several like it) consists of putting your horse in a rope halter that is designed to give the person more control. A regular halter has a wide nose band and if a horse desires, can pull a person in the direction of his choosing. The animal is worked off a special twelve foot rope. In this manner the horse can be taught to respect your space, have his own space to a point, but you still have control of him in a small area.

Eli started Samson on Parelli's "Seven Games." All of these games were to teach Samson that Eli, or the person on the other end of the rope was the dominant creature in this twosome. The "Friendly Game" was first. The purpose was to teach the mule although his species is a prey animal, meaning they get eaten by predators, Eli was not one of them. This game is the foundation of all the training.

Eli touched Samson all over his body with his hands. Now this would seem positively enjoyable, after all, my mule was not a wild horse and was used to lots of touching. Apparently Samson had some resentment issues because while he didn't move his feet, his tail went swish, swish, swish. His tail would prove to be a great barometer to his acceptance level throughout his "reclamation."

After using his hands, Eli used the Parelli "carrot stick" which is about a three foot long stick and is orange like a carrot with a soft rope attached to the end. Pat Parelli says it is a myth that treats spoil a horse. "Carrots and kindness are the way to gain a horse's heart." I liked that thought as I use lots of apples and carrots for treats after a workout or trail ride, or even after leaving the show ring. All my Tennessee Walker show horses learned to look for their apple after they had returned to their horse show stalls!

The stick is used as an extension of the human arm and the soft rope could be flicked over and on the animal. Parelli says having an "arm" that reaches so far about the animal impresses them. He says this long reach "baffles and impresses" the animals. Samson responded well to his carrot stick stroking, and his tail was swished with less frequency.

On to the Porcupine Game. The goal here was to get the mule to move his body in any direction with eventually a very soft touch. As a spectator sitting in a chair in a corner of my inside arena, I thought Samson looked like *he* was playing games with Eli. The mule stood there quietly as though just waiting to see if could outwait the person, or see how much pressure the man at the end of the rope would really use. I said as much to Eli.

"Oh, yeah, he's playing with me. Horses do these games of dominance in the pasture with each other all the time. Samson isn't convinced I am the leader yet, but he will. I have all night."

Eli's patience was a gentle force to be reckoned with. I, on the other hand, am too much in a hurry and I know my mule would read that too. In fairly short order, Samson was moving as Eli directed and he moved on to The Driving Game.

Here Samson rather quickly learned to move his body around, backwards and forwards with just a point of Eli's carrot stick. The tail swishing always started up again with each new game, but as he caught on to what was desired, it began to lessen, but not stop all together.

The Yo Yo Game was next and my favorite. I think it was ten years earlier when I had one of Parelli's instructors come to the barn for a weekend clinic. I loved it, used my stallion, Praise Hallelujah as my lesson horse, and learned a lot. It deepened my bond with Hallelujah too. I had the clinician handy to help me with my stallion, and I really needed it. Hallelujah was powerful, and while he did not display breeding stallion behavior, he was definitely a dominant horse. It helped to be over six feet tall instead of only five feet four. I enjoyed the yo-yo game immensely.

In this step, the person teaches the horse to back up and then come forward by jiggling the rope attached to the halter. First you start with subtle finger pointing, then since the horse has no idea at this point what you are asking of him, you start shaking the rope, harder and harder. As soon as he takes even one step back, you immediately stop. The idea is to eventually get the horse to back up by only wagging or pointing your finger at his chest and come forward by barely touching the rope as hand over hand you gently stroke the rope back to you.

When the horse has learned the routine, you can back him over poles, between trees, or in my case big blue barrels, into water and so on. If you do all these games correctly, they will indeed be fun for you and your animal. My plan was to have Eli teach these things to Samson and then refresh me on how to do them. If I couldn't ride because of time or weather, then instead of just letting Samson out to his pasture, we would play a few games—just to remind him who the herd boss was. If I were smarter than I had been with Hallelujah, I would make myself do them. My failing was that I would much rather *ride*!

I watched Samson and Eli work with yo-yoing. I actually had good intentions one day several weeks ago and thought I would do that one game. Samson had been a show mule and had been taught to "park" or pose with his two front feet side by side and the same with the rear ones, hold his head up and look pretty. When I shook the rope at him, he parked out perfectly and gazed at me with a proud look on his face. I had to smile and stopped and petted him. I didn't have the heart to shake him out of his pose. He was sure he was fulfilling my request. At that time he was a good mule and I had no real purpose in pursuing it.

Now he was doing the same with Eli—posing. Eli gently kept shaking the rope, but he had to chuckle. After a couple minutes, I asked Eli, "He really knows what you want, doesn't he? He just isn't obliging very fast."

Eli allowed that he thought that was the case too. Sort of a quiet disobedience. Samson didn't dance about, throw his head up and around—he just wouldn't move his feet. "I still have all night," Eli said, staying calm. Now if I had been at the rope's end I know my impatience and frustration would have shown. Eli just kept shaking the rope harder and harder until the snap that attached to the rope halter under Samson's chin clunked him again and again. *Finally* Samson figured he'd best move something besides his tail which was switching back and forth in great annoyance, and back up *one* front foot. That was enough for the moment.

One of the signs that a horse or mule is "giving in," whether they are being chased around in the round pen or working on the rope, is licking their lips and making chewing motions. When they do that, you know you have gotten through to their minds. Samson actually "licked and chewed" fairly quickly. Although, he thought he was a head honcho and big boss mule, he acquiesced quite easily. I was very happy to see that trait displayed.

In a few more minutes Eli had Samson backing up a couple steps, but he still had to clunk him under the chin. Eli seemed to possess either "mule savvy" or he communicated well with any animal, but I think he did everything perfectly with my mule. Mule trainers seem to be of two opposing opinions on training, which makes it harder for a novice like me to figure out what to do.

One side says: Don't overdo anything with a mule. Once they have done it, they know, don't make them mad by repeating it over and over.

Another opinion is: Keep at it until they get it *really* well, just like a horse.

Eli only did each of the games for a few minutes. He did not insist Samson do them all perfectly over and over, but he covered all of them in the first evening, accepting baby steps in each.

The Circling Game was next and since he had more or less incorporated that into some of the other games, this one was easy. Samson was to circle around Eli and not stop until he was told to stop. If he did quit, there was no yelling or waving the carrot stick with the rope attached to get him back to circling, but rather, Eli gently tugged him back toward him and then shook the rope to make Samson back up a few steps to send him on his way again. What this taught Samson was that it was easier to keep going than stop, come in, back up, and go again. A few minutes of this and Eli started the last game for the evening—the Sideways Game.

I sort of cringed when I saw this one start because in my mind it is the hardest of them all. I sure had a hard time getting Hallelujah to do it during the clinic. He was all over the place with me. The idea is to get the horse to move sideways. It sounds easy, but I think it is confusing. Using the side of the arena, Eli positioned Samson perpendicular to it and by swinging his rope toward his rear and then shoulders from the side, attempted to drive him sideways.

This was the first I saw Samson actually rebel. He ducked his head down, turned it away to the other direction, and took off. He didn't understand, but instead of just standing there, he made "bad choices" as my four year old granddaughter, Alexis, would say. He got enough of a jump on Eli that he was pulled along a few strides before getting Samson's head turned back toward him and stopped. Three more times Eli tried and with the same results except Eli got him stopped immediately. At this rate I was beginning to see the possibility that it *might* take all night….

Then suddenly, Samson got his feet going in the right direction and took three steps to the side just as nice as you please. I heaved a big sigh of relief, and Eli said, "Time to quit!"

The Squeeze Game was the last on the list, but because Samson was doing the circling and driving games so well, it had been incorporated into the former game playing. Horses and mules, maybe to a lesser degree, are claustrophobic. They don't like small places. It is their "flight" instinct. If a horse flees when chased by a wolf into a cave, it would not be able to escape. Guiding your horse between you and obstacles by simply pointing a finger in that direction, is the eventual goal. Your imagination is the limit on this one, but it has a wonderful end result in that it is easy to load your horse into any trailer after he learns to trust and go where you point him.

I had a big smile on my face at the end of the session. I watched Samson become more adjusted to his role of second place. His tail switched with less force and frequency and his eyes gained that mellow appearance again. Samson wasn't a wild creature or a rogue so it hadn't taken a lot of time to remind him of his status. Eli came two more times that week and by the third visit Samson was going through the games and working on his slight, or maybe not so slight, spookiness.

When I purchased Samson and rode him that first summer and fall, he had displayed very little startle instinct. He might look, or pause, but then went on. That was what I had loved and why I trusted him so much. Now he jumped and spun at real or imagined sights. When Eli dragged out the big blue tarp used to cover equipment, Samson blew through his nose and abruptly backed up. Good Heavens! That was a Miss Ellie, my spookier mule's, reaction.

Eli got the longer twenty-two-foot rope attached to Samson. As he walked, dragging the tarp, which not only looked daunting, but made rustling noises, Samson walked far behind at the end of the long rope.

"This is his comfort zone right now," Eli commented. After five minutes the mule was walking closer and in another few minutes Samson stood to have the tarp flapped about him and over his back.

The next task was to have Samson walk over the tarp, which of course, he refused. Again, here is where I realized I needed to slow down when I worked with him. My immediate tendency would have been to "drive" him more strongly, hopefully over the tarp and not over myself. Eli let him skirt around it a few times, then stopped him, backed him up with the rope and made him stand at the edge of the blue monster. After pawing close to it, he placed one foot upon it and then walked over, calm as could be. Oh, goody. I was sure now that I could play these games with him. After one or two more times with Eli, I wanted to give it a try. I would just need to remind myself, "Patience, patience!"

The goal of the exercises was not just to get Samson to walk over blue plastic, between barrels, back over poles and so forth, but to get his mind thinking again. I wanted him to walk up to frightening objects, real or imagined, assess the situation as a good mule should, and then walk by or over if I was sure it was safe. If I wasn't sure, then I would be smart to trust my mule. How would Eli's training equate to the "real world?"

The next morning when I put the horses out, Samson was to go in with the cows. I wanted him to get used to these frightening monster-like creatures and their pasture was adjacent to the other horses and mules, so he would have companionship. The easiest way would be to put him in the cow stall which opened out to their pasture, but they were packed in it. Samson willingly came up to the door of the stall and stood quietly. I was impressed. His erstwhile behavior would have been to snort and back up with his eyes bugging out like he'd seen a ghost, but I decided that trying to get him into the stall was foolish and let him in the pasture gate instead. This was great progress and I was starting to get that silly "mule smile" back on my face.

Chapter Twenty: The Cow Pony

Eli had started coming out to work with Samson on a regular basis, but one week, large severe thunderstorms storms raced through northern Indiana during our late afternoon training time. Erica came in the barn saying, "Geez, I just heard a tornado warning on my radio for some western Indiana counties!" Many days we had severe thunderstorm watches, but a warning was serious, and a tornado warning was cause for alarm.

We looked out the barn doors to the west and saw ominous dark clouds rolling toward us. I went to the house and checked the weather station. There was no warning for our immediate area, but that could change suddenly. Eli had gotten Samson out of his stall, and had all the training props set up, but decided he should go home instead. Driving through rain so heavy it was hard to see the road, he arrived at his farm to see trees down and discover he had no electric power.

Erica stayed to ride her mule and horse and encountered a distressing sight upon her home arrival. It was worse than Eli's homecoming as more trees were down, some upon the road, and she also had no electricity or phone service. Our farm had been spared any damage. This turn of events made it necessary for Eli to take that week's session of training off as he tended to his own horses.

I was feeling healed and confident enough by now that I decided to ride Samson in the evening with another rider. I was the first rider in the twosome, so Samson had company, but more importantly, so did I. He still had to be the scout, the animal with his ears up and eyes alert, looking for danger. If he spooked now I would be very disappointed, but it was a good test and I should be safe with another rider.

It was evening and time that the deer could be out, and sure enough, going around a bend in the path, there stood a doe about twenty feet from us. Samson stopped, took one step to the right, and then stood still. Deciding it was just a deer, he walked quietly on. This was very good; he was thinking again.

All the next week I rode him with another rider and each time he became more like my old Samson. One time we walked into a patch of sun dappled grass in a deeply wooded area. He hesitated, put his nose to the ground and then calmly walked through. I was delighted. In rethinking my fall, I was really sure that as we had begun to make the descent into the dry creek bed, he saw a sun spot on the shaded dirt, spooked and dumped the unprepared me. I could see that happening. He had been "blowing his nose" at similar places in the recent past. What I hated about it was that his reasoning reflex had deserted us, and he had reacted instead of just checking it out.

The next week, Eli was back on schedule, and I had a lesson getting Samson to move away from my training stick while touching his neck and rear. Eli did more desensitizing and reviewing the training program. The mule seemed very at ease and content. By now, he really trusted Eli and was willing to work for him. The next day we turned two beef steers into the arena where Eli was working with Samson. Although the mule was much better with the cows, I wanted to push his limit. After Eli was finished with his training visits, I didn't want any more cow spooks if I could help it.

The steers, true to cow nature, had a blast running around the arena, knocking over the blue barrels, eating my pretend trees salvaged from limbs of a wind damaged tree and running up into the sawdust piles in the corner of the arena, causing dust to fly and the pile to change its shape and position. Samson hardly looked at them. Previously he would have been charging around the arena trying to escape. Eli herded the cows by leading Samson around next to them. That all seemed to be no big deal, so with a couple people to wave arms and help guide, Samson and Eli gently herded the steers back out the barn door. This was huge! What a change from the mule who had run out his stall door when he simply had smelled cow on my hands, spooking and running off with me in the saddle when he saw them lying in the pasture. I felt like jumping up and down in glee.

The third and final day of that week's training, we planned for me to work more with Samson, but we did something better. Samson became a cow horse. I wanted the cows down from the pasture to check one of them, so I asked Eli if he wanted to go play cowboy and round them up. I thought that would be great mule training. He agreed, but before we got everything ready, the cows came up to the barn by themselves. Still, it offered a great opportunity: I opened the gate and Eli walked the mule through the herd of six cows. I knew the cows wouldn't scare him by running at him, so this would be a close encounter of the sane kind. I still found it hard to believe the set of circumstances that began his fear of cows.

His previous owner and some riding buddies had ridden into a field with many cattle, and wanted to see how close they could get to them. Cows, being super curious creatures, came running toward the riders. This would frighten me, let alone a horse or mule, so of course, they all bolted off. Samson had never forgotten.

Samson seemed totally unperturbed as Eli walked him to the open gate. One of the small calves was lying down in the way, and the bigger ones stood there, docile and chewing their cuds. Samson took several tentative steps among them, the calf got up, and the cows sauntered off several steps, but Samson never quivered a muscle. Eli got behind the cows and herded them into the paddock. Big Red, aptly named as she *was* big, wasn't afraid of Samson and refused to budge.

"I'll let her alone; she is too big," Eli remarked. But before he moved on, Samson put his head down, touched and smelled Big Red's rear end. How much better could it get? That grin on my face was getting bigger and bigger by the minute. Eli and Samson gently walked among the cattle, moving one a few steps here and there; no one was excited about anything. The cows seemed to think it just dandy a mule was walking about them and Samson had decided he might just like to become a cow pony!

Chapter Twenty-one: On Again, Off Again

"Bad things come in threes" and "Only those who never ride, never fall" were a couple of old sayings that kept repeating in my mind after yet another fall off Samson in less than thirty days. This one was my worst equine injury in three years. Eli had been working with Samson, and I had begun getting my courage back to ride him, but only with riding buddies, not alone.

This particular beautiful late summer Sunday, three of us planned on a pleasant ride. I was saddled and ready first, so I wandered around the inside arena where Eli had placed different training aids such as the barrels, tree branches stuck in buckets and a small foot high jump—two poles only one foot off the ground. Eli had been playing the "driving game" over these poles with Samson. The mule easily went over them, sometimes at a walk, sometimes at a jump. It was fun to watch him hop over.

I walked Samson up to the jump, fully expecting him to step over it. He put his nose to the pole, touched it and then things went dramatically wrong. My reins were loose because I had let them slip through my fingers so he could touch the pole with his nose, and the next thing I knew I was sailing through the air. I landed with a thud on the hard arena dirt, but instead of landing more or less square on my seat, then shoulders and finally the back of my helmeted head as I always had before, I landed with a twist to the side onto my left buttock. The pain to my lower back was excruciating.

Quickly, I moved my legs to be sure I could, but trying to move anything more brought tears.

"Are you all right?" one of the gals called out.

"Do you have any sharp pain?" This from Ann who last year had been ejected from her horse, and had broken her collar bone.

"No, but my back is hurt. Oh my poor, poor back."

My lower back is my "Achilles heel." It is the reason I ride gaited animals. I had always been so very grateful in all my other falls I somehow had never hurt it, not in the least. But now I had, because instead of landing straight, I had twisted and wrenched it.

"Call Hal!" Ann shouted to Pat.

Pat took Samson who, I later was told, had not moved from my side. As soon as I fell, he stopped and stood still. I was in pain, but nothing was broken, a real miracle, especially at my age. I remember saying, "Thank God for my helmet." Again it had saved my head. I told Pat to put Samson back in the pasture after unsaddling him. A week later I found my riding gloves I thought I had lost, in the pocket of the jeans I wore that day. Somehow, I'd had the presence of mind to remove and stuff them in there. They were my favorite gloves. Strange what the mind does.

Hal appeared with the golf cart and I was able to roll over, crawl to it and with help, sit down. I was shaking with pain and shock. In the garage, I found I couldn't support my weight standing because of the pain in my left sacroiliac joint. This was an injury that would not have allowed me to get home without help. Thankfully, it had happened in the barn and not out on the trails. An x-ray would later show an acute fracture of my third lumbar vertebrae, which would painfully heal on its own.

What had happened to cause this latest ejection from my animal's backside? The good thing about this fall was that it was not Samson's fault and I kept telling everyone that fact. When we approached the poles, I had no idea that he would jump them, nor would I have worried about it. My horses jumped low objects from a standstill and it was easy enough to stay seated. But let me tell you about a mule's jumping from a standstill. Mule folk reading this will likely shake their heads in commiseration, non-mule folk will be astonished.

Several years ago, I went to the local fair with my daughter Michal. We just happened to be present when the llamas were being jumped over a pole that was elevated higher and higher until the participants were eliminated. The llamas were led up to the jump at a slow, unconcerned walk; they stopped, and then sprang over the pole like a deer, landing on the other side inches from the pole. A horse jumps in an arc—takeoffs are farther away and the landings are feet from the jump. A mule can jump like the llamas. (He can also be taught to jump in regular-horse-fashion and be shown in jumping competitions.)

The old timers used the mule's ability to jump high from a standstill to clear fences while they were coon hunting. A raccoon doesn't stop at fences; man can crawl through or over, but how do you get your mule along with you? You build upon his natural ability to jump from a standstill. Samson had "coon jumped" a foot high pole and it was like riding a bucking horse.

He had his head down to sniff, I loosened the reins, and before I could take a breath, he had balanced himself high on his hind feet and then launched himself over, but as his rear end popped over the poles it ejected me out of the saddle with great force. I must have looked like a grandma rag doll flying through the air. It was only God's mercy that kept me from being badly injured.

I say it wasn't Samson's fault because Eli had been jumping him over the same pole and I didn't give Samson any direction *not* to jump, so he made a choice. In the woods and over many logs he had never jumped one. Now I knew that he or any mule must never jump like that with me on its back. It was good to find this out in the barn.

The September '07 issue of *Mules and More* magazine had a picture on the cover of a mule and rider jumping a relatively low, perhaps two foot high object. The mule is caught perfectly in the photo high up in the air, and his rider is holding on to the Western saddle horn. Now, that is the way to ride such a jump. I, on the other hand, was in a small English show saddle with nothing to hold on to, had no rein contact at all and no idea that my mule was going to be shooting straight up into the air.

This latest fall was the third in a series of accidents in less than thirty days. First, I had fallen while riding Samson on the trail by a very naughty stop and spin; next Bob had a more disastrous accident with Miss Ellie, which left him with a broken rib, and now this. And while it was true that I could have fallen down some stairs or tripped and also injured my back, I tended to blame myself because "Only those who never ride, never fall." This could have been avoided if I didn't ride anymore. Just how guilty should I be feeling, and what should I do about it?

Loren Basham and Hoosier Daddy competing at the 2007 Craig Cameron Extreme Cowboy Race in Kansas City photo compliments of *Mules and More* magazine

Chapter Twenty-two: Soul Searching

As I sat in the easy chair or lay on the couch, I did a lot of questioning, "Why?" I could understand falling off sporadically, but two times in a month was cause for some concern in my eyes. In both of the accidents I really couldn't blame myself for doing something foolish or even careless, except that from here on I would do my meditating while sitting on the ground, instead of on an animal, and I would never have totally loose reins or let my mule coon-jump an obstacle.

I needed to focus more as I rode instead of woolgathering, as Mom would have put it, or meditating. That was sad to me. It had been very enjoyable riding and not thinking about anything in particular. However, I never did it riding my show horses. They required more concentration and apparently, riding mules wasn't totally different.

At one time, I owned a show stallion I called Charlie who absolutely demanded that his riders pay attention when he was ridden. He was a big, black, very talented horse with a mind of his own. I wasn't brave enough to trail ride him; instead, I chose to work him in the inside or outside arenas where I felt relatively safe. If I started thinking about something else, he lost his concentration too. His gait, which we were perfecting and strengthening, fell apart and he stumbled or veered off the outside perimeter of the oval arena tracks.

Occasionally, he puffed himself up and made you pay attention before he decided to spook. My first Erica had noticed it also. Since many times she had another horse in the same arena where I rode Charlie, she made note that Charlie had to be sending horse messages to the other horses, because they became agitated, put their ears back, switched their tails and lost concentration. He did this in the show rings also, several times causing the other horse to "screw up." Charlie was into mind control—and his rider had best have the stronger mind of that twosome.

I could accept this as a riding lesson: focus on what you are doing when riding horse or mule—but three semi-serious injuries in a short time had me rattled. Was I doing something wrong? Was "Someone Up There" trying to give me a message? And was that message that I shouldn't ride anymore for some reason? The physical pain of the fall was nothing compared to the emotional trauma.

Even Hal must have wondered, because when I tearfully asked him what he thought, he said quietly, "Maybe you should consider a lifestyle change." Not what I wanted to hear. Hal and I both believe God opens and closes doors, guides and directs in many ways—was He closing this door?

Ever since I was a child of four years, I knew I had a calling to work with animals, especially horses. In the elapsed time of thirty plus years, I had given my animals up twice. Once to get married and start a family, and again after our family suffered through an Indiana tornado. Both times God had blessed my return to loving and sharing my life with animals in an amazing way. Surely, He wouldn't be telling me to stop now.

Three days after my fall, and being in great pain when standing or sitting, I was lying in bed watching television. I was also crying. Watch some television, cry, blow my nose, sniff, and wipe tears. I had pretty much worked myself up into quite a stew.

One of the programs was a Hallmark story called *Love Comes Softly* about a young western pioneer woman whose husband had died suddenly, and she then married for convenience at the invitation of a gentleman. Later in the story, she was crying and asked her new husband why God had let her husband die.

The man answered that God was like he was as a father to his own young daughter. He couldn't protect her from all pain, but he could be there for her as she went through it. *God* hadn't let her husband die.

I stopped crying and got still. Was God answering my question on a television show? I felt at peace, and as I looked back again at my life with animals, I was reminded again and again how many times I had been through mishaps and been protected.

I remembered back when I was fifteen and our newly gifted Holstein yearling heifer calf had wrapped her tether chain about my waist as I was excitedly, but not thinking, showing her off to a neighbor. Fortunately, this neighbor rescued me in time to avoid being squeezed in half. At the same age, I had hooked a horse up to a hay rake. The horse ran away with me, the big wheel of the rake hit a large stone, and the jolt bounced me off near the barn. I cut my head on a rock, requiring stitches, but otherwise survived in fine shape. All was quiet for several years until Hal, I, Sharon who was four and Roger who was two, survived a tornado, which left us homeless, but alive and physically relatively unscathed. Emotionally we were all scarred in some way.

Later, when I was around thirty and Sharon was twelve, she just "had to have a horse." I bought a green, or almost broke young horse (big mistake) for her. Apache gave me several lessons in the school of hard knocks when as a big, untrained and somewhat ill-humored horse, he had dumped me on the ground a couple miles from home, and kicked at my head as I went off (I felt the air). Mercifully, he had missed.

Two years later, I had the great good fortune to buy an older Arabian gelding. He was delightfully trained, loving and beautiful, but the owner somehow forgot to tell me he was a halter puller, meaning you couldn't tie him up. He pulled back until he broke something, in this case my shoulder as I stood beside him. But it had happened on a weekend while Hal was home, so he rescued me, and took me to the hospital for surgery.

Then there was a nice long, nearly twenty year respite from injuries. It seemed I led a charmed life as I learned more and more about horses. I read an article about the law of averages as it applied to horse and owner. The more you were around them and the more you had, the more likely you were to someday be injured.

Riding my horses was like a blessed addiction, but I have a cranky back—a bad disc and several muscles that spasm and even tear. One summer, when we had first moved to our present horse farm, I moved just right to re-injure an old muscle tear. I was in agony and in bed for a week, but having a husband-chiropractor was the ticket to recovery. The very first day that I was able to walk normally, I went to the barn, saddled up a horse and rode, hoping that Mom who lived next door wouldn't see me. She would have had a fit. I just had to see if I could do it, or if I was ruined forever.

When I was in my late fifties, I found and bought the horse of my dreams. Praise Hallelujah was the sorrel stallion who set our farm upon the path to glory and sired many talented colts. I was getting older and moved slower, but the horses were getting more spirited. These were show horses and more panache was required to accomplish my goal. At a horse show one July, I was showing one of Hallelujah's offspring. After the class as we were exiting the ring, the horse tripped and went down to his knees and nose. I started to fall gracefully off his back when he was only inches from the ground, but before I had reached the ground he flung up his head and neck and then his body to save himself, and hurled me down with force. I remember my neck being bent towards my chest when I landed on it.

As I lay there, several fellow exhibitors ran to me. One of them was a doctor. Holding up his fingers he demanded, "Rose, how many do you see?" I saw only the two he had held up, had no dizziness and left the arena with a little help and a limp.

Next, began a series of spooks and consequent falls from various horses. Once, Hallelujah and I were riding in the woods. I spotted the buck first, but not soon enough to do anything about my horse's abrupt spin as he ignominiously dumped me and took off crashing through the trees back toward the barn, snatching both stirrups from the English saddle on tree branches on his frantic gallop home.

I had only sprained my ankle, and hobbled out of the woods. As I got to the field, I saw Bob coming as fast as he could drive his truck over the bumpy hay field to pick up the pieces. Fortunately, I was still in one piece. He had spotted my horse galloping hell-bent-for-leather to the barn without me. It was after this fall that I started wearing protective head gear. Good thing too, because more falls were about to occur.

The last few years I experienced the basic same type fall: horse stops, spins, I fall, hit my rear then shoulders, and finally my helmeted head, but none of them really hurt me. I get up, dust off my seat, and either get back on if a log is handy, or lead my horse home, unless it left without me. I was amazed and grateful I never got hurt.

On my birthday in January, a few years ago, I decided to have a quick ride in the inside arena, "just for fun." I hadn't been riding much that winter, but a short ride would be exhilarating. I was so happy at the prospect of riding that I forgot my protective helmet. Hallelujah was very spirited that day, but I was coping with him easily. Two other riders were also enjoying the arena.

As I rounded a corner where some water buckets had been dumped and the ground had frozen as solid as cement, one of the barn cats scampered underneath my horse. Hallelujah jumped off to the right, I lost my stirrup, grabbed his mane and almost saved myself, but the darn cat scooted in another direction, and that did it. My horse gave another big jump sideways and I was on the ground. My head hit the frozen dirt and I had no helmet. I saw stars and heard the other riders talking as though from a far away distance. It was only a mild concussion….

The other injury that sidelined me for some time was caused by a horse who was cast (stuck in his stall). He had rolled against the wall and needed help. I thought I could do it by myself, but didn't get out of the way soon enough as his leg swung back, and my right knee was badly hyper extended. Hobbling and sobbing my way to the phone, I called Bob, who ran his business from home, to come get me with the car.

This took much longer to recover and in the process of protecting the right knee, I badly stressed the left one. Would I ride again? Yes, but it was eight months later. Fortunately, it happened during the winter, so I could mend and see the snow fly instead of miss beautiful summer riding weather.

Getting tired of horse injuries, I went to mules and here I was again—still getting hurt. I emailed my friend Connie who is my age, has had two knee replacements, and rides all over creation with her friend Alice. I was embarrassed to tell her of my latest fall off Samson, but I did, and asked her how they managed to keep it together in all the places they went riding.

Mules, Mules and More Mules

It wasn't much later Connie emailed me about Alice and her mule Colonel's latest venture. Seemed the mule had been stung on the nose by some bees and started bucking. Eventually, he unseated his rider. Ouch, that had to hurt! At least I hadn't been bucked off. It is really all in how you land, which is mostly by luck or Divine intervention. Alice got back on and rode another three days before coming home. "See," Connie said, "it does happen to us too!"

The other conflict in my mind was I had gotten hurt having a good time. It was preventable—just don't ride any more. If I had been injured in a car accident, Hal would not have said, "Maybe you should never drive a car again."

My new Erica's mom was in the barn shortly after my fall, and I was telling her where it hurt.

"Yes, I know exactly what you mean. I was rear ended in car accidents twice within seven months, and I have a similar pain," Anita told me.

Sure, I thought, *but yours was "righteous." You weren't having fun.* "Do you think maybe I should stop riding?"

Nearly before I had finished my sentence, Anita said adamantly, "No! It is just a bump in the road. You will soon be in the saddle again."

I really needed to hear that. Any mom who can encourage and support a gung-ho daughter to ride her Thoroughbred in cross country competition is not faint of heart. She understood us passionate and determined horse—and mule—devotees.

After contemplating my life with its past horse incidents, and almost hearing God tell me through a television program to stop crying, that He had been there for me a whole bunch of times, and getting support from horsey friends, and later, Hal, to keep riding, I decided that my glass was definitely half full, not half empty.

I would accentuate the positive in my latest fall. I would soon be riding again. Maybe I would have to work up to riding Samson, but if Alice could be bucked off by her beloved mule Colonel, and not

Rose Miller

hesitate to get back on him, I would address my trepidations where my big mule was concerned too.

Chapter Twenty-three: Ruth Ann

I will never forget the first time I saw Ruth Ann. It was in July at the Mule and Donkey Celebration in Shelbyville, Tennessee. I'd gone hoping to buy a special mule. My first choice was a gaited molly. I'd looked at several mules and as my friend Carolyn and I were leaving to eat supper before the evening show classes, we saw a mule being ridden along the fence beside the road.

Its ears were flopping as its head shook up and down. It gaited like a Walking Horse—much better than any of the gaited mules I had seen earlier—and the man was riding it bareback with only a rope attached to its halter. Carolyn stopped her truck, and I stuck my head out the window and shouted, "Hey, I really like your mule. Do you want to sell it?"

The man stopped his animal and looked up at me. "No, ma'am, she's pretty special to me."

"Yes, she is that," I replied. "Would it be okay to come by your stall and see her anyway?"

"Sure," he answered and told me where his barn was located.

"My goodness," I remarked to Carolyn, "that mule is just what I want. A well gaited molly and just the perfect size. Just my luck that he doesn't want to sell her."

I had already found Samson and liked him very much, but he was a john, and he was so very big. Carolyn agreed that this molly was a great mule specimen. We grabbed something to eat and went back to the barn to find the gentleman and his mule. We located the stall, and the mule was standing quietly, dozing with one hind leg cocked as she rested. Her ears were in a relaxed position, and she paid us absolutely no mind.

"Not very friendly, is she?" I asked Carolyn. With the exception of one other john mule I looked at, the rest of the mules had seemed interested in my advances. Samson had been quite welcoming, ears forward and nose extended, eyes bright and kind as he let me stroke his neck.

I opened the molly's door just a bit, and peered inside. She stood still and I ventured a pet on her neck. She didn't seem to care one way or the other. Carolyn and I decided to wait a bit and see if the owner would show up, so I could chat with him. In about thirty minutes, he arrived.

We introduced ourselves. His name was Mark and the mule was Ruth Ann. It turned out Carolyn and I had seen her in several earlier classes. She always placed very well out of large classes of at least twelve. I noticed her as her walking gait was superb.

Mark, Brenda and Ruth Ann photo courtesy of Avalon Photography

Something unique about mule people, I discovered, was they all loved talking about their animals whether they were for sale or not, and Mark was no exception. He told me that Ruth was thirteen, and he had had her since she was thirteen months old. She had some arthritis, and when she stood in a stall for a while she got stiff, and she had very sensitive skin and was prone to getting girth sores.

Ruth had perked up when Mark arrived on the scene. It was easy to see she loved him. He told stories about her, such as the time the family had been on a trail ride and it was time to load the mules in the trailer to come home. He looked for Ruth and couldn't locate her; she had been loose and grazing nearby. Peering into the trailer, he saw she had loaded herself and was ready for home.

His trailer was a stock trailer, and the mules were loaded side by side with no partition between. He said he loaded Ruth last, because even though the other mules had swung their butts over and taken up all the room, she would jump in anyway and push them over. Mark and she had a partnership that was quite plain to see. No wonder he didn't want to sell her.

Later that afternoon, Mark found me standing around Samson's stall. He told me he and his wife had talked it over, and they would sell Ruth as they had younger mules that were not getting the attention they deserved or required, because Ruth was so easy to use. I was expecting her to be priced high, after all she was proving herself in the show ring, and he really didn't want to sell her. And she was. Still, I wanted to see her more closely and ride her. She seemed to be exactly what I wanted. Perhaps I would have to sell one of my horses to get money to purchase her, but maybe it would be worth it.

I had taken my own saddle to ride on the mules I was considering, so Carolyn and I lugged it to Ruth's stall. She seemed none too pleased to be saddled, her girth area already had a sore, and Mark lamented he had forgotten to bring her special salve. Putting the saddle on, he rode her to the work-out arena and took her around once. She was perfect. I got on and we started our circle. I couldn't get her to go faster than pokey walk; her ears were not back in anger, but back a little as in "I am unhappy, please just get off."

Mark shouted to use the end of the reins to slap her; I did, but nothing much happened. As we went by the entrance into the work arena, Ruth tried to duck out. This was not going well. Ruth had no intention of being sold. I could see it in her body language and actually hear her communicate in a mind-to-mind fashion with mine that she did not want me to purchase her. I dismounted and told Mark I thought he should keep her always. She definitely belonged to him, heart, mind and body. I hadn't gotten those vibes from any of the other mules. There was no way, I told myself. She was more expensive than Samson, she had arthritis, but worst of all, buying her would be a problem since she loved Mark so much. It would be like selling a favorite dog one had for thirteen years. It would never work.

I watched Ruth Ann and Mark show that evening, and true to form, they got their customary nice ribbons in each class. Ruth Ann might have had a girth sore, been a little stiff from arthritis, but she carried Mark proudly and happily. I had just told Samson's owner that I would purchase his big black mule, and felt good about it. At least Samson wanted to go home with me.

Ruth Ann and Mark photo courtesy of Avalon Photography

Feeling Ruth Ann's emotions was such a unique experience for me, I wanted to share it with Mark, and so I called to talk with him several days after we arrived home. Telling other people that their animal "talked" to you, is rather weird. All my close horse friends know about my animal communicator friend, Mary Long, and many have used her to talk to their horses. As I have, they also have become more in tune with their horses and can sometimes feel their thoughts better than before.

It is like learning to ride. The more you practice, the better you get. Just wanting to communicate with your animals is a first step, and then listening for them to impress you with a feeling is next. Be quiet and listen, don't think you need to always be the one to do the talking. How would Mark respond? Maybe he would think me strange, but I wanted to share the love I felt from Ruth for him.

As I gave him my thoughts about his mule, Mark was pretty quiet, but I didn't get the sense that he thought I was nuts. I think he enjoyed hearing that his mule truly loved him. Later in September, I called Mark again. I was searching for another mule, this one for Bob, and I wasn't having much luck finding a gentle, gaited mule. Many mules advertised sounded bombproof, as in, totally dependable, but even some advertised as gaited didn't travel fast enough to keep up with Samson. I turned my thoughts again to Ruth Ann. The problems would be the same, but I was desperate.

Mark said he guessed they were not interested in selling now. They had been invited to take Ruth Ann to Shelbyville to the Tennessee Walking Horse Celebration, the biggest Walking Horse show in the country, and present Ruth Ann in a demonstration ride. Brenda, his wife, had ridden her, and had such a great time, that Mark was sure she wouldn't part with the mule now.

The next summer, I received an email from Brenda telling me that Mark had definitely decided to sell Ruth, and would I be interested? I wasn't, because I had found Miss Ellie for Bob, and Ruth's problems were still there. The price was lowered into the expensive but doable range, but she still had arthritis and I was sure she still loved her family of nearly thirteen years. I tried to talk them out of it, reminding Brenda how much Ruth loved Mark.

Brenda emailed me asking about Mary Long. I gave her the information and warned her that if she talked to the mule via Mary, it might make it difficult to think of Ruth as just a mule after that. She emailed back stating that Mark didn't want her to pursue it; he was selling her regardless; he had made up his mind. Brenda thought I would give Ruth Ann a great retirement home, and Mark wanted her to go to an animal person, but I still saw problems.

We exchanged "Ruth Ann" emails now and then during the next year. In July they took her to Shelbyville again to the big mule show. I felt sorry for Ruth. I was quite certain they would sell her at the show and not everyone takes great care of a show mule, or horse. People want the ribbons and who knew what could happen to her in order for the new owner to keep getting them. More training? More living in a stall? She needed walking room for her arthritis.

For anyone wanting a show mule, which I didn't, she would be a bargain. Ruth pulled out her customary good ribbon placements in large classes, but she ended up coming home with them. Brenda told me by the time she mentioned to Mark that they should advertise the mule, the show was over. Maybe subconsciously they really didn't wish to sell her at a big show.

In the meantime, our home mule adventures were continuing. I had fallen off Samson when he did his big spook, stop and spin, and shortly thereafter, Bob fell off Miss Ellie. In reconstructing Bob's fall, I am pretty certain that Miss Ellie didn't clearly see a garden hose in the plant nursery where we rode, because we had a fly mask on her face. I heard Bob yell, and quickly turning around in my saddle to look, saw Miss Ellie jump straight up into the air. I went back later to look and right in that spot lay the light colored hose.

Bob went off over her right shoulder, and all could have turned out all right, but because of the close proximity of the nursery bushes and Samson, when she turned around to leave, she stepped on Bob and broke his rib. We were close enough to home to get him in a car. Miss

Ellie sauntered back to the barn on her own when Samson and I went for help.

Having such a fall would be bad enough for a seasoned, committed rider, but I wondered how Bob would feel about riding again. I sure didn't want to lose my riding buddy. He had only been riding a year, and riding wasn't his life as it is to some of us.

Talking to him later after he healed for three weeks, he mentioned that he wasn't sure about riding Miss Ellie again. Miss Ellie had come a very long way in her training since we got her, but I didn't think she was the mule for Bob any longer. My thoughts turned once again to Ruth Ann—the bombproof mule.

If Mark would consider a trade with Miss Ellie for Ruth Ann along with additional funds, I decided to do it. Little Susie Q was still the ideal mule and with Ruth Ann we would have two mollies that we could take on longer trail riding away from the house. Ruth Ann was not just a show mule; Mark had hunted, packed and ridden her alone a lot. She taught all Mark's kids to ride. Brenda, a new wife and rider, rode Ruth with confidence. She would be a perfect addition.

Bob questioned my sanity on spending more for another mule, but I knew how hard it was to find quiet, well-gaited mules. After falling off Samson, even I wanted something smaller and more dependable, especially for off-the-farm trail riding. As a new mule owner of barely two years, I was getting educated in mule ownership. I had gone from blind trust and love in Samson—which had worked for quite a spell—to skepticism.

Now I knew mules had their quirks and weaknesses too. You would think that after thirty plus years with horses I would have known better, but I so desired something safe and dependable, I was blinded to reality. I wanted Ruth Ann to be my last mule purchase. In those two years, I had bought six mules and so far kept two—Samson and Susie Q.

I made arrangements for Erica to make the nine-hour drive to exchange Miss Ellie and Ruth Ann. Before she went, I called Mary Long again. This time I wanted to talk to Ruth and be sure she realized

I was rescuing her, so to speak, giving her a great new home, I was not the reason she was leaving her old one.

**Miss Ellie with Brenda, happy and successful in her new home
Photo compliments of Quadropod Photography
2010 Mule and Donkey Celebration**

Erica rode both mules at Mark's place; both behaved well. Mark showed Erica how Ruth would lie down for a rider to mount or dismount. Another plus for Ruth. I could sure use that if I had to get off on a trail. Getting off wasn't a big problem, but getting back on definitely would be. When Erica unloaded Ruth from the trailer at our barn, I observed she was extremely stiff, and she needed her shoes reset before I could even think of riding her, because her very long feet were growing over the shoes. She also stood strangely with her right front leg pointed off to the right with little weight upon it. Oh, great.

Erica had ridden her and she hadn't been lame, or I know she would have told me before bringing her home, but I don't know how a mule could stand like that and not walk or ride lame. It was a good thing my farrier liked me and had a sense of humor, because I kept getting projects for him in newly purchased animals. Samson's feet after eighteen months were getting better, but still were not good mule feet. Ruth Ann's were not matched; one was higher than the other.

Since I wouldn't be riding her, I turned her out with my other mules and horses to let her settle in. She was friendly, easy to catch, came up as one of the first to the barn, and hung her head over the stall door for anyone to pet. I was still recovering from my coon jump experience with Samson and didn't feel spry enough to do much with Ruth other then give her apples, which she had to learn to eat, and carrots, which she ate immediately. Finally the farrier came and fixed her feet. He thought she would begin to stand normally after she was trimmed level.

The day of the first ride finally came. Erica rode Ruth Ann and I rode Susie Q. I wanted to test out my new bombproof mule by observation, not riding. I had Erica go first. I'd specifically asked Mark about Ruth's possible spookiness. Spooky I did not need. He assured me she was fine. If she looked at something, he just told her to go on past. She had taught all his children to ride….

Ruth started out hesitantly. I wanted her to go first as a test and she didn't like it one bit. When we got to the scary corner where the neighbor's dog was sometimes outside, she put on the brakes and turned around quickly, banging into Susie and me. You can imagine what I was thinking as I took Susie first.

Even then Ruth didn't want to go. We had made a mistake in not taking a riding crop. I seldom rode without one, and it was only used as a backup, but not knowing how Ruth might react to one, Erica didn't take it. She had ridden her at Mark's by herself with nothing, and Ruth had traveled down the road like a trooper. Not here.

Getting across the culvert bridge was another obstacle, and Susie was in front. Yes, I was very disappointed. The next part of riding in the hay field, across another smaller bridge and into the woods went without a hitch. We changed leaders again and Ruth was in front when we came upon two hunters. Ruth stopped again and wouldn't go. Susie took the lead again.

All was well until we were coming home and had to pass some large tree stumps. Again, Ruth stopped and looked intently at the trees as though a monster would jump out at any moment. Susie passed her and Ruth continued looking intently. In a way, it was funny. Ruth was the first animal I ever had that wouldn't follow the braver horse. She had to be sure for herself.

As soon as I got in the house I called Mark. This was a problem I had never expected. While she hadn't been dangerous, she certainly was not bombproof. I'd seen the mule at the big show, I knew Mark wouldn't lie about her, and Erica had ridden her just fine at her home, but now she was transformed into a different mule.

Mark's first question was, "Who was riding her?" I suspect he imagined if it was me, then it was a rider problem, but when I answered that it was Erica, he said, "Hmm. I always ride with spurs and when she stops at something, or acts like she will, I just use the spur and say, 'Ruth, go on.'"

Big spurs were definitely "back up," but I hoped he was referring to a little hesitating, not the outright stopping of today's ride. My contingency plan was Eli. He was still coming three times a week to work with Samson, and now Ruth Ann was going to be at the top of his list.

On one of Eli's earlier visits he had gotten Ruth out and did some desensitizing with the training stick and then a stick with a plastic bag attached. She didn't move. I said, "This is *excellent*. She is supposed to be bombproof."

He called her dull, explaining she wasn't really thinking about what he was doing. Maybe that wasn't so good.

After Erica's and my ride, and Ruth Ann's attention to everything except her rider, Eli started her lessons in earnest. When he took her out of the stall and led her into the arena, her ears were as stiff as pokers, and she was looking for things to bugger at. Her body was also rigid.

This was no relaxed mule. It was mid-afternoon; the big double doors at the end of the arena were open, so she saw all kinds of activity, real or imagined. To say she didn't have her mind on Eli, was an understatement. Watching them, I was very happy Eli was working with her and not me.

After being gentle with his commands and getting nowhere—she was still gazing intently out the back door—he did what I would equate to a face slap to a person that was having a breakdown, just to snap them out of it.

He began by raising the carrot stick high and bringing it within inches of her face, getting her to turn about, back up and pay attention to him. He never said anything and was not angry, but he had to get through to her mind, which was closed. After fifteen minutes, I could see Ruth Ann starting to relax just a little. She was so busy moving her feet this way and that, she couldn't keep her mind on the back door and her ears began to soften, no longer ramrod stiff. Soon, she walked around the arena beside Eli, ears flopping and body relaxed. We put her away. This was a good first step—one I would never have thought necessary.

The next training visit went very well. Ruth Ann started backing up and coming forward again on command. Eli drove her through barrels, and she walked over the big plastic tarp with no hesitation. She started out somewhat distracted, but very soon connected to Eli. She did so well that I asked him to ride her. They went around the arena, and then to the outside arena. She was a little nervous at the end where the garden center landscaping business was, but nothing explosive. He quit.

The next day's lesson was riding away from the barn and arenas along the spooky path. From the barn it was down a slight hill, so I couldn't see everything that was going on, but I saw Eli dismount and start leading her on the bridle path. That didn't surprise me.

Half an hour later he reappeared, and as he got to the barn and me, he said, "She is not ready for you to ride! She started down the hill and stopped with all her attention toward the garden center. She was rigid with fear; I could even feel her heartbeat. I deepened myself into the saddle (wish I knew how to do that) because I knew she was going to do something. She spun about and bolted off. I knew I wouldn't be able to stop her by pulling back on the reins; her mouth felt like cement. I had to pull her head about in a circle."

Gracious, it was bad enough that she had balked and then turned around, bumping into Susie Q when Erica and I rode, but to do one of those spin and bolt off routines with Eli, well, that was worse than awful. Some bombproof mule!

A lot of thoughts were going through my mind at this point. I knew Ruth Ann had an amazing gait. That alone made her a keeper. I was tired of mule trading and decided that somehow Eli and I would reclaim her heart and along with it, her body. All the same, I was grossly disappointed. After my bad fall from Samson, I was becoming a much less confident rider. You could bet I wouldn't be riding her anytime soon. Bob either. I was embarrassed to tell Hal and Bob what was transpiring with Ruth. I hadn't bought her for Erica and Eli to ride.

The fall riding weather in northern Indiana was fast coming to a close, and my plan of having two dependable molly mules to ride away from the farm was fading before my eyes. I had known there would be some person/mule adjustments to be made when she arrived at our farm; I even asked Mark how to go about winning her heart. He said through food. She loved food of any kind, and that was how his wife, Brenda, had made up with her. (My inner voice reminded me that with Brenda's friendship, Ruth Ann still lived with Mark. It might not be that easy for me.) Whatever the problem we might have encountered, I never figured it would be for her to turn into a very, *very* spooky mule! I made another call to Mary Long.

After I had explained our situation, Mary said, "She keeps asking, 'Where is Mark?' She is confused and doesn't understand what her job is anymore. With Mark she knew."

I recognized that I must start bonding with her on the ground. She needed to know I was her new companion. As we were conversing with Ruth, Susie Q piped up. "I just love it when you buy more mules. The more you get, the better *I* look." Mary and I both had a belly laugh. Oh, how very true those words were. Little Susie was the best mule I had. I purchased a stall plaque for her door which says: *Susie Q Little Miss Perfect*. Susie was a keeper.

For thirty years, our family has had dogs, and in the later years I finally came to the realization that if they were obedience trained, they were much better adjusted dogs. I went to classes with two of my Dobermans and Muffitt, my Miniature Schnauzer. We always won the obedience trial at the end of each class. The reason I took formal education with them was twofold: I wanted to learn, but knowing myself, I knew if I didn't have a goal to reach and required lessons to complete, the training would fall to the wayside as other things got in the way. One of my greatest training aids was the dog biscuit.

I kept pieces in my jean pocket to use as rewards. Farm dogs really need to come when called, and my system was to use bribery with dog biscuits. After some formal leash training, and using treats as a reward now and then, the dogs, especially my hard headed Giant Schnauzer, Lady Blue, decided coming when summoned was exceedingly pleasurable. The idea of giving the treat only some of the time was so the dogs wouldn't become treat demons. They didn't know exactly when they would get one, so each time they received a treat, it was a joy.

Another bit of training wisdom I learned and used, was lots of praise when earned. Less discipline, but lots of praise. Rebuke the bad behavior, but make a big fuss over the good things they did. Mules are like dogs, it is said, so I needed to get inventive where Ruth was concerned.

With my pocket filled with cut up horse cookies, some dog biscuits, my training halter and rope in hand, I got Ruth Ann out of her stall. In the arena I started having her back up and then return to me. She was paying attention; her ears were relaxed. I led her through the barrels, over plastic, a sheet of plywood, and some poles. No problem. Gave her a cookie. *That* was a big success.

We went out to the big outside arena and did the same simple tasks. Gave her another cookie. Now she was hooked. I was a best buddy. Ruth certainly does love food. We went down to the frightening end of the outside arena. She stopped and looked ears stiff and forward. I jiggled the lead rope to remind her I was standing beside her.

Lady Blue was rustling about in the weeds. I called Blue to me. Gave *her* a dog biscuit, and next gave Ruth another cookie. Then I got a big smile on my face. I was thinking that this was a great idea. Just don't overdo the cookies.

Horse whisper-type trainer die-hards are surely shaking their heads, but I think this is just a better version of bonding. I also realized a person needs to know their mule or horse. I wouldn't use cookies on Samson; I knew he would get pushy and insistent immediately, nor would I use them on Sunday, my horse who lived to eat. I did lots of patting and excitedly saying "*Good* girl, Ruth," along with the cookies. Over time the cookies would become fewer and fewer; they wouldn't be needed. Ruth would know that perhaps I had cookies in my pocket, but we would have developed mutual respect and fondness. At least that was my hope.

Eli's following visits progressively built on her trust issues. He took her to the hill behind the barn area where she had spun and bolted off; she was quieter, but very alert. She felt comfortable enough to graze. Eli told me that was good therapy for her, and I could bring her down there and allow her to eat. As he started leading her along the fearsome path, she stopped, ears stiff. He put slack in the rope and let her sort it out. She didn't turn tail to run, and soon they were walking again.

Before long, I couldn't see them anymore and returned to the barn to wait. When he got back, it was with a great report. They had walked to the garden center with the caged birds, bushes, hoses, cars, wet mucky ground, and she hardly batted an eye. They went down into the dry creek bed and walked in it. Returning home along her spooky path, she sauntered along first, and Eli trailed behind holding the rope.

On the subsequent session, he rode her. I was babysitting Ava, my granddaughter, and could not watch any part of their workout. After Eli put Ruth away, he came to the house to brag on her accomplishment. He had ridden her to the intimidating hill, which remained her sticking point, and where true to form, she stopped. He dismounted and let her stand there; when she relaxed, he remounted and they went on. When they got to the middle bridge across the creek, she stopped and Eli said she would have turned and headed in the other direction, but her reaction wasn't violent and he stopped her without difficulty.

I was displeased she was still trying to head in another direction. Next, he said she decided to back up. Eli said to Ruth, "Okay, you want to back up, we will back up and stop when I say to." Then he turned her about and backed to the bridge again. By then, he related, she was licking and chewing as if to say, "Darn, this isn't at all what I had in mind. I give in."

The rest of the ride, which took them fairly close to a busy highway, up and down hills, across logs, into the rain swollen creek and home again, she did without error. It seemed she was a good trail mule; however, getting her to the trail was still a slight problem. But she was improving and Eli never hit her with a spur or used a crop—he didn't have them. He let her see that she didn't need to be frightened.

The trick would be for her to feel safe with me. I was itching to ride her, but knew I shouldn't yet. I told Eli that next week's sessions would include me. He would ride Ruth and I would ride Susie. In the meantime, I needed to keep up my ground work with Ruth.

Now one of the hardest parts of the ground work was finding different objects to go over, around and past. There was a limit to the junk stored in the machine shed. Each day I rearranged the blue barrels, the blue plastic, the poles, and other props to make it appear different. My next session with Ruth was on a beautiful fall day. I ventured out to the front of the house, down the drive and around my brother-in-law's landscaping machinery and the horse trailers. She followed me like a well trained dog.

I went in through the gate to our back yard where Cagney and Lacy, the geese, lived around the pond area and out another gate. She was perfect. She was so good I went down to her scary spot but took a slightly different path. I was a little nervous; I wanted her to do well and I especially wanted *me* to remain unhurt. She started slowing down and looked back toward the barn. I jiggled the rope saying, "No, Ruth.

This way." And tugged her farther along, using the end of the rope to drive her shoulders when she "stuck."

Eventually, we got to the worst corner and she would go no further. We turned about and came home. Next day, I told Eli I wanted him to ride her and this time use spurs as Mark told me to do. We had tried the easy approach and now push was coming to shove. Time for Ruth to do as she was told.

We started down the path with Ruth and Eli in the front, Susie Q and me bringing up the rear. My back still hurt from my fractured vertebra, but it was healing and I was riding again, albeit carefully. Ruth stopped and backed up, but went on when Eli used the spurs. I don't know that I would have felt comfortable using spurs on Ruth without talking to Mark first, but he had said she was used to them and she never reared, bucked or pitched a fit. Of course, he also had said she was bombproof....

When we got to the corner where the other day I had to turn around, Ruth stopped. Really stopped. Eli used the spurs, hit her rear with the crop and she just backed up faster. This was a dilemma. Eli turned to me and said, "I don't feel comfortable continuing in this way. Let's turn around and ride in the other direction."

I agreed. Eli and I both were flummoxed in dealing with mules. It was something new to both of us. How far to push? When to stop and try something else? We both recalled the saying, "You cannot force a mule."

We rode the mules back and forth in the first part of the scary path with Ruth in the lead until she no longer held her ears poker stiff, then we took another trail around the farm. She was perfect. You can bet I planned another call to Mark.

I felt I knew Mark well enough to realize he had not sold me a bad mule. I knew he loved Ruth Ann and wanted a good home for her. He had not misrepresented her—at least as *he* knew her. When he returned my call, I assured him Eli was a competent trainer and rider; he was not letting Ruth get away with being naughty, but she seemed genuinely frightened. How should we proceed?

Poor Mark, I hoped he was not getting exasperated with me. Ruth's behavior just didn't belong to a bombproof mule. I guess there were a few bombs she hadn't been exposed to—and apparently some of them could be found along the scary path. His response was as before. "When she stops or slows down to look at something, I hit her with my spur. And, I have very large spurs."

Maybe Eli hadn't been definite enough, and for sure, his spurs were not exceptionally large. Then Mark told me a story that helped me understand mules a little better. I asked him about the saying "You can't make a mule do anything it doesn't want to do."

"Well," he said in his slow voice, "one summer I had a young mule that was really barn sour. She would only go to a certain spot down the trail. Her sticking spot happened to be beside some large logs that were in a pile. She went to a log and tried to scrape me off. She just leaned on those old poles. One day I spent two hours trying to get her to get off of it and go on. Finally, I gave it up and rode back to the barn. But the next day when she tried the same stunt and I jabbed her sides with my spurs, she jumped ahead and kept on a goin'. You see, her sides were so sore from the day before that when she realized standing there was going to cause her some hurt—well, she figured it out in a hurry."

Okay, maybe Rome wasn't built in one day, or a mule trained all in one session. Eli and I would have another go at Ruth Ann and be more definite with the spurs. In the meantime, I had been riding her, following behind Bob and Samson. She was perfect for me. Her ears flopped and she gaited just like I dreamed she would.

Apparently, it would be some time before I could ride her alone, but that wasn't required. I had others for such riding. Life closed in on our riding plans. Eli got busy, I got sick with the flu, the weather gave us a taste of nasty November winds and rain, and then Ruth Ann came up lame.

Since it appeared my outside riding was on hold for a week or so, I turned to the unorganized mess on my desk. When the weather is wonderful, any rider worth his salt has to ride. Rainy, dreary days were meant for office work. On my "to do" list was a call to Sue Cole, editor of *Mules and More* magazine. We chatted about mule lore and how they are such interesting animals. Sue and her family have had mules forever, compared to me, a newcomer, but she could relate to my tales of woe and laughter. I told her about Ruth Ann—my "bombproof mule" and she reinforced what I was getting around to thinking about Ruth. "She just didn't trust you," she said. Then she told me about her son, Loren Basham, and his daughter Cori's mule.

Craig Cameron sponsored an event called the Extreme Cowboy Race. In this contest, equine and rider must compete doing extremely difficult activities. Loren decided he wanted to compete with daughter Cori's mule, Hoosier Daddy. The enlightening part of the story wasn't that Loren and Hoosier finished tenth out of a large group of horses, a very impressive placing, but that he had to steal his daughter's mule for six weeks to bond with Hoosier to train for the race. The mule was in the family, but Hoosier Daddy's heart didn't belong to Cori's dad. It belonged to Cori.

Aha, I thought. That could surely explain Ruth. Mark thought I could win her heart with apples and carrots, but that didn't transfer to riding her. After belonging in their family for nearly thirteen years, a few days or even weeks wasn't enough to transfer her trust to me.

Sue went on to explain, "Loren trains mules and he needs weeks to bond with a new mule before he can start riding it. When he sends the mule home, he tells the owner to be sure and spend time on the ground working and rebonding with the mule. "Don't just get on and ride." By this time the mule has bonded with the trainer. More often than not, Sue told me, the owners don't listen and Loren gets a call stating they can't ride their mule. That sounded familiar!

A week later I had recovered from the flu, and Tuesday dawned sunny and warmer. I took Ruth Ann out of her stall and put the training halter on her head. I was going to take my mule for a walk. She was still recovering from her lameness, so I couldn't ride her. We started out heading toward our scary path. She got half way there and stopped, looking off toward the most frightening part—the culvert and the sneaky dog.

When I tugged her rope and said, "Ruth, come," she started walking again. We proceeded like this all the way to the corner before the most frightening part. Walk, stop, tug the rope and proceed, but I was pleased because this was the first time I had been able to get her down the path without near hysterics. Then, wouldn't you know it—the darn dog started barking. He was there hidden behind the trees.

Ruth, however, acted sensibly. She froze and looked, but didn't snort or try to turn around. After a minute of sizing up the problem with me assuring her it was only a dog, even though we couldn't see it, and saying, "Ruth, come!" she walked forward. We walked the few yards more onto the culvert bridge, stopped and turned around.

Our trip home was uneventful except she was in a hurry. Ruth also remembered the horse cookies I'd had in my pocket last time we were out, and kept sniffing my pocket. This time I had forgotten them. To make up for the oversight, I allowed her to eat lush grass when we got back to the gate.

Frankly, I was overjoyed. I considered it as quite a breakthrough. If this kept up, soon she would earn the barn name I had put on her stall plaque. *Queen.*

Chapter Twenty-four: Born to Jump

Erica and Mirabella were a great pair. Mirabella was sweet and a brat all at the same time. Her strange sense of humor was saved for the unwary when they led her into her stall from the pasture. If you didn't get her all the way in before you let loose of the halter, she ducked her head down, turned right, and trotted down the barn aisle and out into the arena and the hay stack. She kicked the stall if she wasn't let out soon enough to suit her, but she had the science down to perfection. She kicked with both feet, but only hard enough to make lots of noise. She never kicked a board loose.

Erica just didn't care about the brattiness. If Mirabella didn't want to do something such as come out of her stall to be ridden, Erica said, "You *are* coming out. It *will* be fun." Erica was perfect for the little mule. She loved her and kept Mirabella's mind busy. One day she proudly related how Mirabella had lain down in her freshly bedded stall to have a good roll and ended up against the side of the stall under the water bucket holder. A horse would have been stuck—cast. As Erica watched, Mirabella scootched herself sideways until she could roll over and get her feet underneath herself. Having been around horses for many years, Erica recognized the intelligence of her mule.

Erica and Mirabella

I called Eli and thanked him for all the canter work he had done with Mirabella while she was at his farm.

"Oh yes, we cantered for miles on the dirt roads. She loved it."

She returned home with a much better canter and stop than when she left. I think it was the fact Mirabella loved to canter that really sold her to Erica. And canter they did—through the woods and around the fields. The day Erica told me she had been jumping her mule over logs in the woods as well as the ravine that drained water from the highway, I was flabbergasted.

"How I wish I could have seen that!" I said.

"Mirabella isn't afraid of anything. She just jumps it."

I told Mary Long, my animal communicator friend, about Mirabella and Erica. "I have some cross country clients." she said, "And they do not know fear. It just isn't in their makeup." I appreciated

Erica's gutsy riding and remembered way back when I thought I was invincible too. Those years were long gone.

One fall day, Erica told me, "I want to show Mirabella in some jumping and someday, dressage classes." Her dressage instructor told her Joe, her Thoroughbred, was good enough to compete at higher dressage levels, but she should stop jumping him and concentrate on dressage. Erica did some checking on rules and found out she could show a mule in jumping and dressage, but not cross country eventing. They were banned from that event. I told her I bet it was because a great mule had beaten the horses.

Lo and behold, the next issue of *Mules and More (*August 2007*)* had the story told by Pat Drugger, of the very mule who had been a cross country star and in the 1980s had beaten too many horses. Her name was Kit and she was a sorrel saddle mule standing 15'3 hands, of unknown origin. Edith Conyers bought Kit and started foxhunting her. Although Kit had no formal jumping training, she excelled. After a successful foxhunting season, where the pair was a huge success, Cathy took Kit to the Mumford Farm Horse Trials in Evansville the following May. There had been little time to prepare and train, but Kit was a natural. She did so well that over time she was featured in *Times Sports, Wall Street Journal* and *Equus* magazine which called her "The Eventing Mule."

Acceptance of Kit in the world of eventing was achieved over time, but there were a few exceptions. Eventually, Cathy sold Kit to a gentleman from Kansas City who had noticed that she wasn't being competed as often as earlier, and made an offer that Cathy couldn't refuse. Realizing that the talented mule would now be back into serious eventing competition, one of the competitors who often lost to Kit managed to get the American Horse Show Association (USEF) to ban mules from eventing. And there it was. No eventing for Mirabella!

Now that Erica had a goal with Mirabella, I saw jumps appearing in the arena again. The first day she planned to jump her, all the boarders who were presently at the barn, came out to watch. The jump was only a cross pole eight inches high in the middle. Mirabella sailed over it with ease, but the interesting thing to me was how she positioned herself to jump.

Xanadu, my Tennessee Walking Horse versatility champion, had the ability to jump. I wasn't able to jump him because of my back problems, but one of daughter Michal's friends did some jumping with her Quarter Horse and she helped us out. He had a terrible time getting to the jumps in the right space. He was either too far back when he started his jump, or too close. Neither was pretty, and on large jumps could be dangerous. Mindy had a good eye and could help Xanadu get to the right spot for takeoff. I might have been able to jump him if he could get there on his own as I didn't have a good eye for take-offs either. Watching Mirabella rate and position herself was a delight.

The jumps got more numerous and higher as the months went on. Still Mirabella sailed over with ease. At first stopping after a jump to regroup was a problem, but the mule got more handle on her, and soon was making turns around the arena and jumping the course of several different looking and height obstacles. Erica stuck to her like glue. I was envious. I did, however, have to give myself a pat on the back. I *knew* that little mule had more in her than being a trail mule.

Mirabella was four now and her back had leveled out—finally. Erica used a mule pad with wither shims, but she no longer looked like she was running down hill and riding her was more pleasant. I'm certain her more grown-up conformation helped with jumping. Being rump high wouldn't be an aid in jumping fences. Mirabella was a natural. It was not hard getting her to jump like a horse and not to "coon jump" or spring over like a deer. After the first jump, when she hesitated and thought about stopping and then jumping, she never did it again.

It was November 9, and Erica was going to a show two hours south of us where she could compete with Joe and Mirabella. The day before the show Erica was practice jumping in the arena, and I watched from the kitchen. Mirabella was concentrating; her ears were back in attentiveness like the race horses. I think she knew some excitement was about to be added to her life. After their workout, Erica called me on her cell phone.

"Mirabella is so smart. She just taught herself to do a flying lead change!"

That was exceptional. In jumping a course the contestants need to change directions. The most efficient way is to change leads, or change which front foot is leading the gallop. Younger or less experienced rider and animal may drop to a trot and then pick up the other lead, or just keep going in the wrong lead. Sometimes teaching flying lead changes can take a lot of time and effort on the part of both rider and animal. And here sassy Mirabella had figured it out for herself. Horses galloping loose with no rider change leads frequently and easily, but working with a rider can make all that naturalness disappear. I was enthusiastic along with Erica. Mirabella had a job and she was going to excel.

The show weekend dawned cold but clear. The show was outside and not for the faint of heart. When they arrived at the show grounds, Joe was anxious, but Mirabella was happy to eat hay. She was content to remain in the trailer while Erica rode Joe. That is a wonderful attribute in any show animal. Having separation anxiety at a show either when leaving or being left by a trailer buddy can cause all sorts of concern for the rider. Mirabella didn't care.

This was the first time for Mirabella to see real jumps. Some were white, some had bushes or flowers along the side, one jump was a "jump up" onto a higher level and then go on. She never batted her lovely, long eyelashes or flicked her impressive mule ears at any of them. This was a fun show for beginner riders and animals as well as practice for the more experienced. No one took themselves too seriously, and everyone had smiles and chuckles for the mule who jumped.

The course was judged on time and faults, but the goal was to jump the course close to two minutes and go clean. The other horses trotted, but Mirabella wanted to canter the course, and Erica let her. She jumped nearly all of them clean, but was too fast. Still, they ended the day with 3 fourth place ribbons. Before the end of the day, Erica received three offers to buy Mirabella. They were not fools—seeing the mule refuse nothing was even more impressive after she told them they did not have real jumps for practice at home, and Mirabella was only four years old.

The winter months dragged for everyone. It had been predicted to be a "La Nina" winter; one with temperatures up and down and with more snow, and the sun forgot how to shine. For once, the forecasters were correct. It was a long dreary and tiresome winter. In February, Erica announced she was taking Mirabella to the Held Equestrian Center in Albion, Michigan to an indoor jumping competition.

"There was another show I considered and I called to see if they would allow me to bring a mule. The lady said she would check with the other instructors. When she called back she told me I could bring Mirabella if I could promise she would not bray and scare the horses!"

Erica explained it was a show for children and it certainly wouldn't do for the young riders' horses to be spooked by a mule. She decided not to go. Who can predict what a mule might do?

The jumping competition in Albion was put on by Albion College and would not be a shabby affair. The college teams compete in varsity-level shows in the Intercollegiate Horse Shows Association. The horses here would be better trained and Mirabella would have stiff competition. Erica couldn't practice jump her at our barn because we are not a jumping facility—especially in the winter. The best she could do was a cross pole which made an easy X type jump and a straight pole about two feet off the ground. No jumping course, no flowers, no white boxes, no double jumps called oxers and no distractions such as strange horses, people and a new place. Erica seemed confident. I recalled her telling me about their jumping the big drainage culvert in the woods by the busy highway. I guessed if Mirabella would do that, she could do anything.

Pulling into the college equestrian center, Erica was surprised to see only four horse trailers parked in a row. Where were all the competition horses? The show started in one hour, was she in the right place—did she have the right day? Turned out the rest of the trailers were parked in the back and indeed there were horses—lots of horses. Mirabella's classes would have twelve to fifteen competitors.

The horses were lined up ready to start. Erica volunteered to go first. Mirabella spooked just a tiny bit at the big observation window in the arena, but kept on going. She jumped the first eighteen-inch-high cross rail obstacle, and then slowed down, ready to stop. After all, that is what they did at home—jump the obstacle and stop. "No, *no*, Mirabella, keep going," Erica admonished, tapping her with the crop.

After a couple more jumps, the mule got the picture. There were ten cross rail jumps in all, and Mirabella went clean. This meant they would do a jump-off of the same course, but with only five jumps. Unfortunately, the jump-off was right after the regular round, no time to rest. Mirabella hadn't been conditioning all winter for this, but she pulled it off. Between the classes was about forty minutes of resting time. Good thing because they jumped in five classes, each with a jump-off.

It is a tribute to Mirabella's common sense that she never looked askance at any of the jumps, which were beautifully arranged with gay flowers, brightly painted poles and a complicated course. (That is where Erica excelled!) Mirabella wasn't perfect—she trotted some, cantered some, but refused nothing. She knocked a pole or two when the later classes consisted of oxers and pole jumps that were two feet and three inches. Their crowning achievement was a first in a jump-off.

The jump-offs were timed, so the faster time won. Erica, who had done this before, was smart and cut in front of one of the jumps, which gave her the best time. Even after seeing her do this, no one else followed her example. They ended the day with a first place blue ribbon, a second place red one and a third place yellow ribbon, and a whopping $27.75. It was a total success. No one wanted to buy the mule this time, but one lady walked away in disbelief after hearing that Erica and Mirabella didn't practice at home.

Erica and Mirabella
Photo courtesy of Linda von Uhl Photography

Chapter Twenty-five: Not This Again!

Soon after I got my mules, a new mule friend who owned several of them, advised me against working with Samson and trailer loading, saying, "He did it once, he should remember. Too much repetition causes aggravation." As it turned out, it would be me and Bob who were aggravated.

For some reason, Bob and I hadn't had the time to trailer off the farm and ride the parks this fall. Finally, a beautiful day arrived and Bob wasn't snowed under with work. We packed the trailer and started to load the mules. Samson first. And Samson wasn't going into the trailer. Eli had been working with me and Samson to get the mule's respect and loyalty. It had been going well, but I wasn't far enough into the training to know what to do about this trailer situation. After half hour, I decided to wait until Eli's training visit the next day and then, by golly this dang mule was going into the trailer. Not once or twice, but until I said to stop. (Or Eli, having a less irritated state of mind, said to stop.)

I left the trailer in the big inside arena all ready for Eli and Samson's lesson. It was pitiful really, at least for my self confidence as a "trainer." After Eli worked the mule for about five minutes, he pointed Samson's head in the trailer and he popped in nice as you please. Then I did it. He was perfect and we both decided to stop.

For each of the next three-day training sessions we worked with Samson in the trailer. Each time he loaded without fuss when the trailer was where we had left it. However, we moved the trailer into a field and again Samson was naughty. He went around the side, backed up and went around the other side, but Eli kept his cool and Samson gave up and went in. I did it, and we stopped.

The next day we moved the trailer to another new spot and Eli told me to do it first and alone. Boy, I was all geared up. This mule was going *in*. The trailer was parked beside the machine shed with a flower bed between the trailer and the shed. That was better than an open field.

I held the rope with the haltered mule in my left hand and the training stick with the rope lash attached, in my right. First off, I got tangled in the long lead rope. I just was not handy with these things. Eli gave me a shorter lead rope. Samson saw a fun game appearing as he went around the side of the trailer and into my flower bed.

I tugged him out and tried again. He sniffed the trailer floor and then went into the flower bed again. I could just hear him laughing gleefully. I tried again. This time he put one foot in the trailer and then stepped out and again headed for the flower bed. By now I was mad. I had lost my horse-whisper-cool.

With Eli standing on the other side of the trailer, looking horrified, no doubt, I yanked on the rope, shouting at Samson in my loudest, meanest voice and hit him with the training stick and rope. He dashed into the trailer. I shut the door and stood there panting, trying to get my breath back.

I looked sheepishly at Eli. "I got mad."

"Whatever works." he said with a small smile.

Later, I talked to my animal communicator friend, Mary, and confessed I had probably broken a horsemanship rule and done a bad thing. I was trying so hard to do this right and had blown it.

"Not really," she said. "He just thought you finally really meant it. Sometimes it takes our getting mad for them to see the picture. In this case: "The Game Was Up!" I felt much better. Samson hadn't been frightened in the least; he was having a good time at my expense.

Next training session, the trailer was back in the field and headed in a different direction. This time I was going to load my beast, my way, which was to be a combination of "horsemanship" and Rose. I was going to reward Samson mightily. I put three broken up big fat carrots and three juicy red apples in the trailer stall feed tub. When he got in he would have a great treat.

I led him to the trailer door, holding the rope in my left hand, the training stick rope "whip" in my right. I pointed with my hand holding the lead. I loved pointing which way for the mules to go. They were so good at it. I pointed them into their stalls, pointed them into the wash rack, around and into training obstacles, and now into the trailer.

Samson walked up sprightly enough. I pointed to the trailer opening, he put his nose down to sniff the floor, but before he could even think of stopping, *whack* went the training stick lash on the ground inches behind his heels. He never took a breath before he quietly hopped in. With Samson munching his goodies, Eli gave me my "goodie."

"You did that exactly right!" he said with a grin. I knew what he meant. The timing had to be perfect. Just a second too late and Samson might have backed up and then we would have our argument again.

That was the last of the training sessions with the trailer. We put it away for the winter, and I hoped next time both Samson and I would remember how we did this.

With the mules turned out for the winter, or at least not ridden, Samson didn't have enough to do. The grass was gone and boredom set in. I'd been putting him in a small pasture with Sunday, my bitchy mare, who seemed able to keep him in line, but he was pushing it. The first days I put them together, he respected the swish of her tail and the raising of a hind foot aimed in his direction. But after a few days he tried to herd her around the pasture. She was such a food-hound that she usually ignored his attempts and kept searching for those few blades of grass left uneaten. I turned the rest of the herd of six out into the large pasture beside Sunday and Samson's small one.

At chore time one evening, Bob brought Hallelujah in the barn saying, "He has blood on his hind leg and is limping a little." It wasn't hard to guess what happened. Hallelujah had been up to his old stunts again: kicking through the wire fence at Samson. Hallelujah's fence kicking was one of the reasons I gelded my stallion. I didn't want to raise babies anymore, and his habit of backing up to the fence and kicking through it at the farm-boarded geldings that were anywhere near, was dangerous for him. The previous winter I had kept him and Samson together in the same pasture, where they had become the proverbial "bad boys."

Hallelujah seemed to know he had a herd, and Samson had a herd of one. I watched as Hallelujah went over to Samson's fence and pooped along it. (Over several days he had piled quite a row.) He was marking his turf and daring Samson to cross it. Then he squealed and backed up to the fence, hiking a leg as though to kick. Samson was not impressed. Samson was too smart to get himself caught in the fence, but he egged Hallelujah on by standing there with his head and neck on Hallelujah's side of the fence.

Quite obviously when we were not around, Hallelujah had carried out his kicking threat and got hung up in the field fence wire. He had extracted himself, but his hock and lower leg showed signs of injury. Neither of my boys was cooperating. Hallelujah still acted like a stallion—and so did Samson. Samson carried his stud role to the extreme of actually "breeding" Sunday when she came in heat. All his gelding mule parts worked to perform the act.

I came up with another plan. I'd put Hallelujah and Ruth Ann together in a field, as both were on the injured list, and turn Samson out with the rest of the mules and mares. It was winter; none would be coming in heat. It would give him a chance to run in a big field and scrounge up more grass.

That evening at chore time I got an excited phone call from Erica. "Nugget is on the ground and making strange loud noises. All the horses are grouped around her, and Samson is biting her!"

My heart jumped into my mouth. I envisioned broken legs. Why couldn't she get up? Erica was talking to me as she walked to the pasture. I told her to get Samson away from the mare, dashed downstairs, grabbed my winter jacket, and ran out to the barnyard. Sure enough there was Nugget, my older and dearly loved mare, lying on the ground with Erica sitting by her head.

As I approached Nugget from the rear, she raised her head and looked at me beseechingly. "Help," she seemed to say. She looked all in one piece. I picked up each leg as she lay with them stretched out straight, and moved them. Nothing seemed broken. She had on her winter blanket for warmth. I unbuckled the chest straps and undid the belly straps. I hoped that the blanket was binding her and she thought she couldn't get up. When it was loose, she gave a mighty heave, righted herself, and then struggled to her feet and limped toward the barn.

Oh, that is just great, I thought. What had Samson been doing? I'd bet my bottom dollar that he had something to do with her being on the ground. By the time Nugget reached the barn, she was traveling fairly well. I gave her a shot of Banamine, "horse Advil," and by morning she looked all right.

Nugget had been a great show mare in her day, and after being retired was one of my best trail horses. She didn't bugger at things, and she had a smooth, rolling canter that I could still ride even with my injured back. Nugget's one failing was that she was aloof. She never wanted to be a pet horse. I blamed it on her upbringing. She had been bred and raised to be a show animal and trained as such. There was no time for fondling, stroking and sweet words whispered into her baby ears. She was more or less a machine until I had the good fortune to purchase her when she was around seven.

Because of her hard life as a young show mare (ridden at too early an age and too long on hard surfaces), her joints had been damaged and she had early-onset-arthritis. It didn't matter how many carrots or apples I gave her or how many pats on the neck, she didn't seem to care. She also was hard to catch in the pasture or even the paddock. She was the boss mare and would chase the others away from the barn door at feed time, but wouldn't come in herself. It was infuriating.

An old fashioned way of taming horses was to throw them down, tie their legs and then proceed to touch them, and make noises to condition them to strange things while the horse was helpless. Some horses it probably helped, some were made worse. Eli told me his dad had one of their young Belgium draft mares broke by this method.

"How did it work out?" I asked.

"It didn't. She was more dangerous and spooky after it. She couldn't stand noises and things frightened her badly. She even became a runaway." (My guess is that the mare became more frightened because when she was down and helpless, the "conditioning" was unrelenting. The new horsemanship method is to advance and retreat until the animal feels comfortable with new situations. This makes them calmer. The other way terrifies them more.)

Putting this in the perspective of Nugget's experience, I had a thought. Perhaps she would see me as her savior who rescued her from her stuck and helpless position and would now like me more. Two things I noticed the next day. She kept her head stuck over her stall door as I walked by—usually she turned it back inside—and when I went to bring her in for supper, she stood still. She was the last horse, but normally she turned and walked away from me. (Sadly, her new-found friendliness didn't last long.)

When we got Nugget and the rest of the horses in the barn that evening, Erica told me that Mirabella had been trying to protect her buddy, Nugget, as she lay on the ground, but was ineffective. Samson was just too big. Poor Nugget had bite marks on her face and ears. What had he been thinking?

The next day I put Samson out alone in the old stud pasture where he spent the day slowly walking forlornly back and forth along the fence line. I could only hope he was contemplating his misdeed.

Rose and Nugget photo courtesy of Brian Richman

Chapter Twenty-six: Rescues

By now it was November, and the great riding days of fall had flown by all too quickly.

Our barn has a big inside riding arena and I used it daily up until three years ago. When I retired from showing the Tennessee Walking Horses, I also retired from riding in the winter months. It was too cold, too cloudy and too dismal—did the sun ever shine in northern Indiana in the winter?

When I was younger I'd turn on the inside lights, turn on the tape or CD player as loud as I could without shattering my eardrums, and keep riding. Then I was on a mission: to train the horses and keep them and consequently me, in shape. Now I was content to brave the frigid mornings to feed the twenty-five or so animals, go back out in a couple hours to put them out, and back out for evening feedings. That was enough outside for me.

Ruth Ann was still lame, and the best anyone could figure was that she had strained a ligament in her lower left front leg. For two weeks I kept her in a small paddock with a companion horse or mule. Whoever was chosen to be her companion was disgruntled and disgusted, as the rest of the herd was out grazing on winter- browned grass. I gave her aspirin disguised as a tasty powder, put support boots on her each day and crossed my fingers.

When a partially sunny and warmer day occurred, I tried riding her. She was all right at the walk, but faster, she limped. We came home. Bummer. I looked through the vet supply catalogues and found a product made to heal ligaments. She had to be sound by spring or I was really going to be upset.

I don't claim to have fame by my animal rescues, but I have been involved with several. Many were dogs and cats that I fostered from the local humane shelter and then either adopted myself or found homes for them. My biggest rescues were in saving the offspring of my stallion, Praise Hallelujah, born from outside mares. I was proud to be a breeder of fine Tennessee Walkers, but not every one of Hallelujah's and my efforts ended up with a perfect home. When I heard about these horses, I bought them.

There was little Melody who was near starved and stunted, and Sport, a big 16'3 hand gelding that started bucking the riders off his back. I surmised his saddles didn't fit and he wasn't charitable in suffering pain. He was sent to a trainer who hooked him between two huge draft horses and hitched them to a metal drag used to smooth over plowed fields. Sport, in a frenzy of fear and claustrophobia, began kicking and kicking. He managed to get himself tangled in the metal drag and cut himself badly. My friend Carol who knew of him, called and asked, "Will you buy him for $500? Otherwise he is going to the killers. His owners are finished with him." How could I refuse?

She kept Sport for several weeks, tending his wounds and then brought him to me where I tried to tend his psychological wounds. Eventually, I gave him to a first time horse owner. It shouldn't have worked—they should have killed each other. Sport was still half crazy, the new owner was a little crazy. The things they did together shouldn't have panned out, but somehow they did.

Lordy was another rescue, this time from a trainer in Tennessee who beat the young horse when he didn't understand and according to a probably true rumor, used the painful soring method on his legs to make him step high. When Lordy retaliated by kicking the trainer, he was put up for sale for dog food. Lordy was a big mess and it took a year to retrain him and get his mind back to some form of sanity. After these and other rescues, I decided that breeding horses wasn't something I wanted to do any longer. I didn't want to be responsible for more horses needing rescuing. *I* wanted to be rescued—by my mules. I wanted to retire from raising, training, showing and selling horses and foals. Bring on the serene life of trail riding!

Mules were not supposed to be as likely to go lame, or so I'd heard. They were tough. Maybe the Grand Canyon mules only had so many trips up and down the canyon in them, but my mules were never worked that hard. I know Ruth had been ridden a lot, and I was told she had arthritis, but a pulled ligament in a leg can be really bad news. She might never be able to go the places I wanted. Or perhaps with my hurt and injured back, a nice sedate walk might be all *I* could muster. I sincerely hoped Ruth Ann would not be just another very expensive rescue, living out her days in a pasture.

Chapter Twenty-seven: Ah, Spring

Finally, after the long, gray and dismal winter, the tulips and daffodils began to bloom, the flowering trees graced our backyard, the grass started turning green and Ruth Ann wasn't lame anymore. Her recovery was not accomplished without trouble, however.

One of my human doctors used a type of therapy on my knees called prolotherapy. It consisted of injecting the muscle and ligaments around the knee, vertebra or hips with a substance, which caused the areas to tighten and strengthen.

I got so much relief that I asked my veterinarian if he had ever heard of it for equines. After some research, he agreed that it might help Ruth Ann's shoulder. It would be sort of experimental, but since she had been lame since October and it was now seven months later, something had to be done. The mule was more or less paddock sound, meaning if she didn't do anything else but eat and walk about a small area, she didn't limp.

I was very nervous when the vet arrived, but excited at the same time. Something had to work for Ruth Ann. Poor mule and poor me. I made it through the winter months hoping that each day, then each month, would bring improvement and healing, but it hadn't happened. Now the sensational spring days were here, and darn it, I wanted to ride my mule!

We thought we had finally pinpointed Ruth's painful area. After first thinking it was a lower leg tendon issue, we discovered her left shoulder was extremely painful. Perhaps she had stepped into a woodchuck hole in the pasture and strained the whole shoulder girdle. I tried professional massage, chiropractic, acupuncture and cold laser. These things had helped, but I still couldn't ride her.

After scrubbing her shoulder area intensely, Dr. Hammond injected a solution of dextrose and lidocane into several points around the top of the shoulder blade where she seemed to be exceptionally sore. The procedure was a lot like blistering stifles in my Walking Horses when they had stressed them, causing one hind leg to stride less far, resulting in a "hitch." I always had good results with that treatment and sincerely hoped it would help Ruth recover. In the case of my knees and back, they were quite painful the next day, but over a couple days, the soreness eased, leaving the area much less tender and stronger.

Ruth Ann didn't seem sore the next day, and lo and behold, she also didn't seem as lame. I gave her a week to recover and then I had Erica ride her so I could watch. She had a very slight hesitation in her left front leg coming forward, but that was all. I watched Erica ride her one time around the arena and we stopped. Dare I hope she was on the road to recovery? A couple of days later, I watched Erica ride her again and nearly shouted in delight. She looked great. I remembered back when I saw her ridden in the field at the mule show in Tennessee two years ago. She had picked up her front feet and glided along so effortlessly. She looked the same now.

Erica and I went on a trail ride, which lasted all of thirty minutes, but it was exhilarating to see Ruth Ann so happy to move forward. My own doctor recommended doing the prolotherapy several times in the same area to continue the healing. I figured I should do the same for my mule, so set up another appointment with the vet. This time things didn't go as well.

The morning after her injections, I started pulling my feed cart down the aisle, feeding horses and mules as I went. When I arrived at Ruth's stall I saw her stuck in one place. She didn't turn and put her head in her feed tub as always. All she did was turn her head and give a soft mule nicker. Oh, boy. I knew what the problem was.

When I'd had stifles injected in the past, sometimes one would have a similar painful reaction. I gave those horses some pain medication, and in a day or two, the discomfort was gone. When I had complained to my own doctor that a particular injection had really been sore for several days, he countered with, "Great, we got a really good reaction!" I figured Ruth would be fine in a day or two. Such wasn't the case.

As long as I gave her the pain medicine, she acted normally. When I thought she was well, I stopped, and she got worse again. This was going on too long to be normal. In three days, the shoulder began to swell and she got a small lymphatic drainage swelling in her girth area. The vet suggested oral antibiotics.

To make matters worse, I was scheduled to leave on a four-day trip. I'd been giving her twice a day anti-pain injections for four days and began to feel sorry about poking her so much. I asked my niece, "Doc Gabriella," who lived next door, to give her the medicine in the jugular vein while I was gone, and keep an eagle eye on her. Every time I called home, I asked, "How are Ruth and Muffitt (my fourteen-and-a-half-year-old Miniature Schnauzer dog) doing?"The reports were always positive.

When I got home, I found a note from Gabriella saying that if Ruth Ann needed more pain medication, I should consider using the paste form (which I tried and was a total disaster because Ruth Ann was sure I was poisoning her), as she had already had a lot of needles. Her former owner, Mark, had assured me Ruth was good with injections such as vaccines. That was a godsend.

Mirabella was not good at all, and Erica and I joked that it was a lucky thing it was Ruth and not her mule we were sticking with needles. I looked at the shoulder and it still appeared swollen, but perhaps a little better. It was warm, but not real hot. I thought we were out of the woods.

Dr. Hammond came in a few days to give some vaccines to the herd and looked at her. He was afraid there was infection perhaps behind the shoulder blade. She wasn't lame, the original problem seemed cured, but the shoulder was painful when palpated. He decided she should be on a different antibiotic. Injectable ones. Oh, dear, not needles again.

She needed two shots, one in the morning and one at night for one week. I thought the week would never end, and so did Ruth. I dreaded going to the barn and seeing her. I filled my pockets with horse cookies and snapped the lead on her halter. At first she came out of her stall easily, later not so readily. I could understand. I gave her a horse cookie then gave the shot, then another cookie, then the other shot, then two cookies, and then an apple. I was trying my best to be a good briber.

Every time I gave her another injection, I told her, "Only a few more days; you are such a good, good girl." Ruth Ann started holding the first cookie bribe in her mouth until after I gave the shot, then she chewed it slowly, her jaw working in slow motion, awaiting the second injection. I felt so bad about the many shots, I began to shed a few tears toward the end of the treatment.

She must have begun to feel better because one day when I led her out to the pasture where Lady Blue, my dog, was sniffing about, Ruth Ann charged toward her with her head down.

"Ruth, *no*," I screamed. The dog was oblivious. When the mule got close enough for Blue to feel Ruth's breath on her behind, she looked up from her horse poop treasure just in time to scoot out of the way. I was surprised at Ruth. I didn't know whether to be pleased she felt like chasing my dog, or dismayed that she did. I really didn't want a dog chasing mule.

Even with all the injections, Ruth Ann and I seemed to be developing a close bond. Bless her heart, she seemed to realize I was trying to help, and not torturing her for no reason. She was in a smaller pasture by the barn and one day as I rode Susie Q, Ruth Ann walked down to the fence line and looked at me plaintively. "I want to go for a ride." The message was clear.

When I got back from my ride, I got Ruth from the pasture and led her along the lane. She walked right along with no lameness. We walked on the scary path that she had hated so much in the beginning. This was super, I thought. Mule people had told me my problems with her were very likely because she didn't know or trust me yet. We seemed to be building this trust.

I kept my mule on her oral antibiotics, which were a piece of cake for both Ruth and me. They were tasteless and dissolved in water and I poured them on her grain. A week later both Erica and I noticed Ruth's shoulder looked normal and I asked her to ride Ruth bareback with no saddle to avoid pressing on the area. I rode Susie, and Ruth with Erica walked right beside us, no lameness at all. I dared to be hopeful once again.

Three days later I saddled her with my dressage saddle, which fit behind her shoulder blade, not on it as a western saddle does, and rode with Bob and Samson. This time we gaited faster than a walk for part of the way. Ruth stumbled some, which worried me, but coming home I put her in front of Samson to be the lead mule.

Ruth pricked up her long ears and picked up her front feet as she did her job to save us all from dangerous mule-eating woodchucks, frightening rabbits, noisy blackbirds and rustling leaves. Then Samson started stumbling along with his ears flopping side to side and half asleep. Truly, the lead animal has an important job; the others just go along for the "ride." Some horses and mules love to lead, some love to follow, but the best don't care. I was very proud of Ruth Ann. It was a graduation of sorts for us. Not only was she not lame, but she would go first. I truly needed that assurance after my horse and mule fall fiascos. I was really falling in love with Ruth Ann.

Unfortunately, our next ride three days later, left me despondent, disappointed and in despair. I thought she seemed a little stiff coming into the barn that evening and again coming out of her stall to be saddled, but decided to ride her anyway. Bad idea. After going several yards she felt stiff and was stumbling again. We turned around and went back to the barn. On the way back, Ruth seemed perfectly fine—not stiff and certainly not stumbling. Her ears were perked up and she was in great spirits. What was up with that?

On one hand I was glad, but not enough that I wasn't almost mad at Ruth. Of course it wasn't her fault, but I was more than upset. What the heck was going on with her? She was more trouble than she was worth, I thought angrily. Yanking off the saddle and shoving her back in her stall without a treat, I got out Susie Q and saddled her. Glancing back to Ruth's stall, I saw her looking at me with her big eyes. "I'm so sorry," she seemed to be telling me. But I was still miffed.

My ride with Bob was rather silent as I despaired of ever having Ruth healthy enough to count on riding. Summer was about here, and we wanted to haul the mules to the parks. I wanted to take Ruth. What was the sense of having a wonderfully gaited, dependable mule that I was getting real fond of, if I couldn't enjoy her? Supper was also a quiet affair. Bob asked me if I was upset about Ruth, and getting a short, curt affirmative reply, said no more. Hal wasn't home, so he wasn't on the receiving end of my ill temper.

The problem with Ruth was that we didn't know *what* her problem was. I thought she was cured. I rode her with great pleasure, all of three times, and she seemed to be feeling great in the pasture. The last two days I turned her out she had actually run and bucked with joy with the other two mules, cantering around and around their small pasture.

Usually, she walked slowly and methodically, heading for the grass but with no real elation at being turned out after a night of fasting in her stall. I thought back to those days and how I had a grateful smile on my face. Then it hit me. The day I tried to ride her, I had given her two vaccines, one in each side of her neck. Could that have made her stiff? It was at least a hopeful idea. Sometimes that happened.

The next morning I got her out to massage and treat her shoulder area and she walked normally. Turning her out to pasture she went through the barn door, spooked and bucked at the cat who may have startled her, and ran into the pasture. Yippee! Alas, that wasn't to last either.

Chapter Twenty-eight: Summer Daze

Spring turned into summer and Ruth Ann was lame again, or better put, *still* lame. Bob and I hauled her an hour away to a different chiropractor. Something was still very wrong. She stood with her left front leg stuck out to the side and walked "all stove up." If she lay down in her stall, she could hardly get up and when up, was really, *really* lame. She reminded me of myself after a long car trip or an evening in my easy chair. I hobbled too.

This vet had a slightly different technique for adjusting than my other chiropractor. He also had many years of practice treating lame horses. He took one look at Ruth and said her seventh cervical vertebra was out. That is the last neck bone before the spine becomes the "back bone." In people it is at the base of the neck, but in equines it is buried deep in the base of the shoulders and hard to adjust. He told me that would make her walk like her two front legs were tied together. She couldn't bring them forward. He also concurred with me that her back was sore also, and her right hip hurt. After her adjustment we loaded her into the trailer and came home.

The next day I hoped for a miracle. I think she was a little better, but not ridable. All through that first fall when she came, winter, spring and now summer, Ruth acted depressed. I thought it more than her just missing her previous owner. She didn't exude joy of living except for the very few times I saw her play in the pasture. She acted dull and uninterested as though she was putting in her time, but really didn't care. Either she was in a great deal of pain or something else was bothering her.

We took her for another chiropractic treatment. The vet adjusted more of her neck vertebra and her back. Ruth never moved, seeming to understand this was more or less the last straw. I was at my wits end where she was concerned. After he was finished she nuzzled the vet's shoulder. She was grateful.

Mules, Mules and More Mules

Two days later I got her out of the stall to check her physical progress. She gimped down the barn aisle just as bad as ever. I broke out into tears. "Ruth Ann, *what* am I going to do with you?"

I thought about putting her down. She was no good to ride; she didn't enjoy her life as far as I could tell, and she probably was in pain of some sort. What was the use? She had been a very expensive mule. A six-time World Champion show mule. What a shame.

After blowing my nose, I got out the clippers and trimmed her ears, mane and muzzle. Then I body clipped all the winter hair that refused to shed. "How beautiful you look!" I told her.

"*I do NOT want to go to a show!*" I heard those words so loud they almost knocked me off the stool I was standing on.

"*I HATE going to shows!*" Well now, that was a revelation. Actually, her former owner's wife had told me she thought Ruth Ann didn't like showing any more. I hadn't bought the mule to show, but if I went to a few, I figured I would take Ruth along and show her in Country Pleasure classes at the Walking Horse shows. At the rate I was not making it to the shows, Ruth had nothing to worry about. When the time came to pack and leave, I discovered I really didn't want to go to the bother.

"Oh, Ruth, you do not have to worry about showing. I don't want to do it either. What I do want is to trail ride. Not many hours-long-rides, just nice jaunts around the farm or to a state park somewhere. Nothing like you used to do."

A week before, I'd put in a call to Mary Long, my animal communicator friend, about another animal. I was getting what I thought were messages, but didn't trust myself. I bounced them off her and she said I was "right on."

"You can talk to them yourself. We have been doing this for a long time together. I will give you the "*Reader's Digest*" version of how to do it. Do you want to talk to one of mine? They are easy to communicate with. They love to talk."

Of course I did!

She said to not look at the animal, but envision it standing somewhere. (Even if I was talking to one of mine.) "Ask them anything, show them what you want in pictures, and then believe you are getting an answer. If you laugh at yourself or what you think they are saying, or don't believe you actually heard them, they will stop talking to you."

I talked to three of her mares, and Mary said I had heard them correctly.

Still, Ruth's announcement that she hated showing came out of the blue. I hadn't asked about showing—but I was sending vibes that I was deeply provoked with her and she had answered.

The same time this happened, I was reading *What the Animals Tell Me,* by Beatrice Lydecker. In 1997 she wrote: "Medicine today tells us that 85 percent of all medical illnesses have emotional roots." She says, "I know that the emotional quality of an animal's life and its physical well-being are directly related. The animal may receive excellent physical care, but if the outward physical symptoms are rooted in an emotional disturbance, healing will not occur. Even death may result. Animals do not have psychosomatically induced physical problems, but they do use physical symptoms as signs to express emotional distress."

Boy, was that Ruth Ann. After all my frustrations, had I finally stumbled upon her real problem, and would assuring her that she didn't need to show anymore, solve it?

Even I wondered at my sanity, but Ruth seemed brighter and happier the next day. She even looked different physically. She stood taller, she carried herself with pride, her eyes looked soft but eager—and yes—she walked sound! I shared the experience with all my horsey friends. None thought, or at least said, that I should be committed. Everyone knew how maddening Ruth Ann's problem had been for me. I had owned her for nine months and had ridden her about a dozen times. That was enough to frustrate a saint.

A few evenings later, Bob and I rode together. He was on Samson and I on Ruth Ann. It was glorious. She bobbed her head like a gaited mule should. Her ears flopped back and forth and she kept pace with the big black Samson—no easy feat. The next morning we rode again and she was sound. Her brown head with perky mule ears and sparkling eyes that followed my every move, hung over the door of her stall as I walked up and down the barn aisle at various times of the day. Ruth Ann had finally come home in mind, spirit and body. Her stall plaque read, *"Ruth Ann, Queen"* but the name Queen never stuck. Ruth Ann she remained.

Chapter Twenty-nine: Divorce

No, not Hal and me, although Hal was certainly putting up with a lot. First one mule comes, another goes, another one comes, and now it was Samson's turn to possibly go. He and I simply were not getting along. Our lovely relationship where he called me "Missus," and promised to take care of me, was no more. In truth, Hal really wasn't upset with all the mule comings and goings. As when I had my show horses, all he wanted was for me to be happy, enjoy them, and stay safe, but staying safe seemed to be a continuing issue.

Understandably, my misgivings with Samson started with my very unpleasant tumble when he went down an embankment, put on the brakes, spun and dumped me unceremoniously in the dirt. Soon following, was my serious fall from him when he "coon jumped" the obstacle in the barn. Even though it really was my fault for not telling him to walk over it instead of jumping it as he had been doing free style on a rope, my subconscious didn't trust Samson as much anymore. I hurt so badly from the jumping episode that I couldn't ride for a long time, during which I lost more of my riding nerve.

When spring came, I told myself I really had to get riding Samson again, but found I was making excuses not to. Finally, I asked Erica to "spring break" him for me: ride him on the paths and be sure he wasn't spooky. She rode him several times, reporting that he had been fantastic. On a warm, sunny and windless day, I saddled him and rode around the inside arena. I felt safe, so I went outside and rode around that arena. Still feeling safe, I started down a path for a short trail ride. That went well and I was beginning to feel comfortable in the saddle on the big mule again. I should have stopped there, but decided to go down another path.

This time Samson stopped at the top of a little knoll that we had to descend. Up went his ears and his body felt rigid. In my earlier days (even last summer), I would have squeezed with my legs and hit him with the crop. Back then, I had the inner feeling I could win. This time

Mules, Mules and More Mules

I sadly turned for the barn. It was too dangerous. I am sure Hal would have approved if he knew I had taken the safe road.

I began riding Sunday Praise, one of my Tennessee Walking mares. Sunday was ten years old, and up until I stopped showing two years ago, had been my best show horse since I retired her sire. I had never fallen off Sunday even thought she was a somewhat spirited show horse. She was a bit spooky, but never spun and ran, so I felt safe riding her alone and started getting my courage back. In a few weeks I began to feel stable and secure in the saddle again.

Since selling Miss Ellie, Bob's mule, Bob had been trail riding Samson around the farm with me in the evenings. They made a good pair. Bob was six feet tall and he looked good on the big black mule. The problem was that Bob had little time to ride, and I wanted animals that I could keep well-trained by riding them. Plus, I loved riding and I had more time. So, I thought I should still keep riding Samson. He and I had been very close the first two years, but now I felt the loss of his dependability and especially his friendship. Bob never rode alone, and Samson was perfect riding in a twosome with me and my other mule.

I had to keep Samson separated from my personal horse herd. Once again in a weak moment, I had tried putting all seven of them together. The herd was made up of two molly mules, three mares, Praise Hallelujah, and Samson. I usually kept Samson with Sunday, one of the mares because she didn't give a darn who she was with, providing she could eat pasture.

Hallelujah had the molly mules and two mares. All was quiet. Figuring my life would be easier if they all were together, I put grazing muzzles on Samson and Hallelujah so they couldn't bite each other and turned them all loose. At first everyone was interested in grazing and quiet prevailed. I came back to the barn a few hours later, and gazed upon a strange scene. Samson had all the females in a bunch, grazing in a corner of the pasture and Hallelujah was munching at the grass all by himself.

It didn't take long to discover what was happening. As I stood watching, Hallelujah ventured closer to the mares and Samson. Samson trotted toward Hallelujah with his head snaked out and down, and his long mule ears plastered flat back against his head. "This is *my* herd now," he was plainly saying. Samson was pleased to play lord and master of the herd. I was not. It decidedly was not fitting that my prize twenty-year-old champion show and breeding horse should be delegated to the bottom of the heap. I was muttering unpleasant things to Samson as I led him back to the barn, retrieved Sunday and put them in their own pasture.

It was about this time that I found another molly mule that I wanted. Mollies would do better in my herd situation. Samson could find a new home. I contacted several of my new mule friends, and I put him in several advertisements. One day after Bob and I had come back from a nice trail ride (where Samson had been "Mr. Perfect), Bob said quietly to Samson as he unsaddled him, "I don't know why we have to sell you."

Oh, my goodness. I didn't think Bob had gotten attached to Samson. Now what to do? I felt guilty. I had sold Miss Ellie after she accidentally stepped on Bob and broke a rib. Not because of the broken rib, but because she had dumped both Bob and me with her spook jumps. The broken rib was the end of it, especially after Bob admitted it would take some nerve for him to ride her again. Should I sell two "Bob mules?"

Then I had another altercation with Samson. The usual turn-out routine was to lead Samson and Sunday into their pasture and then let Hallelujah and the other females out the barn door to run into their field. One day I had a memory lapse and turned the main herd out before Samson. My word! You would have though Samson was coming unglued. He paced back and forth in his stall, spinning his big 16'3 hand body around when he came to end of the large foaling stall. His head was up in the air and his eyes had a mad-frantic look to them. There was no question he was mightily pissed. The fact that Sunday was still in the barn didn't quiet his nerves at all.

I wasn't frightened, but I was disgusted with him. I decided I would teach him a lesson in a quiet non-confrontational "horse-woman-ship" way—no matter how long it took. My plan was to put the rope on his halter and keep shaking it to simply make him back away from the stall doorway when I opened it, and wait until I said he could come out. Thirty minutes later I was still at it, breathing hard, sweating and *not* winning.

My right arm and shoulder were aching from shaking and popping the rope in Samson's face, but that wasn't the worst of it. Several times he got out of the stall door, ducked his head and took off toward the open barn door, which had a gate across it. He stopped, but he had bested me. After pulling him around and going back into his stall, which wasn't easy, I kept at my rope shaking. I was getting nowhere. I angrily called Bob on his cell phone. "Come see why I want to sell this dang mule!" I blurted, trying to catch my breath.

Bob came and he saw. I have to give Bob credit. He really isn't what I would call a "horseman." He loves dogs, especially his Doberman female, Hershey, and my dogs, Muffitt and Blue. He tolerates the horses, but never wanted to ride any, puts up with my beef cows and geese, puts the hay up in the mow (a particularly hot and dirty job), and along with Hal, fixes broken things. He took me to the Grand Canyon to share its beauty, but came home telling me he would ride mules with me. And that was about it—ride them, or more specifically—sit on them as they went down the trails.

However, in this case, even he could see something had to be done. First, he went in the mule's stall, shut the stall door and somehow got the rope training halter on Samson's head. Samson still managed to drag him down the barn aisle a couple times, but Bob took him back to the stall. Bob was stronger than I and pretty soon got the better of the angry mule. Samson actually quieted down some and stood in the doorway of his stall, allowing Bob to lead him out and into the pasture. Something happened that day. Even though Bob hadn't used "the new horsemanship maneuvers," and hadn't done everything exactly right, it had worked. Bob had bested Samson and the mule knew it.

Ah, age. I didn't have the stamina to see the situation through, and I didn't have the mind frame where I knew I could prevail. This state of affairs definitely didn't endear Samson to me.

For the next week, Bob came to the barn in the evening to put Samson out. We made him wait until last. There were a few minor altercations, but for the most part, Samson was fairly cooperative, but not enough that I wanted to tackle him. On the days I had to put the horses out alone, I made sure to put Samson out first. Eli was still coming on a somewhat regular basis and I knew who his next subject was going to be *again*—Samson.

Eli entered the stall to put on the rope training halter and Samson began moving all around. Eli made getting the halter on the mule look like an easy and graceful dance. I was surprised at Samson because he tried to overpower Eli and go out the door. Surely, he should have remembered all the work Eli had done with him before this. Mules don't forget, after all. I knew Eli would "win," but looking in from a distance, it was interesting. Finally, Samson backed off and stood still. I asked Eli what he did.

"I made like I was another horse. I turned my butt to him and kicked with one leg."

Hmm, that was fascinating. I had seen him calm down Ruth Ann by standing still and "cocking" one of his legs as a horse does when at rest, or squatting down, to show he was not worried—not in flight mode. It had always worked. He was speaking "horse."

Eli worked Samson in and out of his stall, and then backed him into the stall. Next, he used a different stall, one with an outside door. Samson bolted through the opening instead of walking politely.

"Oh, shucks," Eli muttered. "Now we will have to work this doorway."

Before the session was over, I was backing Samson in and out, turning him this way and that and going through all the stall doors as I wished. The next day after Eli's session, I put him out last. *I will test myself and the mule*, I thought. It was not perfect but after I "kicked" at him as a horse might, he backed up and stood still. Yep, I was grinning!

As the summer months flew by, Bob and I tried to ride each evening. Now and then I took Ruth Ann, sometimes Susie Q, and Bob always rode big Sam. We were all getting along famously. I still had the mule advertised with my mule contacts, but no one had bought him. The barn gals were planning a trip to a Michigan state forest to ride.

Mules, Mules and More Mules

Did we want to go? Last year we never got off the farm, mostly because Samson wouldn't load into the trailer. Then after Eli worked with him and I practiced, we didn't have another opportunity to go. Farm life on the weekends with a regular job during the day takes lots of time. Bob simply couldn't get away. Yes, we wanted to go! Left to our own devices, we likely wouldn't make it again.

Bob got the trailer hitched and parked in the inside arena so I could load it. The next morning I got Samson out of his stall and headed up the barn aisle to groom him. Samson spotted the trailer and dove into an empty stall, nearly breaking my wrist as he pulled the rope. Dratted mule. I tried mental communication with him. Why was he so vehement in his dislike of the trailer?

Then I remembered his bad ride several summers ago when I first got him. He had been loaded after a ride when he was somewhat hot, not enough that I thought it would be uncomfortable, but when we unloaded, he and the other horse were drenched with sweat. The ride had only been fifteen minutes, but I surmised the air flow hadn't been enough to cool them. He was worse about the trailer after that. I told him I was sorry; it was an accident and wouldn't likely ever happen again as we would be smarter.

I went in the house and told Bob what *his* mule had done, and said, "I sure hope he will load!"

Bob grinned wickedly (for him) and replied, "He will load, don't worry." I decided to take him at his word. Samson was quickly becoming Bob's project. I didn't need a big, black, opinionated mule in my life other than to feed. Let Bob take him on.

Well, the morning we were to go, Bob had Samson in the special training halter with lead rope attached, pointed his hand into the trailer and Samson hopped right in. Loading Susie Q in like manner, we closed the doors and were off to a glorious Sunday ride in the shade of the forest with our friends.

It appeared that Bob had a mule.

Bob and Samson

Chapter Thirty: Lessons Learned

The phone rang. It was Eli and he sounded excited. "Rose, you will never guess what! My wife waited on a man in Eby Pine Restaurant, got to chatting with him, and he turned out to be a mule man. His name is Steve Edwards. Have you ever heard of him? He said he would like to meet you and me!"

My heart sped up a few beats when I heard the name *Steve Edwards*. What mule person new or old hadn't heard of the man? He ran ads in both mule magazines for saddles and seminars—and he wanted to meet me and Eli? Wow.

It turned out Mr. Edwards and his wife, Susan, were in our northern Indiana neck of the woods to get their trailer serviced, and they were sort of looking for things to do to pass the time. Well, no matter, getting to meet this mule man under any circumstances was awesome. Eli couldn't locate the telephone number his wife had given him, but it was in Mr. Edwards' ads. I called and yes, Steve Edwards could come to our farm in half an hour.

I had two mule problems. Both were saddle fitting issues, and this might be the man to solve them. Samson had large shoulders and no western saddle in my boarding barn or my own worked just right for him. My dressage saddle was okay when I rode, but when Bob used his Aussie saddle, Samson's back got sore. I had looked at a trail-riding saddle a few weeks ago on Steve's website and liked the price, weight (it was part cordura instead of all leather), and the looks of it.

The other problem was dear Ruth Ann. She was better, I could ride her some, but she still stumbled and had a stilted walk now and then. Steve and Susan arrived and Eli soon followed. We moseyed to the barn to see the mules. By now, I knew better than to do any bragging about my long eared creatures. First of all, it usually preceded an embarrassing moment as the mule did something to make me cringe, and since this was *Steve Edwards*, I was sure I couldn't impress him anyway. We stood outside Samson's stall talking, and the big mule began pawing and reaching over his stall door for attention. Darn it. Thanks a lot, Samson!

After several minutes of Samson's annoying actions, Steve stepped forward into the mule's face and said, "Stop it. I don't like your attitude!"

I winced. How humiliating. I knew Samson and knew he would be right back making me want to disappear, so I started walking away saying brightly, "And here is Susie Q, my perfect little mule!"

Actually, Susie had been slightly less than perfect that summer. She decided that some slight spooking might be in order, but she was still my best and most dependable mule. I got her out of the stall for Steve to admire.

"She is very nice," Steve observed, "but there are no perfect mules."

I wanted to clap my hands over my ears. *Don't say that,* I thought. But in my heart I knew it was no doubt true, *but I didn't want it to be true. I wanted the perfect mule. Maybe I didn't have one now, but someday....*

Lesson learned: no perfect mules, but working to make one perfect would make me a better mule lady. No point chasing around trying to buy one. I was pretty sure I knew what was making Susie Q somewhat jumpy. It was too much green grass. Steve said mules are carbohydrate junkies. I knew that, so no grain, and my mules wore grazing muzzles which allowed only several blades of grass to be eaten at a time, and they were only allowed in the pasture half the day. Still they were fat and "sassy." I'd have to think more on that solution.

Next, I sort of dragged Ruth Ann out of her stall. She gimped out the door. Today wasn't her best day. I tied her up and Steve stroked her neck. "Oh, my," he said, looking at the hump in her spine. Her hump was right were a person sat and it had worried me ever since I purchased her. Dr. Weaver, the chiropractor vet, said with treatments it would go away in time, but so far it was still visible and sore. When Steve pressed on the hump, Ruth Ann sank toward the ground.

While Steve was talking and touching Ruth Ann's back bump, I stood a little away and observed. It was very strange. Ruth is not a very friendly mule to outsiders; she usually turns her head away, but here was Steve talking to Eli, rubbing Ruth, and Ruth had turned her head all the way around so that her nose almost touched his arm. No one but me would have thought that unusual. In my mind I heard Ruth plead, "Help me." Tears pricked behind my eyes. I knew then I was making a mule saddle purchase.

While talking about Ruth, I told him some about her history and stated she was supposed to be "bombproof" but she wasn't at all. He glanced at me with a slight smile on his face. "There are no bombproof mules either...."

Hearing there were no bombproof or perfect mules didn't really make me upset. Instead, it helped me. "Thank you." I gave Steve Edwards, the mule man, a big hug.

If he didn't know of any totally perfect or bombproof mules, then the fact that I didn't have any was not so terrible. "In fact," Steve continued, "you should ride, paying attention just as you drive your car. If you ride as though your mule is bombproof, it will prove you wrong at the very worst time." That was exactly what had happened with me and Samson.

Lesson learned: Don't be too hard on myself. I should accept the fact my animals were not entirely perfect, but I should keep working to improve. Eli had been a huge help to me. I never quite mastered Samson, but our personalities clashed. I wanted easy at this point in my life. Samson wanted games on one-up-man-ship.

I asked Steve if he had any of the trail pleasure mule saddles with him, and he did, but back in his trailer. He promised to return the next day, bring a saddle, and show me how a mule saddle fit mules better than horse saddles. Giving Ruth Ann a final pat, I put her in the stall. Tomorrow would be like Christmas in September.

I guess Steve Edwards, along with other horse and mule clinicians, must be part entertainer and part teacher. Steve regaled me, Eli, and several friends who came to watch, with stories from his past and present, along with explaining how mule saddle trees are different. I wanted to be sure that the trail saddle I was buying would fit all my mules. My horse saddles did *not* fit all my horses. He assured me it would, and placed his saddle mold over Samson's back. I could see the difference right away.

I had read about the advantage of using a mule saddle, but goodness, how many saddles did I need in my tack room? I already had more horse saddles than I wanted. Now I was to add another one. *Ruth better appreciate this*, I thought. Next, he placed the mold on Ruth Ann and pointed out how it protected the hump in her back. Mules have flatter straighter backs and horse saddles, which have a built-in curve, do not accommodate this element. I had gotten by, but this saddle would be much better.

Samson delighted in using the new saddle. Susie Q and I could hardly keep up with Bob and the big mule as they walked or gaited down the trails. Samson wasn't in a hurry; he just rolled alone with no effort. His back recovered from soreness (instead of gaiting he had begun to trot), and he no longer swished his tail when he was saddled. How in the heck did he know the difference in saddles before it was placed on his back? Maybe there are no perfect mules, but there certainly are very smart ones!

Ruth Ann appreciated the new pad and saddle too. Between more chiropractic treatments and her new gear, the hump started getting smaller and less sore. Ruth Ann had gotten the help she wanted from the mule man.

Lesson learned: Mule saddles are best for mules!

Samson had taught me a very hard and sad lesson: Not every mule (or horse) is right for every rider, and sometimes when you get hurt and frightened, it is best to cut your losses, especially if you are nearly seventy. As much as I had loved and trusted him the first year and a half, he was not the right mule for a "little old lady" who planned to ride until she was a lot older lady. However, he made a marvelous mule for Bob, who tended to simply ignore his shenanigans.

Chapter Thirty-one: A Solution for Ruth

Ruth Ann was another story. Ruth was feeling spunky. Too spunky, in fact. She no longer gimped around, her saddle fit and her back didn't hurt. Her coat was glossy, she was too fat, and getting sassy. I had saddled her in the new saddle and gone for a farm ride. She hesitated going down the scary path. I dug my spurs into her side in no uncertain terms, "Git up, Ruth!" She did, but hesitated nearly every ten steps until we got by the monster dog's yard. Finally, things smoothed out for a nice ride. She was up in the bridle like I had seen her at the mule show. I had mentioned to Steve she held her ears like pokers.

"Yeah, don't you hate that?" he answered.

Yes, I did and I couldn't get her to concentrate, but at least she was moving forward. It was like riding one of my show horses, not at all a relaxing mule ride.

We crossed the culvert and headed into the field. She bolted ahead five steps, but settled down quickly. A few yards farther and going along at a nice clip, she spied a pile of dead branches with dark leaves and took off. I pulled on my reins, first on one side and then the other several times, and managed to pull her head around. She stopped and we walked on. Her head was still up, but I felt she was under control and maybe even perhaps trusted me. I had made her behave and it was fine with her. The difference in what happened with Ruth Ann versus Samson was his size, power and determination. Ruth gave in easily, she wasn't big, and she didn't argue.

Later that week, Eli was out and I told him we needed to work with Ruth some more. He looked in her stall and saw those sparkling eyes. "Hey, this *is* a different mule. There is someone in there now!" He agreed that Ruth had had a shell around her earlier. She was numb. If she was to be ridden and she hurt, she tried to ignore it and turned inward. Her eyes had looked distant, like she was somewhere else. When she had her massages and chiropractic treatments, she didn't respond with the usual licking and chewing. Sometimes it was a delayed reaction—after the treatment was all finished and she was put back into her stall, then she licked her lips. (Licking and chewing is often a sign that something has made an impression, either in training or in treatment.)

Regrettably, the new saddle hadn't solved all of Ruth's problems. Soon she was lame again. I had ridden about half an hour away from the barn when she started limping with her right front leg. I got off and led her home, but she got steadily worse with each step. I called the vet again and he first thought it might be a stone bruise and later an abscess, but it was neither of those things.

Two months later, again despairing to the point of tears that Ruth would ever be sound, I called another vet who had an x-ray machine that took digital pictures we could view immediately at the farm. We saw that her ankles were a mess with arthritis and bony growths, which would make them stiff, hard to bend and easily injured.

The vet injected both of them with cortisone and hyaluronic acid (the natural occurring lubricating substance in joints). When he inserted the needle into her right ankle before seating the syringe into it, blood dripped out. That has happened with my horses when a joint was particularly bad with no lubrication and the bone was grinding upon bone.

Ruth was immediately better, but about a month later was somewhat lame again. I had both ankle joints injected three times over the next three months. I also put her on a product called Arthro-Ionex. It contained special minerals along with substances to support joints. It was expensive, but after all I had been through with Ruth Ann, I decided it was worth it.

That late summer after her injections and new supplement, she began coming into the barn with a spring to her step instead of stumping and stumbling along like she might not make it into her stall, and I began riding her again.

At first, because of her early spookiness, I was very cautions. As the days and rides went along, Ruth Ann transformed more and more into that "bombproof mule" I had been promised. It was as though she woke up one morning and decided she belonged to me.

Mules, Mules and More Mules

I loved Ruth, maybe because we had been through so much together, and she had guts. Through all her pains, she never gave up and never got cranky. Ruth Ann was a real trooper.

Ruth Ann and Rose - Photo by Connie Kleiman

Chapter Thirty-two: Lucinda

The saying I saw on a placard: "Mules Are Like Potato Chips, You Can't Have Just One," was again true in my case. I had three: Samson whom I had given to Bob, Susie Q who was just about perfect, and Ruth Ann who was arthritic and sometimes not ridable. Another mule would fit in just fine, but it *had* to be healthy, sound, and definitely "grandma quiet."

I found several on a website that I had been checking on and off for three years. I'd almost bought a molly last fall, but let her get away. This year I figured if I found what I wanted, I would buy it. Black Diamond had been advertised the previous fall as a "project mule." She was gaited, four years old and didn't have a lot of training, but she cost less.

The following spring she was still the same price and had had a little more riding. I could see from the video she gaited well, which was also extremely important. She had been used for friends to hop on and go with the trail riding group. The seller said she was quiet natured and he was sure she would suit me. She crossed rivers, jumped down stone ledges, stood beside large noisy pay-loaders working on a road. What more did I need?

My young friend, the first Erica, who currently lived near the mule, went to look at and ride Black Diamond, saving me about a 13-hour trip. Erica liked the molly's smooth gait, and she seemed unflappable as a flock of turkeys flew up inches from her feet, so I bought her. A friend of the owner offered to haul her to Indiana, and very soon I had another mule.

I had seen pictures and video of her on the website, but when she was unloaded, I admit I was keenly disappointed. She had wintered outside and had lots of scruffy, long hair; her belly looked big, and her head did too. I certainly couldn't call her pretty. She led into the barn quietly. One thing Erica told me the seller had said about her was that she didn't lead well. Erica had no problem leading her from the paddock, flipping the end of the lead rope at her side for encouragement. I thought that was a minor flaw; better that then spookiness.

Jack, the man who brought her, saddled her up to exhibit her to me the next morning. She startled some as Blue, my big dog, came rushing up beside her, but settled down and demonstrated a superb walking-horse- type gait in the arena. I was pleased. She looked better under saddle than without one, as it sort of camouflaged the big belly. That night when Bob and I went for our evening ride, I decided to ride her. It was anything but a success.

One of the problems I made for myself by not adjusting the stirrups to my correct length. Diamond was a very narrow mule, not rotund and chunky like Susie and my horses. The stirrup length was perfect on my other animals, but because the new mule was narrow, not bulky, they hung too long. The other problem was the mule. She didn't want to move on. Soon we were thirty feet behind Samson, and no amount of leg squeezing or kicking helped. Before long, I had a sour look on my face. This is just great, I thought, a new expensive, ugly mule that won't go. I was sure glad Jack had ridden her for me and I'd seen her gait, or I would have been doubly devastated. Perhaps I was doing something wrong. Thirty-six years of riding apparently hadn't prepared me for Black Diamond!

Bob knew I was unhappy and politely said nothing. He didn't think I needed another mule anyway, and this definitely wasn't the way to impress him, that was for sure. As soon as I got into the house I called her former owner. He said he used a crop (short whip) on her, not his spurs, which she ignored, and he said they never walked, they always gaited unless they were going up, down or across something. That wasn't really much help. To me she seemed dull, dead-sided, and uninterested with little personality at all. Maybe she was quiet, but this sure didn't suit me.

Next I called Erica to inquire more about *her* ride on Diamond. She said the same thing about the crop, but added that after the mule understood what she wanted, she went into her gait and stayed in it. Gaiting is great, but my friends and I walk a lot too, and this mule's walk was slow and actually very bumpy with a side to side movement. It felt pacy. Along with my too long stirrups, her gait was killing my back, knees and legs.

I was alarmed. What if I couldn't ride her because she was uncomfortable at the slow walking gait? That would be embarrassing and costly. I had purposely asked Erica to be sure her gait was smooth for my back, but never thought her slow walk might be a problem! Erica had added, "Her trail walk is sure slow, though." Almost in tears, I hung up the phone.

I was keeping the new mule in a stall with a small turnout pen, because I didn't want to let her out with the herd until I had a chance to do some bonding with her. At the moment I didn't care much for her, but she was mine and I was stuck with her. I had to make something good happen. Diamond had no ground manners, she didn't lead well, wouldn't move over if you pushed on her side and flinched and moved dramatically about when the saddle was placed on her back. (Her seller admitted that he just threw the saddles on his mules—no gentle training.)

Her ears had been trimmed and that was excellent. It meant she was good with her ears; she liked having them stroked and bending them to put into a bridle was no problem. I got out my clippers and began to trim her muzzle hair. She stood still, so I began on her whole head. That done, I clipped the neck. Her face looked a lot smaller without all the hair hanging from her cheeks.

The next day I clipped her whole body and discovered "rain rot" in various places. Rain rot is a common skin infection which affects equines and is caused by dirty and moist conditions, many times under a saddle pad. Her appearance improved a lot without the scraggly winter hair. Maybe she wasn't quite so ugly after all. She enjoyed the petting and brushing and began to make a little progress, giving in to pressure and moving over when I asked. I also changed her name. Black Diamond didn't thrill me, but Lucinda seemed to fit her.

My next call was to Eli who had begun working in another town all week, and was only home on weekends. My only chance to have his help was early Sunday mornings.

Eli worked with her in the arena, getting her more responsive to leading, stopping and turning, and then saddled and rode her outside down the trail. All went extremely well until they arrived back at the barn. At the exact time the twosome was heading toward the large barn door, Blue, my Giant Schnauzer, galloped out of the door with the big horse "jolly ball" in her mouth, making her customary growling noise as she slammed the ball into the ground with every stride. It really made a commotion.

Poor Lucinda. She really didn't have time to think about what that apparition was barreling right at her, but darted off to the side in an explosion of movement. Eli used the one-hand stop, (which she had been previously taught) and they came to a halt several yards away. I sure wished that hadn't happened. Now I was spooked as well as the mule. On the other hand, it was perhaps a good thing for me to see. She definitely was not grandma broke, and best to find it out now and with someone else on her back.

Eli came back the next Sunday and we did more ground work with her. She was catching on fast, and the shell that encased her as well as several of my other new mules, was falling off and in its place was a new mule that saw everything. No more was she dumb to her surroundings; she had awaked from her Rip Van Wrinkle sleep. Now I had a five-year-old reactive mule to train.

I felt foolish, but I didn't have the courage to ride her. I kept telling myself: "tomorrow," but it didn't happen. Perhaps I had a sixth sense of survival. I decided to hire Erica, who had bought Mirabella, to ride her for me in the arena and with me on the trail. That went well except coming home she did a good sideways spook at the lawnmower. Darn, that was very disappointing; I had almost gotten up my nerve to ride her. More Erica rides were in order.

I worked with her on the ground, leading her into the claustrophobic wash area, more leading, backing, moving sideways and ground manners; I was pleased with her "try" and her curiosity.

One day Erica came back from a trail ride and said, "I am sorry, but this mule is a thinker. You might as well accept it. She wants to be sure about any situation herself." I didn't care if she thought, as long as she decided to accept my decisions when we were together.

Next Eli visit, we tried the horse trailer. Lucinda loaded, but I wanted to be sure she would whenever I said to. No horse seems to like a step-up and down trailer, preferring the ones with ramps. Unfortunately, mine was a step-up. Getting up and in wasn't a big issue, but backing out and finding that big, scary step-down made them apprehensive until they had done it enough times that it became routine.

It started out grand. She hopped in but wanted to turn around to come out head first. Eli made her back out, which she did well the first two times. Next time it was "no thank-you, no more trailer loading for me."

Eli said, "I was looking for that."

I was too. The mule had been quite cooperative at everything, but push hadn't yet come to shove. Now she was drawing a line in the sand.

Half an hour later she was hopping in and backing out with perfection. It was interesting to me. I remembered what John, who sold Miss Ellie to us, said: "Only do it until they get it, after that it pisses them off." Lucinda did it fine two times and in her mule mind that was all that made sense; but doing it over and over taught her that when her person said to do something, she better do it. A very good lesson for a young pushy mule to learn. Eli was super. He never raised his voice; he simply used the training stick and rope to keep her from running him over, and persisted in his request.

My first Erica, who had been with me for ten years, came for a short visit. She'd ridden Lucinda before I bought her, and I wanted another young body to ride her some more. I still hadn't gotten on her since the first day. As Erica started through the gate and down the short hill to begin the ride, Lucinda stopped and did a big old turn-around spook and bolted off.

I looked at my friend sitting beside me and said, "Now *that* is why I haven't been riding her…" and patted myself on the back that I'd had the sense to listen to my inner voice, which had been telling me Lucinda wasn't ready for Grammy just yet! Erica's ride had more excitement when Lucinda refused to go past a pole sticking in an old woodchuck hole. Erica dismounted and still had a hard time getting her to go past.

It appeared Lucinda was still a work in progress and Eli working with her once a week wasn't enough. I made plans to send her to a local trainer, another good friend told me about. I liked Lucinda, but she needed more saddle miles while she was "bright-eyed and bushy-tailed," as the old saying goes. Now that she felt good, she needed more education. Another chapter in Lucinda's life was about to unfold.

When my young granddaughters, Alexis and Ava, who loved feeding the horses at chore time, asked where Lucinda was, I explained she was away at "mule school."

"Why?" was the next question. I explained she needed to learn to be a good riding mule and make good choices, a term with which they were very familiar.

I called Gary, the trainer, every week, promising myself I would not be a pest; I would have been happy to call every day. The first comment he made was a lot like Bryan's who'd trained Miss Ellie—"She doesn't stop or steer well, does she?" With each succeeding week, both those talents improved. It was her "looking at everything" that bothered me the most because she would sometimes react by spooking. She was there for five weeks; Gary used her to move his small herd of cattle, rode in the woods, fields, across the creeks, and pastured her with strange critters such as his emu and goats.

When Bob and I went to pick her up, Gary "hauled" her away from the feed bunk with his rope. I noted she didn't lead any better, in fact, worse, than when I left her. She stood in his cross ties with her ears back—not in defiance, but as in, "I do *not* want to do this!" and with a detached, sullen look on her face. After saddling, I rode with Gary for about twenty minutes in his woods. Lucinda followed Gary's horse at a slow pokey pace, and I swear she tried to knock my knee against a tree and managed to snag my foot in a vine that grew close to the path. She wasn't a happy mule, but she was quiet and didn't spook.

I promised myself I would ride her while she was this quiet and perhaps depressed, because I knew it wouldn't last. It never does. Miss Ellie had been the same, only more depressed, and it hadn't taken her long to return to her normal, somewhat ornery, but better trained self. Gary had ridden Lucinda every day at varying lengths of time. She wouldn't get that much riding here because I didn't have the time. I was determined not to let her revert to who she was before mule school.

The next day, Bob sat in the arena while I rode her. She was perfect, but very slow. Plod, plod, plod along. It was not fun, but certainly not dangerous, and I was satisfied. Three days later and she was still plodding, but I had graduated to the outside arena where we practiced our turns, stops, and standing still. I rode her with Bob on the trail following Samson. I tied her up every morning for at least two hours. She was used to it at Gary's and it was good passive training. Now, if I could just convince her to remain safe, quiet, well trained, but move faster!

.

Chapter Thirty-three: Lucinda, Part Two

I continued working with Lucinda every day time allowed, and I was pretty pleased with our progress. I did ground work: leading, stopping, turning and standing still. All the time Lucinda was becoming more and more alert, but not necessarily in a good way. One day she spotted something outside the barn door and tried to run over me. I made her stand by shaking the rope and shutting off her escape route with my training stick. She stood with a disgusted look on her face and stomped her back foot. At first I thought she had a fly as it was a quick hard stomp, but as she continued to do it, I figured out she was having a mild hissy fit.

I had discovered a little riding trick that made me feel much more secure in the saddle. I had read about it in the June 2008 issue of *Mules and More* magazine ("Few Things I Have Learned,") but couldn't figure out exactly what the author, Capt. Joe Vaclavik, was talking about. I even contacted him and still couldn't figure it out. He called it a "night latch," and stated it would help keep you in the saddle if your animal spooked or did other unpleasant acts. Boy, did I need and want one!

One day, months later, as I was trail riding with my right arm hanging by my side and my left hand on the reins, my hand touched the dangling latigo strap that hung from the front of my saddle. It was sort of a God-given reflex that caused me to wrap my hand about this strap. Low and behold, I now had an anchor. By firmly grasping this strap, I was secured in my saddle, but it only worked if the animal would neck rein, not if you needed to use both hands to guide and stop.

Because Lucinda did not neck rein, I had to teach her so I could use my anchor. I felt safest in the inside arena, so that is where we worked. We walked around big barrels, cones, buckets or anything else I could get, to use as visual aids for turning. Lucinda turned like a cement truck even with two hands, but she was intelligent and soon figured out she could turn in small circles around the orange cones, but she was far away from using fingertip aids.

One morning as we walked around the perimeter of the arena, a cat scampered out from behind a board. Lucinda startled just a tad, but not a bad spook. I was pleased. I had my anchor and barely moved. That little strap was working out so well I was almost brave again. Thinking I had made real headway in training my mule, we made another lap around. When we came to the same spot, Lucinda almost came unglued.

She jumped sideways so fast it was unnerving. I was riding with one hand so couldn't pull her head around, but the strap gave me time to get a grip and stay in the saddle. If I hadn't had my hand wrapped around the strap, I would have been sitting in the dirt or worse. I pulled her to a stop and she threw her head up so far it almost hit mine, and that was just the beginning.

We quieted down and began another lap around the arena. When we got near the same place, she bolted way out into the arena and no amount of coxing, prodding or threats of being sold did any good. She wasn't going near. It was the same thing going in the other direction. I was at a big disadvantage since I had to ride with one hand to keep the other wrapped about my strap. I got off and tried it on the ground. She acted like the earth was about to open up and swallow her. Again, no amount of work on my part would convince her that spot was safe.

I kept working with her on the ground and eventually I could lead her past "the spot," but we had to skirt several feet into the arena. I called Eli again. When I sent Lucinda to Gary, Eli had stopped coming, but now I needed his reinforcement.

Eli had her going sideways down the side of the arena like doing a shoulder-in movement if one was riding. She did that both ways without any fuss, but even for him she wouldn't lead past the dreaded spot. The good part of the day's work was that I could now ground-drive her both ways along the side. It took diligence to keep her focused.

On our next session, I was alone with Lucinda. I was not especially coordinated with the training stick, the rope and the mule; I kept stepping on the rope, hitting myself with the training stick and letting Lucinda get ahead of me. However, I was pretty disgusted with her by now and my ire showed with my getting quite proficient with the stick. When she wanted to come off the arena path and knock into me, I brought up the stick and hit her neck, head, nose, whatever part I could reach to make her get over, and it worked. Several days later, I could lead her by the spot.

Next, Lucinda and I had a big argument on the other side of the arena. The big door was open and the lawn sprinkler was on, which made noises as the water sprayed on the plants. Now she was spooked about that. I won. I was proud of myself. Lucinda eventually allowed me to drive her sideways past the sprinkler. We quit.

When Eli came next, I bragged on myself. It was a big breakthrough for me. It was the first time I felt I really had control of the situation—and my training stick! It quickly became my new best friend. Eli worked with the mule some more in the arena, and then took her for a trail ride. I had been riding her with Bob and Samson in the evenings. Sometimes Lucinda was a real gem—quiet, attentive and responsive. I usually followed them, but if she was mellow, I went in front in safe places. I was fairly content as I felt certain I could ride her behind and be safe.

Then one day she started spooking as we were following Samson. I had my anchor and nothing dire happened, except when she quickly went sideways about eight feet, it pulled one of my lower back muscles. The following day she acted so silly I couldn't even think about riding her in front. Then more days went by, and she acted mellow again. She was driving me nuts.

That was why Eli was riding her in the field. He came back with enjoyment written all over his face. "She is a great mule. She did spook at a cat in the grass and a woodchuck running along the path, but it wasn't bad."

Not bad for him, but bad enough for me. I knew the problem with Lucinda was definitely part mine. I was too old for these pranks. Ten years earlier I might have thought little about it. After all, I was riding, showing, and training show horses. They had to have spark to be good show horses. They were not quiet, placid trail horses. Then too, I'd had some rather awful falls off my horses and mules the last few years, and I was still trying to overcome my fears.

Lucinda was a good mule, but maybe not for me; she wasn't proving to be a "grandma mule." I had her on an herbal supplement to make her more mellow, and still she had spooked. I decided a call to Mary Long was in order. It turned out to be quite an eye-opener.

After the first few friendly catching up minutes, Mary said, "Lucinda isn't the same mule we chatted with months ago. She is very dominant."

I agreed. I told her how Lucinda had changed after we did the ground work training and she "came out of her shell." Now she was alive and saw everything and reacted. She needed training all over again.

It's interesting talking to the animals and almost scary when you see how much they are aware of the whole situation. Lucinda chimed in with her ideas. First she thought she was very beautiful and could be a show mule. I had said that to several people (not Mary). She wondered if I sold her, maybe she would have a better home as a show mule. I told her she'd really have to work hard, it wouldn't be vacation place. I said life on our farm was very easy, and if I sold her she'd more likely end up a trail mule working even harder. She didn't think she would like that.

Next Susie Q, my nearly perfect and favorite mule, offered her advice. "Lucinda hasn't learned to soften her mouth yet. It needs to soften past her lips and on to her poll." I could agree with that. Susie went on to say, "With Lucinda you almost have to wait until she acts out and then break down her idea that she can always do what she wants."

Mary added that Lucinda's acts of dominance were to be in control of the situation. She could be pokey slow, spooky, or overreact to my aids to go faster and go too fast. I understood the dominance factor on the ground, and we were working on that. I never considered her dominance could influence her spooking. She did it because she could.

I'm sure there were situations that really did cause her to be anxious, but all this stupid stuff such as acting like a dark spot in the arena where a cat had scampered out was going to kill her, was plain dumb in my mind, and Lucinda was not dumb. She was very intelligent, thought too much and had a memory like an elephant. I was going to have to become smarter and more in charge. Darn, I really didn't want this. All I had wanted was another mule like Susie Q.

Mary had another extremely interesting comment. She works with all kinds of animals—cats and dogs, as well as equines. She has found that they have tuned into a sort of general cosmic consciousness of being the dog or horse that you want while you are working with them, but are subtly waiting until you go away and then they will go back to what they were doing and thinking. In other words, the lessons don't stick. She said she was getting many calls from owners and trainers who "just couldn't seem to get anywhere" with their charges. That sounded a lot like my Lucinda.

My conversation with Mary helped me realize I was reading Lucinda quite rightly. She was very dominant in sly as well as obvious ways. Her spooks were not spins, bolts or rears, just unexpected and aggravating. Her walking gait was superb, and she was beautiful.

Another gorgeous September morning was here and I had a choice: ride my lovely Susie Q on a serene trail ride or work with Lucinda. I chose Lucinda. First we did ground work; she was excellent, walking by her scary spot in both directions. Then I drove her sideways along the arena wall. That went well, but she swished her tail a lot and started trying to go head first in a straight line. I prodded her with the stick and she became agitated. She was saying, "No." Sticking to my resolve to be boss, I decided I could do this for hours if necessary. All I wanted her to do was go nicely without pulling or backing off the track. It didn't have to be perfect. We went back and forth about five times and she finally was softer. I rubbed her head and neck and went back to her scary spot. She did that fine, so I saddled her. Making a silent plea for safety, I headed to the arena.

Lucinda actually was pretty good. We were able to ride past her scary spot in both directions and around the arena. I stopped her at the spot and gave her a horse cookie. Lucinda was also aggressive with her food, and I knew giving treats had to be done judiciously and sparingly. However, I considered this justified one.

Just as I thought we were finished with our training, she decided there was something very wrong with the west end of the arena with the big open double doors. She was looking again and was stiff through her neck and body. About this time I had an epiphany. It was just as Susie Q had said: I needed to push her until she rebelled and then push her some more. I remembered when Eli was teaching her to load in the trailer. She was fine for a while, and then she rebelled. He worked through it, and now I had to do the same thing. I think I had been quitting too soon with my other lessons.

We stood there, turned around, stood some more, walked off around the arena again and when we came back to the doorway, she was again stiff and stared at something only she could see. We did the same thing four times before she finally walked softly past. One more time around and I stopped her at the door and gave her another cookie. I decided the place to give her treats was when she was working well, not after the ride when I gave the other mules a treat. She would be rewarded for working, not coming home.

One late summer morning, Lucinda came into the barn for feeding with a swollen left eye and reeking of skunk. Leave it to Lucinda to get skunked. We have lived here for over thirty years with numerous skunks roaming the pastures and no horse, cow or mule ever bothered them.

Rose Miller

Lucinda

Chapter Thirty-four: Reflection

I grabbed my jacket and headed to the barn for the bed-time check. As I entered the barn, Sunday, my mare, nickered. Sunday loved to eat, and probably was hoping I'd toss her more hay, or maybe offer an apple. The rest of the horses and mules were quiet, some with their heads hanging over their stall doors. Early morning and this bed-check occasion were two of my favorite times. This night everything was peaceful: the daily hubbub and hustle had died down, tummies were full of hay, and eyes blinked sleepily.

Ruth Ann was next in line as I walked the barn aisle. She pulled her head back slightly as I approached. I stuck my hand into her stall, touched her nose, and said, "I love you." She stuck her head out for more. She was the first to come to me in the pasture, and if I had a treat, well, that was just so much better. Ruth was definitely a favorite, and with occasional ankle injections and her special supplement, I continued to ride her occasionally.

Susie was already looking my way, her fuzzy long ears begging for a rub. There was just something about Susie that made me feel relaxed and serene. I felt my tensions fade as I rubbed her head and kissed her nose. In the summer she was as sleek as could be, but now, in the dead of winter, she was a furry, fluffy comfort talisman.

Samson and Lucinda were at the end of the row, and also had their heads poking over their doors. When I approached, Samson pulled his in, shook his head, and flicked his ears.

"Yeah, I know, you bossy thing." I chided him. "You only want petted on your terms." Samson and Bob were a good pair and got along famously. I was content with that.

Lucinda was always friendly. I never saw her with ears back in any fashion when she was looking at a human. She might run over you, bite your fingers when taking a treat, but she did it without malice. I came to the conclusion Lucinda was half donkey and half horse, all right, but a lot of the time she wasn't blended into a mule. I had to pay close attention to exactly which Lucinda I had at the moment. She kept me on my toes.

Everyone was safe and healthy: no colic, no one was cast in their stall, and no one was loose. Closing the barn door behind me, I felt privileged to be in the company of mules—and of course, my horses. In the beginning I had looked at mules through "rose colored glasses." The almost desperate desire for something safe overwhelmed my practical nature. With all my years of equine experience, I should have remembered I had to be part of this new equine equation, and as I had been reminded: there are no perfect mules—but by building a relationship with each one, I was rewarded with a growing bond that could work toward perfection.

Mules and horses *are* different, and in my story, I share my fascination and excitement with these differences. My mules with their more relaxed demeanor and friendliness make me feel fulfilled and content. I cannot now imagine my life without them.

Ruth Ann (foreground) and Susie doing what they do best!

CPSIA information can be obtained at www.ICGtesting.com
Printed in the USA
240485LV00003B/5/P